ESSENTIAL ALLY

America and Britain from Gulf War to Iraq War

Saroj Rath

Reference
Press

4831/24, Ansari Road, Darya Ganj,
New Delhi-110002
Tel. : 23260807, 41563444
Fax : 011-41563334
E-mail: info@essessreference.com
www.essessreference.com

REFERENCE PRESS
4831/24, Ansari Road,
Darya Ganj,
New Delhi-110 002.

Tel.: 23260807, 41563444
Fax: 41563334
E-mail: info@essessreference.com
www.essessreference.com

Rs.825/-

First Published - 2010

ISBN: 978-81-8405-059-2

Cover Design by *Patch Creative Unit*

Published By Reference Press and printed at Salasar Imaging
Systems

PRINTED IN INDIA

Essential Ally
America and Britain from Gulf War to Iraq War

It was the best of times,
It was the worst of times,
It was the age of wisdom,
It was the age of foolishness,
It was the season of light,
It was the season of darkness.

- Introductory lines of Charles Dickens'
"A Tale of Two Cities"-

CONTENTS

Prologue .... (ix)

Acknowledgment .... (xiii)

1 **Tracing History : Remote & Recent** **1**

Essentiality of the Alliance 1

Historical Links 6

Churchill and Formulation of "Alliance" 9

Convergence and Conflict in the US-UK relations 14

The Checkered Phase 17

2 **Touching Thorny Issues: Together & Separate 20**

"The Alliance" Meeting the Challenges 20

Cold War and Anglo-American Alliance 21

European Union and US-UK Alliance 32

Alliances on Multiple Fronts 38

Structure of Transatlantic Relations 41

The Alliance and Enlargement of NATO 43

The Alliance Partner and Ireland Problem 67

3 **Mere Anglo-Saxon Ties or an Alliance on Firm Foundation** **78**

The Alliance in approaching 21st Century 78

The Alliance on Critical Issues 93

Defence and Nuclear Cooperation 109

Defense Relationship 111

The Escalation of Rebellion and Repression 130

Nuclear Cooperation 134

Communications Intelligence 139

Former ground stations 145

**4   Identified Core Commonalities beyond
       Linguistic Oneness** **149**

Economic, Political and Legal Relationship of
the Alliance 149

5   The Best Bonding **182**

September 11 Crisis and Iraq War :
The Essence of Anglo-American Alliance 182

The Alliance on Iraq War 207

Iraq War of 2003 245

Attack on Iraq 252

6   Postscript **259**

The Human Cost of Iraqi Occupation 259

Obama and Brown 261

Gordon Brown and U.S.-U.K. Relations 263

Conclusion 264

References 277

PROLOGUE

Britain's American colonies broke its umbilical connection with the mother country in 1776. Following the Treaty of Paris, the new nation identified itself as the United States of America. Over the next two hundred years, the 13 original states of the United States of America added 37 new states while expanding her across the North American continent and acquiring a number of overseas possessions. During the 20th century, America was greeted by numerous major victories like the World War I, World War II and the decisive end of the Cold War in 1991. The US continued to be remaining as the world's most powerful nation state. The economy is marked by steady growth, low unemployment and inflation, and rapid advances in technology. World's biggest economy, the United States also houses the strongest army of the world. All these easily make the United States as the most powerful country of the world.

The United Kingdom with its maritime and industrial supremacy considered as one of the pioneers of modern civilization. At times the Empire covered almost one-fourth of the surface of the world. In the beginning of the 20th century, the downfall of the empire started and continued for nearly five decades. But during the second half of the same century the realization comes to the Kingdom that alone it can not dominate the world. So in alliance with the European Union and the United States, Britain regained its lost ground and established itself as a modern prosperous European nation. UN security council status, nuclear weapons, G8 economy, a leading democratic state, and membership of the EU, all these added to its power.'

'There is only one thing worse than fighting with allies, and that is fighting without them' said Sir Winston Churchill. Both the countries (the US and the UK) are very popular around the world. Together the powers of both the countries are mythical as their action ensures victory, their inaction confused nations, their diplomacy never failed and their relations excite envy among others. The world politics is being dominated by these two powers, individually or together, for the last hundred years or even more. Sometime shy, sometime sweeping; their inter-personal relations are both open and secret. Together they do things but they never hesitate to criticise each other. There are some areas of mutual relationship clearly demarcated as open and still there are other areas demarcated as secret. The best thing is they are being able to maintain the same without any dilution or difficulty. But despite their huge influence on the affairs of the world, there is absence of information about their interpersonal relations. This book is an earnest effort to provide information and analysis about their mutual relations.

While at the outbreak of cold war the US registered her strong presence on the world stage with Marshall Plan and Truman Doctrine, the British capacity for any action during the same period was not independent of American approval. During the Suez Canal crisis, the Anglo-French forces were forced out of the Middle East because of American disapproval. Similarly during the Cuban Missile crisis, the United States allowed only marginal role of Britain. During the long and intricate involvement of America in the Vietnam War, the relationship cooled down perceptibly. The leaders from both sides like Lyndon Johnson, Richard Nixon and Horald McMillan and Edward Heath did not take steps to improve this relationship. The task of restoring the height of "Special Relationship", as often it is termed, left to President Reagan and Prime Minister Thatcher.

Soon after Reagan had left the White House, and just before Thatcher was ousted, the cold war ended completely with the collapse of the Soviet Union in 1991. It was left to leaders like George Bush senior, Bill Clinton and George Bush junior from the American side and John Major and Tony Blair from the side of Britain to manage the "Special Relationship". These were all done at a time when the United States of America sought to redefine the international system in terms of a "New World Order".

Essentially, this book deals with the developments of US-UK "Special Relationship" in the context of the fast changing international scenario in the post cold war era. The time period from 1991, when the Gulf War engulfed both the nations and the collapse of the Soviet Union ended the cold war, to the attacks of the United States and Britain on Iraq in 2003 was an interesting period in history. Britain was undergoing the suffocating embrace of contesting parties like the United States and the European Union together. NATO's Post Cold War role and enlargement aspects, Bosnia and Kosovo crises, Clinton Administration's Ireland policy and 9/11 attacks on United States were events which tested the relations of America and Britain.

The policy makers, leaders, law enforcing authorities, intelligence officials, legislators, journalists, academics and common people from both sides of the Atlantic decides the relations of both the countries. When the US foreign policy need not to be modified or readjust to accommodate the aspirations of the United Kingdom, the UK has been making its foreign policy flexible in the post World War scenario to remain safe in the closet of the United States. It was often happened that the leaders of both the countries dictated their term and conditions on each other in the name of national interest. There was no dearth of instances of disputes and disagreements between the two. But the underlining philosophy of both the countries has been continued to be 'Essential Ally'.

ACKNOWLEDGEMENTS

After my doctoral degree I was out of Jawaharlal Nehru University with a permanent job at the Embassy of Japan in New Delhi. The activist zeal inside me was refusing to die. Love, knowledge and human suffering blowing me hither and thither in a wayward course when one internationally acclaimed sociologist, Professor P. Radhakrishnan of Madras Institute of Development Studies encouraged me to write a book on the research I have done in India and in the United States. He even volunteered to read the writing and suggest change, if any. A better inspiration is beyond any search and I am humbled with his gesture.

The writing was reaching nowhere but to the very verge of despair till the moment Mony agreed to join me for life with unassuming ecstasy and unstinted bliss. Then onwards life and writing never remained the same as both sought and got gratifications. The high wall of the embassy, the serene inside the wall added value to the writing I must say.

The easy, amiable and researcher friendly environment at the Library of Congress, National Archives and Record Administration, Library of George Washington University all in Washington DC; New York Public Library in New York and Rockefeller Library of Brown University in Providence enabled me to complete my research and acknowledging them is giving me tremendous joy. Finally, the trust of Sumit Sethi, a new generation publisher supplied me the reason to remain honest to the deadline earnestly and come out with the publication of 'Essential Ally' without any difficulty.

1

TRACING HISTORY:
REMOTE & RECENT

ESSENTIALITY OF THE ALLIANCE

Everybody, even the five year old kid around the world with the minimum nursery education, know the sagacious story of London and Washington and their proximity with each other. Their symbiotic relations never ever feel the detachment even after the cut in the umbilical connection. They can command and demand anything and everything from each other even if the command is not received well and the demand is not met adequately. The most important office in Washington DC after the White House is 3100 Massachusetts Ave, Washington DC, the British Embassy in America and similarly the out of ordinary foreign office in London is 24 Grosvenor Sqare, London, the American Embassy in Britain. White House or any other American Government office never refused a visit, planned or unplanned, if it is desired by the officials from the British Embassy in the United States. The eye and ears of America is always open to their most illustrious friend Britain and the British Ambassador may get direct access to the highest US government officials without meeting the protocol. Similarly, the Britishers never hesitate to accommodate any officials from the American Embassy in London as they believe that their survival as a world power rely on the depthness of the US-UK alliance and the voice of America may have the potential to place or displace Britain on the big league of great powers!

To the dismay of many people outside and inside America, many important American foreign policy decisions are often made in the Embassy of Britain in America. The intelligence officials of both the countries are indispensible for each other and the American Government may never hesitate to take decision on vital matters after secret consultation with the Britain. Considering Britain's classified knowledge about many third world countries, which were at some point colonies of Britain, the United Kingdom can offer sagely advice to the American to opt suitable policy that may suit America's interest in most part of the world and that too under the most unlikely condition or situation. The British understanding of countries, their collection of secret information and their manipulative tactics are the stuff, the American always admire and sought to avail. Britain's American colonies broke with the mother country in 1776 and were recognized as the new nation of the United States of America following the Treaty of Paris in 1783. During the 19th and 20th centuries, 37 new states were added to the original 13 as the nation expanded across the North American continent and acquired a number of overseas possessions. The two most traumatic experiences in the nation's history were the Civil War (1861-65) and the Great Depression of the 1930s. Buoyed by victories in World Wars I and II and the end of the Cold War in 1991, the US remains the world's most powerful nation state. The economy is marked by steady growth, low unemployment and inflation, and rapid advances in technology.

As the world progressed, the rise and fall of great empire taken place and Britain was the latest victim of this theory in the post war period. It was nightmarish on the part of Britain, the country where the sun never uses to set, to lose super power status. Britain's gifted diplomats, clever diplomacy and deft statesmanship found way to remain as an influential power even under the direst of the conditions. They befriended America in a big way. Citing some lingual and historical connection, which enabled them to usher the term 'Anglo-American Special Relationship', Britain bargain for a space at the top along with America in exchange of loyal support. Once the greatest colonial power ruling most part of the earth from a tiny land, Britain know well how to use its strength and limitation with equal easiness. As a dominant industrial and maritime power of the 19th century, the United Kingdom of Great Britain and Ireland played a leading role in developing parliamentary democracy and in advancing literature and science. At its zenith, the British Empire stretched over one-fourth of the earth's surface. The first half of the 20th century saw the UK's strength seriously depleted in two World Wars and the Irish republic withdraw from the union. The second half witnessed the dismantling of the Empire and the UK rebuilding itself into a modern and prosperous European nation. As one of five permanent members of the UN Security Council, a founding member of NATO, and of the Commonwealth, the UK pursues a global approach to foreign policy; it currently is weighing the degree of its integration with continental Europe. A member of the EU, it chose to remain outside the Economic and Monetary Union for the time being. Constitutional reform is also a significant issue in the UK. The Scottish Parliament, the National Assembly for Wales, and the Northern Ireland Assembly were established in 1999, but the latter is suspended due to wrangling over the peace process.

If anywhere in the world personality of a person at the helm of affairs decides the contour of diplomacy and inter-personal relations in international relations; it is the US and the UK, which are heavily depended on the personality and personal preference of the person at the top. Fresh from a great bonding with President Ronald Reagan, Prime Minister Margaret Thatcher passed the baton of England onto the hand of John Major. The Reagan-Thatcher bonding was subject of many page-3 story but at the same time the diplomacy and national government of both the countries were as successful as their story in the 3rd page of newspapers. President Ronald Reagan, on the other hand, left the office at Capitol Hill to his successor George Bush and expected that his policies will be continued in the next administration. Now the helm of affairs of both the countries is shifted from a long excellent personal bonding of the leaders at the top – Madam Prime Minister Margaret Thatcher and Film Star turned politician President Ronald Reagan to set of newly elected leaders. The deep rooted understanding between the two nations at various levels remains the same for sometime while the new administration in both the countries still to test each others view and vision! It was at this time that another innings of great personal affinity was ensured by the newly elected President George Bush and Prime Minister John Major and the test of time passed well with the great success of Gulf War with both the leaders essayed an epoch making victory together. The four year of Bush Presidency received unstinted support from the John Major administration and their international relationship achieved another great level and remained as a milestone in US-UK alliance.

The Bush-Major bonding was so strong that the British Prime Minister never hesitated to support the reelection bid of his best buddy Bush at the 1992 US Presidential Election. John Major's support style to the bid of President Bush' reelection was novel and unacceptable to many including President Bush' rival Bill Clinton. John Major revealed the so called damaging personal details of Democrat Presidential contestant Bill Clinton to help George Bush to reelect to the office of the President of the United States. Bill Clinton was a Rhode scholar at the Oxford University in 1968 and his studentship was not normal at Oxford as his view on Vietnam War was something many sees as against the American policy. It was contended that during his Oxford year he has crossed the European border to visit the erstwhile USSR on a three week trip and it was accused that Clinton had hand in globe with Russian authority. Along with this information, his Oxford personal file was transferred to the campaign team of President George Bush. This act was enough for the next President of the United States Bill Clinton to take hard on the British leader John Major. The next few years were the stormiest of all in the relations between the US and the UK. President Clinton never missed a single opportunity to take revenge against the Major administration and as part of this scheme President Clinton touched the Ireland issue and provided visa to the banned Sinn Penn leader Garry Adams to enter into the US. Not only this despite the protest of the British Government, President Clinton again provided Visa for the second time to Garry Adams much to the dismay and embarrassment of the Major administration. It was left to the Churchillian Tony Blair to restore the best of the relations between the US and the UK once he enthroned at the 10, Downing Street. Prime Minister Blair never let the past to loom on the future and he crafted a shrewd set of diplomacy which prompted his critics to term him as more of an American than a British! The close bonding between the two again resumed the bonhomie and again Britain coming close at the shoulder length with the America.

The end of President Clinton's Presidency was witnessed the best of the relations between the US and the UK with one leader only always standing with President Clinton was Prime Minister Tony Blair irrespective of the nature and intensity of the problem or prospect. During the Monika Lewinsky scandal it was Tony Blair who rush to the rescue of his good friend Bill Clinton. With the departure of President Clinton, President George Bush occupied the White House with a US Supreme Court order as the 2004 US Presidential election ended up in a dispute. President Bush heralded somehow a lukewarm administration. Prime Minister Tony Blair never late to welcome the leader whatever may be his stature and this enabled the alliance of the two countries flourished. The September 11 attacks on America changed the dynamic of world politics. It has established President Bush as a world leader and also this event established the US-UK alliance to the highest level never before in the history of both the countries.

The British Prime Minister Tony Blair stands decisively with his American counterpart in the aftermath of September 11 and never hesitated to act as the most reliable partner. The Bush-Blair friendship is now famous beyond their countries and together the two leaders tried to take on the world in the name of War on Terror. Obviously their target was Iraq and after a prolong debate and despite comprehensive opposition around the world the two power went on to War against Iraq.

The war against Iraq proved to be as another Vietnam for America and Britain and all the previous gains of both the countries at the international level are now replaced with a demonic figure of both the countries and leaders. This has although never had an adverse effect on political front and bring back both Tony Blair and George Bush to the office, the sheen of the leaders were no more like the previous term. Also this misadventure in Iraq cost Secretary of State Colin Powell's job as well as that of Prime Minister Tony Blair. Now Gordon Brown replaced Tony Blair riding on a high resistance note against the American adventure and started a slight shift in the close proximity of both the countries. After the departure of George Bush, it is now left to the Obama administration and Gordon Brown to test the time to maintain their much flaunted alliance. Both the new leaders have their own exclusive view for their domestic as well as international policies.

HISTORICAL LINKS

Human history has always been shaped by the growth and migration of populations, by the opportunities and constraints provided by the environment and by the rise of new technologies. After the discovery of the New World by

Columbus, the European began to establish their colonies on the soil of the two continents of America. The people of Spain established prosperous colonies in Mexico and South America. Long after that, early in 17th century, soon after the death of Queen Elizabeth I, the English colonists crossed the Atlantic and reached the soil of North America in search of permanent homes. The first permanent English settlement was established in America in 1607. The name of that place was given as James Town. The region in which that place was situated was called Virginia. The Whole area was fertile for cultivation[1].

James I (March 24, 1603- March 27, 1625) succeeded the last *Tudor* monarch of England and Ireland, as *Elizabeth I*, who died without issue. He then ruled England, Scotland and Ireland for 22 years, until his death at the age of 58. During the time of Elizabeth, Protestantism was well established in England. Among the Protestants, the more austere and more orthodox people were known as the Puritans. The Protestants in general and the Puritans in particular were hostile to Catholicism. But King James I was a Catholic. His religious policy displeased the Puritans so much that they decided to leave England and settle at some new place in order to practice their religious faith freely. They did not like to remain under the English Church.

Those pious Puritans were mostly poor and simple-minded village people. Their sole aim was to follow a religion independent of external control. When they found it impossible to do it in their own country they decided to leave it for good. These people came to be known as the Pilgrims or the Pilgrim Fathers. In the year 1620, the Pilgrim Fathers left England from the port of Plymouth in a ship named May Flower. They sailed towards North America. On arrival there, they established a colony and named it as Plymouth in an area called Massachusetts.

A greater number of the Puritans left England during the reign of Charles I, a devout Catholic like his father James I was the *King of England, King of Scotland,* and *King of Ireland* from *27 March 1625* until his *execution* in 1649. There was the desire to escape the King's religious tyranny as well as burdens of an old social system. There was the temptation of a better economic life on the soil of a more prosperous land. It was not only from England that the pilgrims left for America, but also from Germany, Ireland and Holland. Of course, the number of Englishmen was much greater than the number of other European races. The climate of the new continent and its unlimited expansion proved attractive. The soil of North America was also seen to be very fertile for cultivation of various crops. The new continent, as if, opened for the Englishmen unlimited prospects of a bright future. In course of time, the English settlements became permanent colonies. As many as thirteen English colonies came to exist on the Atlantic coast of America, slowly rising into prosperity and prominence in their own ways.

Now after their material prosperity there was a growing concern among the colonists that they should form a separate identity than to remain a colony of England. Several causes contributed to the separation of America from the main colony. One fact is certain that the relations between America and Britain was from the very beginning. Their culture, language, political behavior and outlook were more or less same in many fronts. On the contrary certain causes, which include a) progressive outlook, b) economic and social newness, c) political and physical separateness from the England, d) Economic exploitation of England and finally e) removal of French fear after the French defeat in 1763 in Canada, encouraged the new settlers in America to think of separation from the mother country.

Under the above mentioned circumstances the American colony has been separated from England. But the impression England has left in that land remains forever. Certain factors led to the establishment of special ties between the US and UK.

The people of America were more or less English or European in composition[2]. So their relationship with Europe in general and England in particular was cordial. With the passing of time both part of the Atlantic growing gradually on all fronts, materially, politically and democratically. As nation state arrived at a position for better relationship with other country, both the countries again came in term in the name of international relations.

CHURCHILL AND FORMULATION OF "ALLIANCE"

Great powers like the US and the UK manufactures myths in international relations. Their relations are particularly prone to myth-making which through the passing of time tend to turn into truth. The relationship between the US and the UK is a case study to prove this maxim. The special relationship between the US and UK is often defined as such as the two speak a common language[3]. It is this fact that combines with a shared history and culture to suggest that there is a natural political affinity between the two nations. The United States was after all, the product of a colonial rebellion against Britain. The creation of a democratic republic under the provisions of a written constitution was an explicit rejection of contemporary British values.

In the inter-war years America allowed a policy of isolationism, seeking to distance herself from European affairs. The Wall Street Crash of 1929 however had a drastic effect on the fragile European economies and is believed to be the origin of the phrase: "When America sneezes Europe catches the cold". The term "special relationship" was first coined to describe the strong ties forged between US President Franklin D Roosevelt and Winston Churchill during World War II. While discussing military and diplomatic strategy, the two struck up a deep friendship and exchanged thousands of messages and phone calls.

At a functional level, in terms of American and British

foreign policy, during the cold war, there were a number of occasions when the special relationship seemed more apparent than real, notably when the questions of taking military action overseas was at stake.

Sir Winston Churchill is often regarded as Britain's soldier, statesman and scholar par excellence, and he is a source of great national pride for many (and shame for others). After World War II, in which his strength and leading role were undeniable, Churchill suffered a landslide defeat to Clement Atlee's Labour Party. But even as Leader of the Opposition Churchill continued to give inspiring speeches around the World.

The origins of the special relationship are usually traced to his speech on "The Sinews of Peace", made in Fulton Missouri, President Harry Truman's home town, on 5 March 1946. In this speech the British wartime leader committed his enormous prestige in the United States to suggest the need for "a fraternal association of the English speaking peoples" a special relationship between the British Commonwealth and Empire and the United States. It was in the same speech that Churchill also famously described the partitioning of Europe between communist and non-communist nations in terms of the "iron curtain" that was descending across the continent. The battle line for cold war thus drawn: of the war-time alliance between America, Britain and the Soviet Union – there is no mention of France in this – the stage was set for Anglo-American agreement on the need to contain Soviet expansionism, not only in Europe, but also in world wide. In Churchill's words, "Now, while still pursuing the method of realizing our overall strategic concept, I come to the crux of what I have traveled here to say. Neither the sure prevention of war, nor the continuous rise of world organization will be gained without what I have called the fraternal association of the English-speaking peoples. This means a special relationship between the British Commonwealth and Empire and the United

States. This is no time for generalities, and I will venture to be precise. Fraternal association requires not only the growing friendship and mutual understanding between our two vast but kindred systems of society, but the continuance of the intimate relationship between our military advisers, leading to common study of potential dangers, the similarity of weapons and manuals of instructions, and to the interchange of officers and cadets at technical colleges. It should carry with it the continuance of the present facilities for mutual security by the joint use of all Naval and Air Force bases in the possession of either country all over the world. This would perhaps double the mobility of the American Navy and Air Force. It would greatly expand that of the British Empire Forces and it might well lead, if and as the world calms down, to important financial savings. Already we use together a large number of islands; more may well be entrusted to our joint care in the near future[4]."

Churchill expressed tremendous faith in English speaking while he said, "If the population of the English-speaking Commonwealths be added to that of the United States with all that such co-operation implies in the air, on the sea, all over the globe and in science and in industry, and in moral force, there will be no quivering, precarious balance of power to offer its temptation to ambition or adventure. On the contrary, there will be an overwhelming assurance of security[5]."

The question of how the United States should engage the world is an old one in American history. The framers confronted the question only four years after ratifying the constitution when England went war with France. President George Washington ultimately opted for neutrality, disappointing partisans on both sides. The hero of Valley Forge calculated that the small and fragile experiment in republican government would likely be crushed if it joined a battle between the world's two greatest powers[6].

America's relationship with Europe remained an issue

throughout Washington's presidency. He discussed the topic at length in his magisterial address announcing his decision to retire to his beloved Mount Vernon. He encouraged his countrymen to pursue peace and commercial relations. "Harmony, liberal intercourse with all nations is recommended by policy, humanity, and interest." But he discouraged them from tying their political fate to the decisions of others. "It is our true policy, to steer clear of permanent alliances with any portion of the foreign world", Washington counseled. His argument for keeping political ties to a minimum was simple: "Europe has a set of primary interests which to us have none or a very remote relation. Hence she must be engaged in frequent controversies, the causes of which are essentially foreign to our concerns[7]."

Washington concluded his Farewell Address by noting, "I dare not hope (that my advice) will make the strong and lasting impression I could wish[8]." His vision of an America that traded happily with Europe but otherwise stood apart from it became the cornerstone of the new nation's foreign policy.

Britain emerged from the Second World War as one of the big three: perhaps not a superpower like the United States and the Soviet Union, but the third wealthiest power in the world. Britain's reputation was higher than perhaps at any time in the twentieth century. But it was clearly exhausted from its efforts. Even in the closing months of the war its strength was visibly declining. In June 1944 British Empire troops deployed in Normandy had equaled those of the Americans: by March 1945 only about a quarter of the troops under the command of the Supreme Allied Commander (SAC) General Eisenhower were British. By the end of the conflict the British wartime debt stood at £22 billion. The post-war debt of the United States was in per capita terms much the same, but the American national income had doubled during the war, and went on in the next five years to double again. The British emerged from the war almost bankrupt. Both countries had learned that the cost of victory comes high, but for the British the cost was so high that it threatened to lower permanently their economy and their standard of living[9].

British power was so rapidly eclipsed during the last months of the war that the United States became convinced that, together with the Soviet Union, it could construct a post war world order largely without British assistance. And yet the UK spent the next 25 years as a major world power. The British retained conscription maintained a relatively large force in uniform (800,000 men and women in 1951) and spent about 10 percent of their GNP on defense (as opposed to 3 percent in pre-war years). This was a remarkable effort at a time when they continued to be beset by shortages, rationing and austerity measures at home. Not until the late 1960s did they begin to see themselves as a medium-sized power.

In short, in the 25 years that followed the surrender of German forces at Luneberg Heath, Britain continued to play the role of a world power, tracing a path that had seemed questionable even at the turn of the century. The next challenge to the European balance was already identifiable. The reality, real or perceived, of the Soviet threat meant there could be no ten-year rule as there had been in the 1920s, when the government had based its defence spending on the assumption that there was no immediate prospect of war with any power or combination of powers.

Secondly, Britain may have emerged from the war economically weak but it was by far the strongest European power. In 1948 British defence spending exceeded that of all European countries. Even as late as 1952 Britain's arms production was greater than that of all other European NATO members combined. As a result the British believed they could not confine their interest to Europe. As the first post-war foreign secretary, Ernest Bevin, remarked, 'Europe is not enough; it is not big enough.'

CONVERGENCE AND CONFLICT IN THE US-UK RELATIONS

The US and the UK, at times they seem like the best of friends, at others they are barely speaking. The graph below is designed to find out more about the highs and lows of the two countries' special relationship.

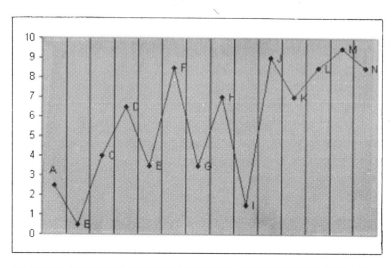

Identified in the graph as	Years	Event/ incident	Point in the Relational Scale (out of 10)
A	1773	Boston Tea Party	2.5
B	1775-81	War of Independence	0.5
C	1861-65	American Civil War	4
D	1914-18	World War I	6.5
E	1929	Wall Street Crash	3.5
F	1946	Churchill and Roosevelt	8.5
G	1956	Suez Canal Crisis	3.5
H	1962	Cuban Missile Crisis	7
I	1965-73	Vietnam War	1.5
J	1985	Thatcher and Reagan	9
K	1991	Gulf War	7

L	1997-2000	Blair and Clinton	8.5
M	2001	After September 11, 2001	9.5
N	2003	Iraq War	8.5

When Thatcher and Reagan assumed leadership of their respective countries, they unfolded an era in the history of their nations, which will go down as one of the most spectacular inter-state relationship. The reason for this lies in their personal factor which was the strong point in their relations. Thatcher and Reagan were ideological twins in the true sense of term. Both leaders were archconservatives and fanatical in their hatred towards communism. Reagan wanted America to stand tall and Thatcher too wanted to boost up Britain's image. The period when the two leaders came to power was also a significant factor, which influenced their policy reactions and overall perceptions.

The Reagan administration took a decisive step towards regaining the American superiority and stealing a march over the Soviet Union was its announcement of the Strategic Defence Initiative in March 1983. This was aimed at ensuring an antimissile shield in space thereby restoring America's nuclear invulnerability. The announcement of the SDI programme came as a surprise to the Thatcher Government for, in this instance, the US had no advance consultation with its allies. Britain criticized the SDI as being impractical and aiming to regain a superiority that was not only not needed but also not realizable. On the whole, the initial reaction of the Thatcher Government was to extend limited support for the SDI programme. There were very few public signals from which one could glean the British response and reactions. Reagan had, for sometime, been pressing for support from the allies and Thatcher could ill-afford to continue to be evasive on a subject, which was increasingly becoming an obsession with Reagan. The '4-point' agreement reached between Reagan and Thatcher in December 1984 was as follows:

1.   The aim of the US and Western Europe was not to achieve superiority, but to maintain balance, taking into account the Soviet moves.

2.   The SDI-related development would, in view of treaty obligations, have to be a matter of negotiations.

3.   The overall aim was to enhance rather than undercut deterrence, and

4.   East-West negotiations should try to achieve security with reduced levels of offensive systems on both sides.

On another occasion the Falklands War was an armed conflict between Argentina and the United Kingdom over the Falkland Islands between March and June 1982. On April 2 1982 General Galtieri's military junta invaded the Falklands. Though surprised by an Argentine attack on the South Atlantic islands, Britain mustered a naval task force to engage the Argentine navy and air force, landed Royal Marines and after heavy combat eventually prevailed and the islands remained in British hands. In Argentina, the conclusion of the war led to the downfall of the military junta.

Legally, the United States had military treaty obligations to both parties in the war, bound to the UK by NATO and to Argentina by the Inter-American Treaty of Reciprocal Assistance. Alexander Haig, the United States Secretary of State, briefly (April 8–April 30, 1982) headed a "shuttle diplomacy" mission before President Ronald Reagan declared U.S. support for Britain and instituted sanctions against Argentina. Support of the USA was initially equivocal, and is reported to be the result of urging by Haig and Caspar Weinberger, who advised the President to support the UK. Reagan famously declared at the time that he could not understand why two allies were arguing over "that little ice-cold bunch of land down there". Reagan sympathized with Galtieri because of his anti-Communist position. He had received a reportedly warm reception when he visited the US.

The Reagan administration had opted for a high-profile stand in its opposition to communism and terrorism. Use of military force and intervention, if necessary, became acceptable instruments. The US intervention in Grenada in October 1983 is one such instance the use of force on the part of America and the fact that Grenada was a Commonwealth country were ample enough reasons why the Thatcher government could not remain mute on this. But it resisted pressure from publicly criticizing the US action for a long time. However, the government was forced to take a firm stand.

THE CHECKERED PHASE

In the checkered history of Anglo-American relations, the decade of the 1980s could well be classified as the high noon of their special relationship in the post-war period when Britain and United States were led by two outstanding leaders – Margaret Thatcher and Ronald Reagan. It is true that their personal chemistry, as in the case of Churchill and Roosevelt in the 1940s, played a significant role in it. As persons both there leaders held each other and their countries in high esteem. While Reagan believed that Britain and America were 'kindred nations of like-minded people' and should face their tests together. Thatcher was moved by a conviction that 'an enduring alliance with America was fundamental for Britain'. They set their agenda for 1980s at their first official meeting it, which took place in Washington in February 1981. In that meeting while Reagan unequivocally stated that "absolute trust between the Prime Minister of the United Kingdom and the President of the United States will continue to be the hallmark of Anglo-American cooperation", Mrs. Thatcher reciprocated by saying that "your problems will be our problems, and when you look for friends, we will be there". The next eight years witnessed how they tried to live up to this agenda which they set for themselves and how, in the process it turned out to be the most spectacular period of Anglo-American special relationship[10].

But, for all their coalescence of ideas and perceptions, the harmony was punctured on more that one occasions by occasional bouts of unilateralism on the part of America. The announcement of the SDI by President Reagan, the Reykjavik Summit and the decision to invade Grenada were all instances which was no prior consultation between Britain and the United States and always nearly with the British position looking woefully exposed as a result of lack of information. Convergence on political issues, barring the occasional tangle, was far easier to achieve that on knotty economic ones. The long-drawn out trade disputes between America and Britain showed Britain sharing more in common with the EEC partners and less with America.

Leaving aside the rhetoric and hyperbole it remains a fact that the relationship is by and large a one-sided affair. Despite the closeness that marked their ties, neither Thatcher nor Reagan were blind to the actual power positions. This was a matter, which no amount of wishing away on Thatcher's part could obliterate. And, as was the case, Reagan did not back away from adopting unilateral postures when American interests demanded likewise. The poignant truth, which these incidents revealed, was that America could afford to by pass Britain, blissful in the knowledge that for Britain the American connection was too strong to be discarded. Since Thatcher and Reagan shared an excellent personal rapport, Thatcher enjoyed the liberty of voicing her opinions in a forthright manner. She had at her immediate disposal direct telephone links with Reagan, making it possible for her to establish communication without loss of time[11].

On the hole, the eight eventful years that marked the Thatcher-Reagan era have been one of the most spectacular and intimate periods in their bilateral relations.

The Reagan and Thatcher era witnessed the best of the relationship between the United States and the United Kingdom. Both of these leaders fully realized the power, prowess and potentials of each other. With this they have also visualized the fact that in close company of each they may dominate the world politics. Their common thinking and outlook on many fronts were taken seriously. The solid foundations built by these two leaders over the period were pronounced as the base for future relationship of these two nations. The two long terms served by both President Reagan and Prime Minister Thatcher provided the time to cement the ties despite the kind of animosity over some of the issues involving the two nations. After the exit of Reagan and Thatcher, two new leaders came into picture of the world politics in the United States and in Great Britain. Bill Clinton and John Major have taken their position as President of United States and as Prime Minister of Great Britain respectively.

Earlier, John Major's support for President George Herbert Bush's election bid had taken the toll on the relationship, as experts stated predicting a rough relationship between these two leaders. But with the passing of time both these leaders shown their mature mind and consider the international affairs seriously over their personal choices. Relations improved gradually with the passing of time and both the countries came to the same table to break the bread together. On the part of the Great Britain, it is always safe and profitable to be sided with superpower United States. Britain's diminishing position in the world affairs made it easy for the United States to take them in to their league easily and at their own discretion.

2

TOUCHING THORNY ISSUES: TOGETHER & SEPARATE

"THE ALLIANCE" MEETING THE CHALLENGES

The term Anglo-American relations refer to bilateral relations between the United Kingdom and the United States. The special relationship is a term used to emphasize the warmth and cordiality of the relationship between the leaders and military forces of the two countries and used to describe Anglo-American relations in a positive light; however, Anglo-American relations have survived times of war and conflict as well as peace with close cooperation. The term transatlantic relations as used in the United Kingdom usually refers to Anglo-American relations, as the United States and the United Kingdom lie on opposite sides of the Atlantic Ocean. As used in the United States, the term can refer to either Anglo-American relations or to relations between the United States and Europe.

The special relationship is the phrase used to characterize what advocates view as the warm political, diplomatic, historical, and cultural relations between the United States and member nations of the Commonwealth of Nations. The phrase is more frequently used by some British and American commentators to mean the relationship between the United Kingdom and the United States, and its advocates view it as is the chief benefit-in-action of the Anglo-sphere.

The United States has close relations with many friendly allied countries, among them Canada, Australia and Israel are prominent. Similarly, the United Kingdom has close relations with such European Union (EU) nations as France and Germany, and of course with major Commonwealth countries (and former British colonies): Singapore, South Africa, Canada, Australia and New Zealand. The most common usage of the term "special relationship" nevertheless usually refers to an Anglo-American relationship.

The special relationship is based on historical, cultural, economic and ideological ties, and is often evoked at times of difficulty for either party. Built on the principle of interdependence, most American commentators had until relatively recently construed the special relationship as a "one-way street", namely that Britain relied heavily on the United States to promote its affairs further in international relations. This was certainly true from the perspective of post-second World War Britain, until the resurgence of the British economy; post Margaret Thatcher's radical economic and social reforms while Prime Minister of Britain. Moreover, Thatcher's exceptionally close political and personal relationship with and influence on US President Ronald Reagan is widely-regarded as having contributed in part to the international political climate which ultimately led to the dissolution of the Soviet Union.

COLD WAR AND ANGLO-AMERICAN ALLIANCE

At the end of World War II, the United States and the United Kingdom became two of the founding members of the United Nations, as well as two of the five permanent members of the Security Council. They were suspicious of the motives of their former ally, the USSR, under Stalin. Rising tensions between the capitalist and communist powers led to the Cold War and an era of close cooperation between the United States and the United Kingdom which included the formation of the North Atlantic Treaty Organization, a mutual-defense alliance. As the British Empire declined throughout the world, the United States became one of two world superpowers along with the Soviet Union, while Britain became the most important and influential alliance partner with the United States on the American side of the Cold War. Forces from both countries were involved in the Korean War, fighting under United Nations command. The United States had become the leading world power and pursued a mixed anti-colonial anti-communist policy, refusing to support the French attempt to retain Indochina and threatening to impose financial sanctions on Britain over Suez. As the Americans concentrated on their technological rivalry with the Soviet Union and waged an unpopular proxy war in Vietnam, Anti-Americanism became a factor in Europe, which partially reached Britain due to Suez and Vietnam. However, Harold Wilson refused to send British troops to Vietnam. Besides protests against the introduction of medium-range weapons which might allow a nuclear war to be confined to Europe became a feature of British politics in the eighties.

In 1969, the USSR, the United States, and about 100 other nations signed a treaty banning the spread of nuclear weapons to countries not possessing them. Strategic Arms Limitation Talks (SALT) between the Soviet Union and the United States began in 1969, and they were continuing in 1973. When President Nixon visited Moscow in 1972, an agreement partially limiting strategic arms was signed (an agreement that was renewed during Nixon's 1974 visit to the USSR), along with accords on cooperation in space exploration, environmental matters, and trade. By this time Soviet-U.S. relations were described as having entered an era of détente and the cold war was said to have ended. In 1973, Brezhnev toured the United States and met with Nixon.

A major objective of Soviet foreign policy in the early 1970s was to gain official recognition of the post–World War II settlement in Europe. In 1972 the USSR, the United States, Great Britain, and France signed an accord regularizing the position of Berlin.

With the inauguration of Richard Nixon as president and the appointment of Henry Kissinger as his President's assistant on national security affairs, the United States tried a new approach toward containment, officially labeled détente. In Kissinger's words, détente sought to create "a vested interest in cooperation and restraint," "an environment in which competitors can regulate and restrain their differences and ultimately move from competition to cooperation."

As both a goal of and a strategy for expanding the superpowers' mutual interest in restraint, détente symbolized an important shift in their global relationship. In diplomatic jargon, relations between the Soviets and Americans were "normalized", as the perception of conflict and war receded. As a strategy of containment, on the other hand, the objective now was "self-containment on the part of the Russians".

Arms control stood at the center of the dialogue surrounding détente. The Strategic Arms Limitation Talks (SALT) became the test of détente's viability. Initiated in 1969, the SALT negotiations sought to restrain the threatening, expensive, and spiraling arms race. They produced two sets of agreements, the first in 1972 (SALT I) and the second in 1979 (SALT II). With their signing, each of the superpowers gained the principal objective it had sought in détente. The Soviet Union gained recognition of its status as the United States' coequal; the United States gained a commitment from the Soviet Union to moderate its quest for preeminent power in the world. The SALT II agreement was not brought to fruition, however. It was signed but never ratified by the US. The failure underscored the real differences that still separated the superpowers.

As part of the emerging East-West détente, in November 1972 talks opened in Helsinki to prepare for a Conference on Security and Cooperation in Europe. On 1 August 1975 leaders from the participating nations signed the Helsinki Final Act. It included three "baskets." Basket I contained a "Declaration on Principles Guiding Relations between Participating States." It legitimated the present borders within Europe, outlawed the use of force, prohibited intervention in the internal affairs of any state, and required respect for human rights and the self-determination of peoples.

Basket II addressed "Cooperation in the Field of Economics, of Science and Technology, and of the Environment." It sought to encourage increased East-West trade, scientific collaboration, and industrial management, and recognized the *interdependence* of societies across Europe.

Basket III dealt with "Cooperation in Humanitarian and other Fields." It provided a basis for increased person-to-person contacts between Eastern and Western Europe, encouraged the freer movement of peoples and ideas, and promised to facilitate the reunification of families long separated by Cold War conflict.

In 1973 European Security Conference, which the USSR hoped would help make permanent the status-quo in Europe, formally opened. A second phase of SALT talks began, as well as negotiations for a mutual and balanced reduction of forces in Europe. The USSR gave considerable assistance to underdeveloped countries during the Brezhnev era. During the 1973 Arab-Israeli War the Soviet Union played a major role in equipping both the Egyptian and Syrian armies yet the Arabs lost.

After the return of the Labour Party to power in the 1974, the essential outlines of British policy towards the Soviet block remained unchanged. Both the Wilson and the Callaghan governments sought to play a constructive role in East-West relations – Wilson made his much publicized trip to Moscow in 1975, for example, where he agreed a 1 billion Pound trade and credits package – but it was becoming increasingly clear even then that the détente process was in serious trouble. As criticism of that process mounted in the West and the rhetoric about a 'new' or 'second' cold war began to be voiced by a rising New Right on both sides of the Atlantic, there was even less opportunity for Britain to play a significant détente role in the second half of the 1970s than there had been in the first. Indeed, the profound ambivalence towards the whole process of East-West détente, which had been a feature of the British approach since the beginning of that decade, was if anything more marked after 1974. The potential costs rather than the benefits of East-West détente appeared to exercise on British more and they dictated a cautious approach.

When, for example, President Carter sought to make human rights the centre-piece of his foreign policy in 1977-78, the British became concerned that such high-profile pressure on the Soviet system could provoke confrontation rather than promote cooperation. Thus, there was a clear preference for a low-key approach on human rights at the Conference on Security and Cooperation in Europe (CSCE) Review Conference in Belgrade. The British fear was that too much emphasis on change in Eastern Europe might not only be counterproductive in terms of its purposes, but could spill over and obstruct or undermine the moves towards accommodation that were being made at the state level. The Callaghan government was prepared to press the Soviet Union to uphold the Final Act commitments, but was 'sensitive to the dangers of pressing too hard too publicly. The CSCE process had turned into a weapon that could be used by the West'.

During the same period, the British role in the Comprehensive Test Ban (CTB) talks, which began in June 1977, provides an interesting illustration of both the extent to which Britain had been marginalized in the détente process and also the tough line that the British now taken on détente. By 1979, according to Ray Garthoff, the British were taking an even harder line that the Americans on the issue of verification. Having attempted unsuccessfully to persuade the British to increase the number of onsite seismic stations they would be prepared to accept, Carter apparently proposed to Brezhnev at the Vienna summit in June that they should proceed with a CTB without Britain if necessary. However, both superpowers had already decided that a strategic arms agreement should take priority over securing a comprehensive test ban treaty.

The tone of speeches by Labour Minister in the mid-1970s show very clearly the continuing British commitment to détente but also, with Western eyes focusing anxiously on Soviet involvement in Southern Africa, the determination to balance contributions to that process by ensuring that the West's ability to deter the Soviet Union was undiminished. A speech in January 1976 by the then Foreign Secretary James Callaghan, for example, expressed his concern that:

In the last few years the Soviet Union has added to its existing numerical advantage over NATO in manpower and conventional weapons in Central Europe, an approximate strategic nuclear parity with the United States in addition to rapidly expanding its navy and improving its air force and missile system[12].

Is conclusion was that 'as long as the Soviet Union and her allies devote so much of their resources to armaments, détente must also be matched by an adequate defence capability that its sufficient to deter.' The contribution of Roy Hattersley to a Commons debate on East-West relations the following month was even more hawkish. Though he was concerned in his speech to defend détente in general and the Helsinkin Accords in particular, he warned the House that 'the policy of détente has to be pursued with the greatest possible caution. It can proceed only on the secure foundation of a strong and effective Western Alliance'.

It is of interest that Hattersley went on to note the absence of any 'disagreement between the two Front Benches' on this balanced approach to détente. Labour spokesmen at this time were to only reacting to a worsening climate of East-West relations after Helsinki, but they were also responding to attempts by the Conservatives, and their new leader Margaret Thatcher in particular, to suggest that the Wilson government was rather too keen on promoting close links with the Soviet Union and was bent on pursuing East-West détente with something less than 'the greatest possible caution'. Although Mrs. Thatcher made few statements on East-West relations in opposition, two speeches she did make not only set out her position on détente very clearly but also established the beginnings of an international recognition on this issue, which would be very significant after she became prime minister in 1979.

She was not against détente, she told Chelsea Conservatives in July 1975, just before the signing of the Helsinki Accords. Indeed, détente sounds a fine word. And to the extent that there has really been a relaxation in international tension, it is a fine thing. But the fact remains that throughout this decade of détente, the armed forces of the Soviet Union have increased, are increasing and show not signs of diminishing.

Tutored by the historian Robert Conquest, a trenchant critic of détente during this period, Mrs Thatcher was already firmly of the New Right view that détente was not merely an illusion about a dangerous Soviet ploy to enable Moscow to extend its influence over the West. The assumption that this tactic was working implied that it was no longer appropriate to pursue a balanced policy of détente and defence. It was necessary to pour all the resources of government into increasing defence expenditure to match the growing soviet threat. Even expanding trade credits to Moscow, as Wilson had done in 1975, was dangerous, because it would enable the Soviet government to divert even more resources to its military machine.

The British-American relationship is based on ties of history and kinship, but also on a unique record of cooperation in the intelligence and nuclear fields stemming from the Second World War. These provide both the rationale and the requirements for bilateral consultation. The relationship with the United Kingdom is not America's only close link with Europe. The United States also has significant common interests and ties with other states, particularly the Federal Republic of Germany. The ties with Britain, however, are in many ways the closest. In the economic field serious issues in finance, trade, taxation, and such difficult issues as civil aviation have been resolved. Thorough consultation preceded the deployment of intermediate-range nuclear weapons in Europe. Although this was a European initiative, the United States clearly took into account the particular circumstances of the United Kingdom, and consulted London bilaterally. Because of the virtual identity of views between President Reagan and Mrs Thatcher on South Africa, consultation on that subject has been close. At the time of the Carter administration the London government worked closely with the Americans on the questions of Rhodesia and Namibia. The United Kingdom, along with Canada, West Germany, France and the United States, were formal members of a 'Contact Group'. The United States and the United Kingdom also consulted closely during the Carter administration on arms sales to China. In the case of the US raid on Libya, prior consultation did take place on the question of the use of the American bases in Britain where the F-111 aircraft were stationed. The Times quoted Mrs. Thatcher:

'President Reagan informed me last week that the US intended to take such action. He sought our support under the consultation arrangements which have continued under successive governments for over 30 years[13].'

The consultation arrangements she referred to were described by Malcolm Rutherford in the Financial Times:

> The known pain of the Anglo-American agreement reached between Mr. Attlee and President Truman in 1951 and endorsed by Winston Churchill in 1952 runs as follows: 'Under arrangements made for the common defence, the US has the use of certain bases in the United Kingdom. We reaffirm the understanding that the use of these bases in an emergency would be a matter for joint decision by Her Majesty's Government and the US Government in the light of the circumstances prevailing at the time.' Consultation with Britain at the time of the Libyan raid, however, was solely on the question of the use of the US bases. The United States had made the decision to attack Libya without prior consultation. American officials, however, believe the matter should not have been a surprise; the United States had given Britain and other Europeans ample evidence of its deep concern over Colonel Muammar Qadhafi's support for terrorism. Efforts have been made to consult and to smooth ruffled feelings after unilateral actions by the United States have created serious problems with its allies. After the decision not to manufacture the neutron bomb in 1978, President Carter sent Secretary of Defense Harold Brown to London to explain' the position. After Reykjavik, British and other allied views were made known through various channels, and President Reagan met Mrs Thatcher at Camp David. Even the Skybolt decision, which provoked such criticism at the time, was followed by a successful meeting at Nassau, and the establishment of cooperation on an alternative system. Yet despite the efforts on both sides of the Atlantic, and

the long period of concern over this issue, serious problems exist which create political difficulties for governmental leaders in both Britain and America[14].

Whatever the reality of consultation, in each of the instances cited above, the public impression in Britain has been of the United States proceeding without paying adequate attention to British official opinion. Such perceptions pose political problems for leaders who are seen as unable to maintain British interests in the relationship with the United States. Unforeseen American policy decisions, especially if they involve military action or are otherwise deemed dangerous, create doubts about US leadership of the Western alliance and strengthen the voices calling for a more independent Europe. This, in turn, affects how Europeans regard the sincerity and policies of the Soviet Union. Even when British and allied concerns are taken into account after consultation, the results may not necessarily quieten apolitical storm. President Carter took European concerns into account in his final decision on the neutron bomb. Richard Burt, then a reporter for the New York Times, wrote:

"Over the last three weeks, Mr Carter's advisers and European leaders, particularly Chancellor Helmut Schmidt of West Germany, had sought to deflect Mr Carter's tentative decision against production, not hoping to reverse it but only to insure that the weapon was not halted altogether. In the end they succeeded and Mr Carter's announcement on his decision called for continued modernization of those weapons that ultimately might be armed with neutron warheads. That concession did not quieten European unhappiness with the decision. There is no lack of communication between the United States and Britain. Much of it stems from the 'special relationship' that was established during and after the Second World War and has been reaffirmed by most American presidents. The United Kingdom is often the first to know of

American intentions and decisions, a fact that endears neither Britain nor the United States to other European allies[15]."

Henry Kissinger refers in his book, *The White House Years*, to the close ties between Britain and America as he examines the beginning premises of the new administration of President Richard Nixon:

"For the special relationship with Britain was peculiarly impervious to abstract theories. It did not depend on formal arrangements; it derived in part from the memory of Britain's heroic wartime effort; it reflected the common language and culture of two sister peoples. It owed no little to the superb self-discipline by which Britain had succeeded in maintaining political influence after its physical power had waned. When Britain emerged from the Second World War too enfeebled to insist on its views, it wasted no time in mourning an irretrievable past. British leaders instead tenaciously elaborated the 'special relationship' with us. This was, in effect, a pattern of consultation so matter-of-factly intimate that it became psychologically impossible to ignore British views. They evolved a habit of meetings so regular that anonymous American action came to seem to violate club rules. Above all, they used effectively an abundance of wisdom and trustworthiness of conduct so exceptional that American leaders saw it in their self-interest obtain British advice before making major decisions. It was an extraordinary relationship because it rested on no legal claims; it was formalized by no document; it was carried forward by succeeding British governments as if no alternative were conceivable. While some may consider this an idealized statement, nevertheless this special relationship is continued through a variety of channels of communication. Embassies of British nations in Washington and London are staffed with experts capable of consulting not only on bilateral matters, but on Europe and other areas of the world as well. In Washington, in a government in which normal access for diplomats above assistant-secretary-of-state level is relatively rare, the British ambassador is able see higher-echelon officials on a regular basis. Personal friendships are formed between British and American diplomats that outlast individual periods of assignment. The closeness of the ties at the middle levels has, at times, helped smooth over problems that have occurred between individuals higher up. The diplomatic contacts are supplemented at frequent intervals by meetings between the American Secretary of State and the British Foreign Secretary. Secure telephones today make possible conversations at the ministerial level between meetings. The American President and the British Prime Minister meet less frequently, but, when they do, the common language and the common heritage make these 'summit' conversations easier than most. Moreover, the practice has developed of 'back channel' communication between foreign policy advisers at No. 10, Downing Street, and national security advisers in the White House. Since the administration of President John F. Kennedy, with the growth in power of the National Security Council staff, this executive channel has been more and more the route for the discussion of sensitive issues, sometimes without the knowledge of the respective foreign offices[16]."

EUROPEAN UNION AND US-UK ALLIANCE

The economic relationship between the European Union and the United States is perhaps the most defining feature of the global economy. The integration is broader and deeper than between any two other political regions in the world. The EU and U.S. account for 37 percent of global merchandise trade and 45 percent of world trade in services. The partnership is also the single most important driver of global economic growth, trade, and prosperity. And bilateral economic ties are increasing every year. The EU and the U.S. are each other's main trading partners in goods and services and account for the largest bilateral trade relationship in the world as well as providing each other the most important source of foreign direct investment (FDI). The huge amount of bilateral trade and investment illustrates the high degree of interdependence of the two economies. Bilateral trade between the EU and U.S. amounts to over $1 billion a day; investment links are even more substantial, totaling over $1.8 trillion a year. Each partner creates jobs for about 6 million workers on each side of the Atlantic, and EU-U.S. trade accounts for almost 40 percent of world trade.

Despite the importance of the relationship, there is a long list of US-EU trade disputes. Quarrels range from unresolved issues, such as the EU refusal to allow imports of hormone treated beef despite a contrary WTO ruling, to those disputes that are only just about to erupt, such as the potential row over the imposition of tariffs on US steel imports. All in all there are currently 14 active bilateral US-EU cases in the WTO. This means that even though EU-US trade accounts for less than 22% of EU trade, it comprises over 47% of the EU's WTO disputes. By contrast, the EU currently has not a single WTO dispute with its preferential non-EU Member State partners in Europe and Africa, although 32% of its trade takes place with these countries. These numbers point to a preference by the US and the EU to settle their bilateral trade differences in the WTO rather than through informal negotiations, and in the past this approach proved rather successful.

The European Union and the United States have ended their long-running battle over bananas in 2001, removing a major irritant from trans-Atlantic relations but leaving other issues outstanding. The compromise proposes to end a dispute that has dragged on since 1993. In 1999, the United States won a case in the World Trade Organization, which agreed that the EU's banana import quota system discriminated against American producers to the benefit of growers in former European colonies. Under the agreement, subject to approval by EU member states, the European Parliament and the WTO, the United States would drop tariffs totaling about $191 million a year that it imposed on a range of European goods in response to the WTO ruling. In return, Europe would make it slightly easier for U.S. companies to export bananas to Europe from plantations in Latin America in the short term. Over the long term, the market would be opened further[17].

The two sides said the agreement ensured fair access to the European market for bananas of all origins while continuing to protect vulnerable producers in Africa, the Pacific and Caribbean, including territories that have no other source of export income. In a joint statement, the EU's trade commissioner, Pascal Lamy, and the U.S. secretary of commerce, Donald Evans, described the agreement as "a significant breakthrough." The statement also was signed by the U.S. trade representative, Robert Zoellick[18].

Another source of friction is the EU ban on American beef produced with growth hormones. The United States contends the ban is discriminatory. The EU argues that it is excluding hormone-treated beef over questions about its safety. The Union is conducting several studies on the impact of hormones on the environment and human health and has offered compensation to the United States pending their outcome.

Trade relations have increasingly moved into the public spotlight, and trade has rapidly become a high-profile business. In addition, while traditional trade disputes were concerned with market access or industrial policy, sometime the EU and the US find themselves entangled above all in ideological clashes. The EU thus opted to disregard the WTO's ruling on its ban on hormone treated beef not because it seeks to protect European farmers, but because there is widespread agreement within Europe that hormone-treated beef is harmful to consumers' health. And the European Parliament decided to create even more stringent rules for the labeling of GMOs, not to keep U.S. products out of the markets, but because European consumers fundamentally distrust genetically altered foods.

Though both powers have always faced protectionist pressures from certain industries and interest groups, George W. Bush seems particularly sensitive to the demands of powerful constituencies. The Bush administration has created barriers to imports of lumber, added new tariffs on foreign steel, and signed into law a new Farm Bill, which increases agricultural subsidies considerably.

Section 301 of the U.S. *Trade Act* describes itself as "the principal *statutory* authority under which the United States may impose *trade sanctions* against foreign countries that maintain acts, policies and practices that violate, or deny U.S. rights or benefits under, trade agreements, or are unjustifiable, unreasonable or discriminatory and burden or restrict U.S. commerce." The provision allows the United States Trade Representative (USTR) to initiate an investigation of the trade practices of another country, either on its own initiative, or upon the request of a U.S. citizen.

The Airbus' stand that it would not launch a new medium-sized jetliner before completing its restructuring plan, but the financing of the A350 could exacerbate tensions between the US and the EU. The cost of launching the A350, a long-haul mid-sized plane with seating for 270 to 350 passengers, has been estimated by European aircraft maker Airbus at eight to nine billion euros ($10 to 12 billion). Airbus has been struggling to overcome costly production delays to its A380 super-jumbo program, which is running two years behind schedule. Airbus chief executive Louis Gallois, after a meeting at the company's headquarters in Toulouse, said a decision about the A350 would be made "before the end of November 2005. We cannot launch a new program if we are not sure of being in a competitive situation," he said.

Funding for the A350 poses a dilemma for the European company and the issue has the potential to intensify trade tensions between the United States and the European Union. Airbus is able to call on loans from European governments to cover part of the development costs of the aircraft, but the arrangement is at the center of a long-standing dispute at the World Trade Organization. The US filed a revised complaint at the World Trade Organization in Geneva, charging that the preferential loans available from the French, German, British, and Spanish governments to fund up to one-third of new Airbus aircraft amount to illegal state aid under WTO rules. For its part, the European Union claims that Boeing benefits from illegal state aid through space and defense contracts from the US government.

Then the EU took the United States to the World Trade Organization over a long-standing U.S. law that provided tax breaks for American exporters. The WTO ruled against the United States, finding that the law violates international trade rules. The WTO has given the EU permission to put $4,000 million of punitive import tariffs on U.S. goods if Congress fails to repeal the export tax subsidy. A bill that aims to conform to WTO norms but which would still give some tax advantages to American manufacturers is now before the U.S. House of Representatives.

In another dispute, the EU has challenged U.S. subsidies on steel, which it says discriminate against imported steel. In yet another case, the European Commission announced last week that it has requested "consultations" with Washington over the way the United States calculates anti-dumping duties. That's the first stage of possible legal action at the WTO.

In a statement, EU Trade Commissioner Pascal Lamy asserted that the U.S. practice — called "zeroing" — results in higher anti-dumping penalties of hundreds of millions of Euros on EU exports to the United States. Lamy, a pugnacious Frenchman known for his hard edge is seen as the driving force behind the EU's tough approach to trade issues in recent years.

In another dispute, U.S. government financial regulators rejected EU requests to exempt EU companies from comprehensive new U.S. rules on corporate governance. The U.S. side also said there could be no negotiations on the issue.

The EU is particularly concerned about the burden the rules would place on European auditing firms, and analysts say this could provoke retaliation from the EU in the form of imposition of rules on U.S. companies operating in Europe.

The biggest of all the disputes must surely be the one over genetically modified organisms (GMOs). The United States last month decided to take the EU to the WTO tribunal over Brussels' de facto moratorium on approving foodstuffs containing GMOs. The United States is the biggest backer of GMOs, which allow the development of plants that are resistant to certain pests and bacteria. The EU asserts that these products could have health risks for humans and could also impact the general environment by upsetting the natural plant and insect world. The Commission points out the refusal of many European consumers to buy GMO products, and a European Parliament committee has just demanded laws rather than voluntary measures to control possible GMO contamination of natural crops. U.S. President George W. Bush, in turn, has accused the EU of contributing to starvation in less-developed nations by making farmers there unsure of whether to plant genetically modified crops.

Thus, the trans-Atlantic trade tensions have a political side to them. For instance, to express their rejection of the French stand against the Iraq war, big U.S. companies and senior military officials have stayed away from the 2005 Paris air show, the biggest trade exhibition of its kind in the world. And Senior U.S. Trade Representative Robert Zoellick recently spoke of the sense of "betrayal" felt by many Americans at the

European opposition to the war.

ALLIANCES ON MULTIPLE FRONTS

The relationship between the two partners, however, goes beyond economic ties. The European Union and the United States increasingly share the opportunities and responsibilities of world leadership. Together they work to promote common values, including peace, freedom, and the rule of law; create conditions for harmonious economic development worldwide; advance the stability of international trade, financial, and monetary systems; and aid the economic integration of developing countries and those in transition. Acting on these shared values, the EU and U.S. have played a significant role in promoting the institutions and international norms that helped bring an end to the Cold War and subsequently encouraged global trends toward democratization and market integration. The EU and the U.S. work together to confront global challenges such as terrorism, threats to security and stability, weapons proliferation, drugs, and organized crime. As partners promoting peace and stability, the EU and the United States recognize the impact of regional conflicts, both in the direct consequences of violence, and the wide-ranging, spin-off impact of crime, terrorism, poverty, and disease that can result from such conflicts. The two partners worked side-by-side to bring stability to the Balkans. The EU and the U.S., through the Organisation for Security and Cooperation in Europe (OSCE), are supporting the new Ukrainian government in adapting legislation, structures, and processes to the requirements of a modern democracy. In Afghanistan, the EU and the United States together have provided the lion's share of the international reconstruction effort. In order to help the reconstruction of a democratic and stable Iraq, the European Commission and U.S. government both donate to the International Reconstruction Fund Facility for Iraq (IRFFI) set up under the United Nations and the World Bank. In addition to financial resources, the EU and the U.S. contribute technical expertise and an unbending commitment to the principles of democracy and freedom.

The European Union has a permanent presence in the United States with delegations in Washington, D.C. and New York City. The Washington office was opened in 1954 at the very outset of the six-nation European Coal and Steel Community that would become the EU. The Washington office, the Community's first overseas presence, opened with two Americans occupying two rooms. It now operates with a staff of more than 80 professionals and serves as the EU's representation to the U.S. government and as an information conduit to Washington and the rest of the United States. It is a diplomatic mission but does not have functions such as consular or military affairs that attach to a standard embassy. The New York office was established in 1964 and became the delegation to the United Nations in 1974. The U.S. government has a permanent presence before the EU in Brussels, home to most of the principal EU institutions[19].

Several channels afford private sector and government leaders the opportunity to participate in policy development that affects both the EU and U.S.

Transatlantic Business Dialogue (TABD): The TABD's goal is to help establish a barrier-free transatlantic market which will serve as a catalyst for global trade liberalization and prosperity. Unified markets are needed to create a business environment that will stimulate innovation, economic growth, and more investment as well as create new jobs. TABD members include leading American and European companies both large and small and with strong transatlantic credentials. The TABD is convened by the U.S. Administration and the European Commission.

Transatlantic Consumers' Dialogue (TACD): The TACD is a forum of EU and U.S. consumer organizations that develops joint consumer policy recommendations and works to promote consumer interest in EU and U.S. policymaking. TACD conferences take place once a year, alternately in the U.S. and the EU and produce recommendations related to food, electronic commerce, trade, health, and intellectual property issues.

Transatlantic Legislators' Dialogue (TLD): The TLD Dialogue involves biannual meetings of the European Parliament and U.S. Congressional delegations along with a series of teleconferences organized on specific topics of mutual concern with a view to fostering an ongoing and uninterrupted dialogue[20].

The EU's Centre of Excellence in the US: The EU supports a network of centers at leading universities across the United States to promote the study of the EU, its institutions and policies, and to foster EU-U.S. relations through teaching programs, scholarly research, and outreach activities. The EU funds this initiative as part of a broader effort to promote the people-to-people ties spelled out in the New Transatlantic Agenda. The centers are located at:

Florida International University and the

University of Miami

Indiana University

University of Michigan

University of North Carolina at Chapel Hill

University of Pittsburgh

Syracuse University

Texas A&M University

University of Washington at Seattle

University of Wisconsin

Washington, D.C., Consortium

American University, George Mason

The George Washington University

Georgetown University

The Johns Hopkins University

To be sure, differences exist, just as they will between any partners. The U.S. death penalty and certain trade disagreements are among the most visible, along with others of varying size and duration. Ninety-eight percent of economic relations between the two partners, however, are dispute-free. The EU and the U.S. share an overarching commitment to the democratic values that underpin their respective ways of life. These values are reinforced through the myriad transatlantic interactions that take place daily among government officials, business leaders, non-governmental organizations, professional associations, academia, civil society, and ordinary citizens, and they are implemented on the world stage through common actions in a variety of policy fields.

STRUCTURE OF TRANSATLANTIC RELATIONS

Transatlantic relations encompass more than EU-U.S. relations. North America and many EU countries provide for their common security in the North Atlantic Treaty Organization (NATO). The U.S. also maintains strong political, economic, and cultural relations with many individual European nations, EU and non-EU countries alike. The European Union and the United States hold regular presidential summits, which were launched with the 1990 Transatlantic Declaration that formalized U.S. relations with what is now the EU. The emergence of an EU Common Foreign and Security Policy in 1993 further solidified the relationship by providing the United States with a stronger partner in areas beyond trade matters. An additional step was taken at the EU-U.S. Summit in December 1995 with the adoption of the New Transatlantic Agenda (NTA), which provided a new framework for the partnership to deal with the growing number of external challenges. The relationship moved from one of consultation to one of joint action in four major fields:

- Promoting peace, stability, democracy, and development.
- Responding to global challenges.
- Contributing to the liberalization and expansion of world trade.
- Improving communication and ensuring a long-term commitment to the partnership.

The NTA was accompanied by a Joint EU-U.S. Action Plan setting out specific actions ranging from promoting political and economic reform in Ukraine to combating AIDS; from reducing barriers to transatlantic trade and investment to promoting links between universities and professional associations. Within the NTA framework, the Transatlantic Economic Partnership (TEP) serves to intensify and extend multilateral and bilateral cooperation and common actions in the field of trade and investment. The TEP sets out a plan identifying areas for common actions with a timetable for achieving specific results. Since the NTA was adopted, the EU and the United States have made good progress in implementing the agreed-upon actions. For example, trade barriers have been reduced, and both sides work together on customs procedures. The EU and the United States also cooperate outside the NTA framework to improve the dialogue between EU and U.S. regulators and provide companies, consumers, and government authorities of both parties access to each other's regulatory procedures. The 2004 EU-U.S. Summit generated a proposal for both sides to invigorate the partnership by working toward the creation of a barrier-free transatlantic marketplace. Officials on both sides hope to reduce regulatory costs to the commercial sector and increase trade opportunities. The Summit sets the tone for eliminating impediments to further economic integration and developing a forward looking strategy to enhance the economic partnership.

Addressing the EU Parliament on 23 June 2005, Mr. Blair said: 'The debate over Europe should not be conducted by trading insults or in terms of personality. It should be an open and frank exchange of ideas.' The Prime Minister added: 'In every crisis there is an opportunity. There is one here for Europe now, if we have the courage to take it.' The Prime Minister added: 'The issue is not about the idea of the European Union. It is about modernization. It is about policy. It is not a debate about how to abandon Europe but how to make it do what it was set up to do: improve the lives of people. And right now, they aren't convinced.

THE ALLIANCE AND ENLARGEMENT OF NATO

U.S. security in the post-cold war scenario requires looking closely at NATO, which is already the strongest security alliance in history, and finding ways to make it even stronger. To confront and eliminate such global threats as terrorism and proliferation of weapons of mass destruction, it is pertinent for the US to ally with countries that share its values and act effectively. Since the end of the Cold War, Europe's newest democracies have proven themselves as able partners, whether securing stability in the Balkans or fighting terrorism in Afghanistan. The enlargement of NATO may cement these benefits for the United States and its Allies, making the whole of NATO much stronger than the sum of the capabilities of individual members. NATO enlargement will help to enhance the political and economic stability for all countries in the Euro-Atlantic area. By helping Europe's newer democracies as they strengthen good governance, rule of law, and human rights, NATO will also facilitate a better long-term environment for American trade and investment.

The US decision to support NATO enlargement was largely bipartisan and, as with most foreign policy initiatives, not a priority issue for the public. In contrast to public interest, executive and legislative policymakers viewed the enlargement of NATO as a major national security decision with substantial implications for fundamental U.S. interests and relationships. As a result, enlargement prompted interagency debate up to the time of a presidential decision in mid-1994 and a robust congressional discussion at the time of the required Senate ratification for treaty revision in 1998.

The security dilemmas of the 1990s posed entirely new challenges for the United States. With the fall of the Berlin Wall in 1989, the United States began the slow process of reevaluating and responding to the consequent changes both on the European continent and globally. After the disintegration of the Soviet Union in 1991, the United States became the World's single super power, and the potential for an East-West nuclear war receded almost overnight. The U.S. and many foreign publics breathed a collective sigh of relief.

The larger question was whether NATO, as an organization established to counter the Soviet Union, would remain the cornerstone of Western security. After a brief flirtation with the idea of replacing NATO with the conference for Security and Cooperation in Europe, NATO members turned instead adopting NATO to the demands of the post-cold war[21].

In 1991 the State Department circulated and then submitted a proposal to NATO that resulted in the establishment of a North Atlantic Cooperation Council (NACC) at the Rome summit in November 1991 as part of the new "strategic concept". The rationale was to provide a forum within the alliance for the new democracies and NATO members to address common problems. When the Clinton administration entered office, attention focused on the options for a more satisfactory inclusion of selected Central and Eastern European countries in the Atlantic security community.

The enlargement of NATO became one of the major policy initiatives for the Clinton administration. From 1993, the new administration found itself quickly embroiled internally in a discussion of the benefits and costs of enlargement to which it responded in fall of 1993 with a proposal for a Partnership for Peace (PfP). NATO formally established PfP in January 1994 to include all the states of the former Warsaw Pact and the newly independent former republics of the Soviet Union (initially, with the exception of Tajikistan) in a program for common exercises and military coordination. Partnership for Peace (PfP) is a *North Atlantic Treaty Organisation* (NATO) project aimed at creating trust between NATO and other states in *Europe* and the former *Soviet Union*; 23 nations are members. It was created in *1994*, soon after the collapse of the former *Eastern bloc.* Ten states which are members (*Bulgaria, Czech Republic, Estonia, Hungary, Latvia, Lithuania, Poland, Romania, Slovakia* and *Slovenia*) have since joined NATO. On April 26, 1995, *Malta* became a member of PfP; it left in October 1996 in order to keep their *neutrality* intact.

But almost before NATO even started its PfP program, President Clinton announced in speeches given in January and July 1994, in Prague and Warsaw respectively, a commitment to NATO membership for eligible Central European aspirants. The United States then turned to defining how enlargement would occur in the NATO alliance, which states would be offered membership, and when NATO would enlarge. Beginning in early 1994, Republicans in Congress also began to discuss the need for enlargement. The Senate offered its first expression of interest in late January 1994, and the House followed in April. As the Atlantic alliance coalesced around a policy of enlargement in 1995-1996, the decision encountered increasingly more opposition from both states outside the alliance and their own expert communities, particularly the intellectual community of Russian experts and scholars. This opposition became more vocal with the Madrid decision in July 1997 and played a significant role in the next year's Senate ratification debate.

The U.S. National Security Strategy document issued in

1994 with the title "Engagement and Enlargement" prompted heated debate, fundamentally between the State and Defence Departments, requiring the National Security Council to mediate[22]. For most Europeanists in the State Department, NATO enlargement was a logical step in this effort, although enlargement had its detractors as well; for the Defence Department, the prospect of extending the NATO nuclear and conventional defence guarantee to a group of nascent democracies was sobering, and there was veiled, at times even vehement, opposition from the military downsizing under way, DoD was struggling to maintain coherence in its force structures and deployments; any additional commitment with the extension of the U.S. nuclear guarantee to other countries was viewed skeptically.

A compromise for which Deputy Assistant Secretary of Defence Joe Kruzel took responsibility was the announcement in January 1994 at the Brussels NATO summit of the PfP program[23]. While the states for whom NATO membership was clearly a long-shot were enthusiastic about PfP as a manner in which to be at the table, albeit without a vote, other states who desired membership looked suspiciously at PfP as shield for the West to avoid real commitment.

President Clinton's trip to Eastern Europe moved the United States on this debate. In January 1994 in Prague and again even more forcefully in July in Warsaw, Clinton announced that it was no longer a question of whether; rather, it was a question of when, how and which countries were now ready to assume the responsibilities of NATO membership. The remarks in Warsaw committed United States more forcefully to enlargement than Clinton had in Prague, but still without a timeline. There is substantial speculation about Clinton's motives. Some attribute his announcement to the ethnic communities' pressure in the year before a midterm election, others to an attempt to preempt the Republican adoption of

NATO enlargement as official party policy. Certainly neither of these potential motivations discouraged the Clinton decision. But it is also difficult to attribute the decision strictly to political motives – the ethnic constituency is modest and the broad public appeal of any foreign policy issue short of war is questionable at best. Much more in character was the explanation he gave, which Deputy Secretary of State Strobe Talbott reiterated, that it was time to recognize the hardships these countries endured on the "other side of the East-West divide," and ring qualified states in to the NATO alliance as soon as possible[24].

The presidential decision obviously silenced a substantial degree of the inter-agency opposition, but it also generated strict admonishments from the newly appointed Assistant Secretary of State Richard Holbrooke to Department of Defence officials where vocal opposition arises in fall of 1994. The importance of Richard Holbrooke as a champion for the NATO enlargement cause was not inconsequential in the final U.S. support and eventual December 1994 NATO summit adoption of this new direction for the alliance[25]. Also important was the support of Deputy Secretary Talbott, who also worked to reconcile NATO and Russian policy within the government. Security advisor Anthony Lake was most receptive to enlargement. The Pentagon opposed a quick decision; new commitments should not be taken at a time when the defence budget and the US presence in Europe was declining. Furthermore, Russia, on the other hand, Defence Secretary, Les Aspin remarked, could on no account become a military threat for eastern central Europe before the turn of the century. At the same time, he felt that caution was advisable when assuming security obligations in view of conflicts in the region. The state department on the other hand, was opposed to a fast track approach on providing membership to the East Central Europeans. Secretary State Warren Christopher felt that NATO was open to new members in the foreseeable future if they fulfilled certain criteria.

However, Strobe Talbott's arguments carried the day. The then special presidential adviser on the successor States of the Soviet Union, who became the real architect of American policy on Russia due to his close friendship with the president, declared that if NATO was enlarged, then the most democratically developed states – Poland, Hungary and Czech Republic – were the most probable candidate, whereas Russia and the Ukraine could not be taken into account for many years to come. In such a case, he felt a new dividing line would be created in Europe, adding fuel to fears in Moscow that NATO wanted to contain and isolate Russia.

The American Senate on 16 December 1997 identified and submitted at least four reasons why NATO enlargement has emerged as cardinal in the U.S. foreign policy. The reasons were very dear to the US strategy to wield influence around the world through multilateral agencies. The four reasons why NATO enlargement is in the U.S. national interest are as follow:

- Enlarging NATO will make it stronger;
- Enlargement will secure the democratic gains in Eastern Europe;
- The NATO enlargement will foster regional stability;
- And finally the enlargement will erase Stalin's artificial dividing lines[26].

After the NATO summit agreement, the alliance began the process of drafting guidelines of the eventual membership process. The period 1995-1997 marked the consolidation and design of a process whereby three new members joined NATO in 1999. There were three major issues address in this period by the United States and NATO:

1) Intra-alliance consensus-building from the December 1994 summit decision to the September 1995 agreement on the Enlargement Study;

2) Negotiations with potential members; and

3) Initiatives undertaken to mollify opposition to enlargement, particularly by Russia.

On the first issue, following the 1994 decision to pursue the objective of enlargement, the alliance partners entered a phase of negotiation on admission requirements for new members. The process was vintage NATO – slow and frustrating but ultimately successful. NATO released an incredibly crafted consensus document in September 1995 outlining the basic requirements of enlargement – democratic governance, free market reform, and civilian control of the military as well as resolution of outstanding border disputes.

While intra-alliance cooperative efforts leading up to the Enlargement Study completed in September 1995 and agreed on a the summit produced allied consensus on the requirements for new members, that consensus became fragile in the weeks prior to the July 1997 Madrid summit and was nearly overturned in Madrid. At the summit France, Germany and Italy attempted to reverse what the United States had considered a done deal by proposing Romania (France) and Slovenia (Germany and Italy) respectively for inclusion in the first phase of new membership. Driven by the conviction both that more than three new members could undermine the necessary U.S. congressional support for the treaty revision and that these two countries would stretch U.S. and NATO resources beyond their capabilities to bring new members up to NATO standards, the United States expended its influence to convince allies of the folly of more than three members in the first phase. In return, the United States agreed to a clause in the Madrid communiqué committing NATO to future enlargements and taking the unusual step of mentioning Romania and Slovenia explicitly as examples for future membership.

With respect to the second issue of negotiation and agreement with potential members, the Enlargement Study offered all interested countries and individual briefing of the necessary steps to potential membership. NATO assigned several teams to conduct these briefings to discuss the general and specific expectation. While the process proved to be a learning experience in many aspects, it also sparked a number of necessary reforms, for instance the shift to civilian control of military in Poland.

To respond particularly to the domestic skeptics who feared that the United States would be confronted with the need to resolve standing disputes soon after enlargement study also stipulated that all border challenges and disputes be resolved before NATO membership. This led, for instance, to a constructive Hungarian-Romanian agreement on contentious border issues. In sum, while not a perfect process, the attempt to hold potential members to generally specified guidelines proved useful in meeting the oft-stated U.S. objective that new members needed to be "not just consumers (of security), but also producers".

The third and most challenging issue in this period was mollifying the opposition to enlargement, or "NATO expansion". There was both a slowly gathering domestic opposition and an opposition outside the alliance. The major external opposition came predominantly from Russia. Despite an unexpected interest in Russian membership in NATO expressed by President Yeltsin at one point, there was general condemnation by Russia by pointing out as the continuation as well as expansion of the NATO threat. Repeated U.S. and NATO assurances that enlargement would provide enhanced stability on the continent and not create dividing lines did not seem to quiet Russian fears.

On the bilateral level, the United States pursued two initiatives to reassure the Russians that the NATO decision to extend its membership did not indicated any attempt to create divisions: one, in arms control and, two, in support of Russian membership in a number of organizations dealings with trade.

The first offered discussions on Strategic Arms Reduction Talks (START) III (while waiting for START II ratification), and the second offered to support Russian efforts to gain membership in the Organizations for Economic Cooperation and Development (OECD, the World Trade Organization (WTO), and in some form the Group of Seven (G-7).

On a third initiative, the United States crafted a response, adopted by NATO, of three "no's" to assure the Russians: NATO had "no intention, no plan, and no reason to deploy nuclear weapons on the territory of new members, nor any need to change any aspect of NATO's nuclear posture or nuclear policy – and (did) not foresee any future need to do so." In December 1996 at a NATO foreign ministers meeting in Brussels, Secretary of State Madeleine Albright continued to underscore these assurances in a number of public addresses, adding often "we do not contemplate permanently stationing substantial combat forces." To assure those worried about defence of NATO territory, the three no's did not extend to conflict situations, so there would be no Russian veto when national interests were threatened.

US policymakers recognized the thin line this policy forced them to walk in terms of their commitment to potential full member states, but they were needed to assure the Russian state, which had undergone a tremendous transformation since the days of the Cold War[27]. Nevertheless, the US and NATO alliances did not desire to be seen to dictate the terms of enlargement. In blunt Kissinger style, the former secretary of state voiced his own misgivings:

"I will hold my nose and support enlargement even though... dangerous. .... Whoever heard of a military alliance begging with a weakened adversary? NATO should not be turned into an instrument to conciliate Russia or Russia will undermine it."

Meanwhile, when US and NATO allies were all set for

enlargement, the Russian opposition grew shriller as the July 1997 Madrid summit neared. The European allies were also increasingly nervous about the impact of enlargement on Russia. Proposals for an appropriate response ranged from support for the Russian concept of an alliance of sixteen-plus-one to an agreement for a forum for closer consultation and coordination. The result of the subsequent discussion of various options was the May 1997 NATO-Russian Founding Act establishing a Permanent Joint Council (PJC) in Brussels for discussions, but no veto power given to Russian on alliance issues.

NATO enlargement did not loom prominently in public debate after Madrid summit. In fact, the decision did not register to any extent with the broad U.S. public. The discussion remained a largely elite debate yet one that drew more attention beginning in later spring 1997. To assure Senate passage of the required NATO treaty revision the administration had Jeremy Rosner, special officer on NATO enlargement, set up office in March 1997 at the State Department to oversee the campaign for enlargement. Over the next year he worked to broaden support, not only from ethnic communities but also from other groups. Critical backing came from Republicans, who had run in 1994 on the Contract with America and supported the NATO Enlargement Facilitation Act of 1996, which passed the Senate 81 to 16.

President Clinton has yet to make a speech to the country or Congress laying out in substantive and concrete fashion his reasons for believing that NATO enlargement is in the US national interest. Whatever detailed case he may later make, he forced the alliance into accepting his Madrid initiative without Prior justification or debate. His style is to wait until debate starts in the Senate before bringing his formidable powers and instruments of persuasion to bear. His speech to the graduating class at West Point on May 31, 1997, is as good a point of departure as any. It raised the same points he has repeated time and again – always briefly, often verbatim. First there is the cost factor. Clinton said NATO enlargement was not "without cost" or risk, but gave no specifics. In a report to Congress on February 24, 1997, he held that the cost would be modest, averaging no more than $150 million to $200 million a year for the first ten years, bashing his estimate on an in-house State Department study. But even staunch NATO-boosters are disinclined to agree with this minimalist figure. Several years ago, the highly respected Rand Corporation, known for its close ties to the Pentagon, calculated the cost at $3-5 billion per year over a ten-year period, with the U.S. share being $1-1.2 billion annually. The Congressional Budget Office posits costs greater than Rand's by a factor of two or three, depending upon the assumptions used.

A second justification made by Clinton in his West Point speech is that the admission of new members will strengthen the alliance and that the "gains decisively outweigh the burdens". As evidence he cited only the assistance of Poland, the Czech Republic, and Hungary in NATO's operations in Bosnia. Yet historically, no alliance has strengthened itself by embracing weak, dependent, resource-poor, geographically vulnerable new members, none of whom is in immediate or foreseeable danger of attack by any power. In its present geographical and military position, the United States does not need the territory, know-how, or capability offered by the Central and East European Countries (CEEC). Not is the security of any other NATO country significantly enhanced by the three invitees whose defense only adds unnecessarily to every NATO country's burden. Rather, an enlarged NATO would benefit only the "Brussels-crats" – the generals and diplomats, staffers and office personnel, and mushrooming committees and conferences based at the headquarters.

Clinton's third point is that NATO enlargement will foster democracy in the CEEC, encourage the peaceful resolution of disputes, and help build a peaceful undivided Europe. He rejects the view that enlargement would create a new fault line in Europe closer to Russia's own borders. It may well be that its proponents hope that NATO enlargement will unify and heal Europe. But if so, then the Senate should ask why the West European members of NATO do not admit the CEEC to the European Union to facilitate their economic as well as military integration, and thereby deepen their political ties to the democracies of Western Europe. As matters stand, the EU has no immediate plans for the admission of new members, even though most CEEC members are more eager to join the EU than NATO.

President Clinton's laudable aims rest on the dubious assumption that NATO, a military alliance, can help further them. The diplomatic correspondent of the New York Times, R.W. Apple Jr., writes:

"What the aliens must guard against, the Administration believes, are terrorism, illegal drugs, nationalist extremism and regional conflict fueled by ethnic, racial and religious hatreds. Yet Mr. Clinton has not spelled out what means would be used to do so. Warplanes are of little use against terrorism and drug smuggling, and naval power is of little help in fighting racism[28]."

After the July 1997 NATO decision of enlargement, U.S. scholarly opposition increased and became more vocal, Michael Mandelbaum voiced one of the most outspoken opinions, warning of the dire consequences to the US-Russian relationship. Susan Eisenhower added her concerns about the potential for Russia to turn away from reforms. Other prominent opponents included George F. Kennan and Senator Sam Nunn.

For the remainder of 1997 and until the final vote, the administration focused on ensuring bipartisan support for enlargement and a positive Senate vote. Republican Senate majority leader Trent Lott established the Senate NATO Observer Group, which supported enlargement. Finally, administration officials testified frequently over the year in

Congress: Secretaries Madeleine Albright (State) and William Cohen (DoD), among others such as Chairman of the Joint Chiefs of Staff General Henry Shelton, appeared in October 1997 before House Committees and again before the Senate Foreign Relations Committee. The House and Senate testimony attempted to reassure particularly on the issue of cost, and the final spring 1998 Senate hearings found a very receptive Senate chair, Jasse Helms.

Perhaps the more skeptical congressional opposition came from the House of Representatives, which does not have a vote in treaty ratification but held hearings in fall 1997 before the final Senate hearing in sprint 1998. The major concern in the House deliberations was the extension of US military commitments, but the potential cost of enlargement also worried members. The range of estimates was striking, from US $13 billion over fourteen years by the Congressional Budget Office (CBO) to US$5-6 billion over fifteen years from RAND to US $1.5-2 billion over twelve years by the Department of Defence. The CBO and RAND studies assumed four new members, including Slovakia, while the DoD assumed only three, but was officially classified. The leading Democratic member of the Senate Foreign Relations Committee, Senator Joseph Biden, took the lead in responding to the various attempts to derail enlargement. In the end, the 30 April 1998 U.S. Senate vote (80 to 19) clearly supported the treaty revision without any crippling amendments and with a comfortable margin over the required 67 votes.

During the U.S. debate, charges were leveled at two interest groups for undue influence in the U.S. decision to seek NATO enlargement – the Eastern European ethnic communities and the defence industry. In the former case, it is revealing that the Polish-American community actively petitioned officials both in the Government and in the Republican Party for NATO enlargement. The Polish-American Congress was actively involved in lobbying. Its president, Edward J. Moskal, wrote President Clinton in October 1995 by pointing at his concern that "Time is not on our side", and that the answer to who? And when? Might be "No one and never." The cause also attracted influential support from personalities such as former National Security Advisor Zbigniew Brzezinski. The smaller Czech- and Hungarian-American communities, meanwhile, were not as organized or effective and their impact was less substantial.

In the case of influence by the defence industry it has been observed that companies were attempting to sell their arms and platforms to the emerging democracies. If new members do increase defence spending to upgrade their military capabilities, it will come at the expense of economic and social investment, because none of their budgets could afford the large extra expenditures required. Notwithstanding Secretary of State Albright's assurance to a Senate Committee that "NATO enlargement is not a scholarship program," that is precisely what it is likely to resemble: long-term government guaranteed loans to enable recipients to pay for costly goods and services with a promise of eventual repayment. Prospective members would thus be forced to purchase weapons they cannot afford and do not need, but which they must acquire as the entry fee for membership in the NATO club. The only winners would be US arms merchants for which enlargement would be the boon of the decade.

At the time of the 12 March 1999 admittance of the three new member states to NATO, the United States reiterated its commitment to an open process of enlargement. Just over a week later, NATO became involved in an air war in Kosovo. This first conflict for NATO since its inception in 1949 turned attention to the Balkans. Even the long-awaited NATO fiftieth anniversary celebrations in Washington were muted and focused on the conflict. But the alliance agreed to a

Membership Action Plan (MAP), which explicitly stated the intention of NATO to expand and listed the potential states. There was also a clearer definition of the requirements of membership, albeit not exact standards. While there was U.S. support for the MAP and for a clear signal to the disappointed states "in-waiting", the Kosovo crisis might be seen as almost fortuitous in its impact – the United States could signal support for further enlargement, which had wide domestic support, but delay immediate decisions due to the burdens of the Balkan war.

For all the differences between the foreign policies of the Bush administration and the Clinton administration, policy toward NATO enlargement has been one area of significant continuity. The core of the Clinton strategy was to promote peace and stability on the European continent through the integration of the new Central and Eastern European democracies into a wider Euro-Atlantic community, in which the United States would remain deeply engaged. A revitalized NATO was an important tool for the maintenance of American engagement and leadership, and its expansion to the new democracies— especially given the delays in their efforts to join the European Union (EU)—was a key part of the strategy. President Clinton expressed his support for enlarging NATO as early as 1994—following the creation of NATO's "Partnership for Peace," designed to strengthen relations with the former Warsaw Pact states—and at the Madrid summit in 1997, Alliance leaders decided to invite Poland, the Czech Republic, and Hungary to join. The process was continued at NATO's April 1999 50th anniversary summit in Washington, D.C. There, leaders not only welcomed the new members but pledged to leave open the possibility of expansion to more countries and offered to help them prepare for membership.

President Bush has largely picked up where Clinton left off. Bush committed to the enlargement strategy on his first official trip to Europe in June 2001, putting an end to speculation during the 2000 presidential election campaign that he might withdraw American troops from the Balkans and back away from NATO enlargement in an effort to secure Russian acquiescence to missile defense. The new president not only reiterated the Clinton "in together, out together" pledge in the Balkans but forcefully made the case for NATO's continued expansion. In a major speech in Warsaw, Poland, Bush asserted that "all of Europe's new democracies," from the Baltic to the Black Sea, should have an equal chance to join Western institutions. He suggested that the failure to allow them to do so would amount to the moral equivalent of the World War II Yalta and Munich conferences and appealed to NATO leaders to take a forward leaning approach to enlargement at their November 2002 summit in Prague. At America's urging, Alliance leaders agreed to allow NATO Secretary General George Robertson to announce that NATO expected to launch the next round of enlargement at the Prague Summit in 2002[29].

Russia's reaction to the new momentum behind NATO enlargement has not been as hostile as many expected. Indeed, just 24 hours after the Bush speech, Russian President Vladimir Putin warmly embraced the American president at a summit in Bled, Slovenia, strongly implying that he did not intend to let enlargement undermine the potential for U.S.-Russia cooperation. Later in the summer, Putin took a further step toward acknowledging the inevitability of enlargement by expressing the view that Russia might itself want to join NATO, as an alternative to his preferred option of seeing NATO disappear. Putin went even further in October 2001, as Russian-American cooperation on terrorism was moving forward, saying that if NATO were to continue "becoming more political than military" Russia might reconsider its opposition to enlargement. This was hardly an expression of Russian support for enlargement, but it was the strongest signal yet that Moscow wants to find a way to accommodate a development that it does not like but knows it cannot stop. At their November 2001 summit in Crawford, Texas, Putin did not press Bush on the issue.

The United Kingdom moved relatively rapidly to adjust its defence policy to its perception of the new security needs after the end of the Cold War. Throughout the Cold War, the UK had taken pride in being a significant player in NATO and is spending more than the European average percentage of gross domestic product on defence.

The UK government published a fundamental review of its defence policy in 1990 known as "Options for Change". It was undertaken to gain a firm understanding of the new security context. It was assumed that a resurgent Russia had the potential to threaten the West, and that traditional UK support for a strong NATO would be the primary requirement of British defence policy. Then Defence Secretary Tom King wrote in April 1990:

"History shows that periods of great political upheaval are also likely to be periods of insecurity. Whilst we look forward to a new security order in Europe, we have no right to assume it. New arrangements must be worked at and constructed through patient negotiation and agreement. NATO provides the focus through which its members .... coordinate and pursue arms control and other ways of managing international security. But NATO can only succeed if it can continue to demonstrate a willingness and ability to defend itself for so long as there remains a potential for military exploitation in Europe[30]."

The British planners adopted with alacrity the new NATO Strategic Concept and divided up their remaining forces into the three required degrees of readiness: rapid reaction, main defence and augmentation forces[31].

The 1994 government's annual defence policy statement warmly endorsed the outcome of the NATO Brussels summit of January that year and used it as the first opportunity to trail the longer-term possibility of NATO enlargement:

"NATO is also a focus for stability, valued not only by its members but also by the newly democratic states of central and Eastern Europe. The work of the North Atlantic Co-operation Council has done much to cement relations. ....
"Partnership for Peace" will deepen the ties ..... through close co-operation on a range of military and political issues and open up the prospect of enlargement of the Alliance in the longer term[32]."

In the US during this time NATO enlargement was hotly debated behind closed doors within the Government and particularly between the State and Defence Departments until summer 1994, when President Clinton made it clear he would support enlargement.

In the year 1995 the Conservative government inclined more toward a transatlantic relationship than toward closer integration with Europe. However, it would see that a diluting of the membership of NATO might weaken the bonds that held the United States engaged. The Foreign Office of the UK released a statement in May 1995 said:

"We place great value on.... A balance between partnership and membership in the development of the wider Europe we wish to see. But there is an unhelpful preoccupation with the latter and in particular with membership of NATO and the European Union. Playing down the value of co-operation and playing up the significance of decisions on membership will risk re-creating the type of divide in Europe which we wish to avoid[33]."

By now the main thrust of defence policy was attached to wider security policy, not to mention Britain's interests in a stable world. The annual statement on defence policy by the conservative government was published in May 1996. The opening statement declares:

"The goal of our security policy is to maintain the freedom and territorial integrity of the United Kingdom and its Dependent Territories, and the ability to pursue its legitimate interests at home and abroad[34]."

The British Defence Secretary Michael Portillo was well known for his lack of enthusiasm for greater integration of the European Union. In his introduction to the annual statement, he welcomes the enlargement of NATO and said, "We shall argue vigorously at the European Union's Inter-Governmental Conference that European defence arrangements must be based on sustaining NATO's strength and effectiveness." NATO enlargement is given prominence for the first time. There is no discussion of the issues or even an indication of the United Kingdom's view on the desirability of enlargement. The paper reports that ministers will assess progress at the Brussels meeting in December 1996 and consider the way forward.

At a time when NATO was agonizing over its future, little discussion took place within the UK apart from within the strategic studies elites. Unlike the US Congress no significant debate on the issues took place in Parliament either. The House of Commons had a brief debate in February 1997 followed by an even shorter debate in the House of Lords the following month.

The House of Commons spared an hour and a half to debate NATO enlargement on 26 February 1997. The debate was opened by Bill Walker, a conservative Member of Parliament, who expressed reservations about enlargement and advocated keeping the current NATO membership strong and ensuring that the transatlantic bond was not weakened. Members raised the question of potential cost but unlike the American argument which provided convincing reason to enlargement, no hard evidence was provided for Members of Parliament. The debate did not divide along political party lines as in the US where the support was bipartisan for enlargement; some Labor and Conservative members expressed concerns about the potential weakening of the alliance through the process of expansion, while others were broadly supportive. Tony Lloyd, who would become a Foreign Office minister in the Labour government, explained that the Labour Party strongly supported NATO and would also support, with some qualifications, enlargement. The debate was concluded, without any vote being taken. In addressing the cost issues the Foreign Office Minister Sir Nicholas Bosnor suggested that the lower estimates of $35 billion were nearer the mark than suggestions of $125 billion.

In contrast, there were no significant debates of enlargement in the U.S. Congress until the final stages of the hearing process. This had several causes. Except for very specific communities with large Polish-American, and to a much lesser extent Czech- and Hungarian American, populations, the issue had virtually no visibility for the public until the very last stages of congressional debate. In addition, the Republicans had adopted the objective of enlargement before the 1994 election in their Contract with America. They had joined with the Democrats in a 94 to 3 Senate vote in January 1994 after the President's remarks in Prague.

In the UK the House of Lords provided a forum for a discussion of all aspects of NATO enlargement after two weeks of House of Commons' debate. On 14 March 1997 (a Friday afternoon when low-priority business is done), Lord Kennet opened the debate by asking the government for its policy on the proposal. In a strong opening speech, he expressed great concern about the potential of enlargement causing a re-division of Europe, an alienation of Russia, and a remilitarization of Europe. He also complained about the lack of parliamentary debate before the government decided on its policy toward NATO expansion. In the brief debate, the process of enlargement had more supporters than opponents. Lord Wallace, speaking as a Liberal Democrat, wished to see

Slovenia and Romania included in the first wave of enlargement. Many speakers, meanwhile, regretted the lack of public debate about the important strategic issues involved, blaming the government for conducting its policy development behind closed doors. Lord Williams, the Labor Party spokesman, explained that his party supported enlargement for Poland, the Czech Republic, Hungary, and possibly Slovenia, but not for Romania in the first wave. He also highlighted the importance of working with Russia, and he supported the approach proposed by the United States. Winding up the debate for the Conservative government, Lord Chesham did little more than restate its support for the principle of enlargement. The debate lasted fewer than ninety minutes and caused no ripple of interest among the British public.

The primary NATO meeting on enlargement policy would take place in July 1997 in Madrid. Despite limited time and competing priorities for reform, the new government did address the NATO issue. Robin Cook becomes the foreign secretary on 1st of May 1997. Within two weeks of taking office Robin Cook, the new foreign secretary, gave a major briefing on the priorities of British foreign policy. In this mission statement, he listed four goals of foreign policy, with security through NATO at the top:

"The first goal of foreign policy is security for nations. Our security will remain based on NATO. We must manage the enlargement of NATO to ensure that a wider alliance is also a stronger alliance and that the process reduces rather than increases tensions between East and West[35]."

This early statement of support for enlargement was not followed by any great public discussion. Before the Madrid summit of July 1997 George Robertson, the new Defence Secretary, indicated the UK favored full membership for Poland, the Czech Republic, and Hungary and had sympathy for the Slovenian case but was less enthusiastic about Romania as part of the first wave of new members. The government believed that enlargement was a good thing, but that it needed to be managed carefully so as not to cause divisions within NATO and increase tensions in the rest of Europe.

In the US in the 1996 presidential election, Republican candidate Robert Dole and incumbent Clinton differed only in timing. The Republicans pushed for an accelerated timetable while Clinton cautioned that the NATO process needed to be deliberate. This fundamental bipartisanship carried over into the Congressional debate of the treaty revisions in 1998, with only two Senate Foreign Relations Committee votes (one each on left and right) registered enlargement (16 to 2) and a more than comfortable two-thirds majority vote (80 to 19) on the Senate floor in favor of treaty revisions to enlarge the alliance. Despite the fact that Congress considered the issue seriously only during the final year of a five-year process, Senator Lott cited forty hours of Senate debate, fifty senatorial statements, and twenty defeated amendments, leaving no question of Senate advice and consent.

The outcome of the Madrid summit in July 1997 was on the expected result what the US and UK aimed at regarding the UK. Tony Blair reported to Parliament on 9 July 1997, singling out for clarifying the stand of UK on the membership of Slovenia and Romania:

"I should say a particular word about Romania and Slovenia, whose applications were especially closely considered even though there was no consensus to invite them on this occasion. Both countries have indeed made remarkable progress. Romania's new Government deserves particular congratulation on the steps taken since they took office last November. A number of allies would have liked to see Romania and Slovenia including among those invited at Madrid. All, including ourselves, saw them as strong candidates for any future enlargement, but we felt that Poland, the Czech Republic and Hungary were the limit for current enlargement[36]".

Discussion in the main academic centres was more critical of the concept of enlargement. Senior military officers and distinguished professors used every opportunity to say that the West's policy was misguided. The Times, London carried an editorial against expansion:

The most urgent reason for European to rise to the Albright challenge is that the centre piece of her European strategy, the enlargement of NATO by 1999, is dangerously misjudged. Far from enhancing the security of the European continent, this imminent decision risks creating fresh sources of insecurity, inviting confrontation with Russia and impairing the alliance's capacity to respond to new dangers that wiser policies might avert[37].

In the US it was in the final stages that the most vigorous public debate took place, primarily by those who feared repercussions from Russia. Russia had indeed expressed its displeasure over enlargement, and although its opposition had been shrill at points, it was reduced with time.

In January 1998, the Defence Committee began taking evidence about the UK policy on NATO Enlargement with the title "Third Report on NATO Enlargement" and published its report in March 1998[38].

The committee took oral evidence from the defence secretary, the minister of state at the Foreign Office, the Prime Minster of Hungary, and the Defence Minister of Poland. They also took written submissions from the embassies of Bulgaria, the Czech Republic, Estonia, Hungary, Latvia, Macedonia, Poland, Romania, Slovakia, and Slovenia. As with all select committee investigations, this one invited submissions from interested parties. The resulting report is the most coherent UK document on the issues of NATO enlargement. Like related discussions in Parliament, however, it received little publicity and no public debate.

While the British parliamentary role is limited in treaty matters, its Defence Committee report gave clear support to enlargement. Acknowledging the need to consult with Russia, the committee also rejected a veto by Russia over NATO affairs. It backed the three candidates and counseled caution on future enlargement.

The House of Commons started its debate on NATO enlargement at 9.37 AM on Friday, 17 July 1998, and had finished by 11 AM that morning[39]. The debate opened with Robin Cook making a strong argument about the rights as democratic European states of Poland, the Czech Republic, and Hungary to join NATO. He made it clear that this would increase the UK's commitments, but he also placed obligations on the new members and reminded members of the principle of collective defence in Article 5 of the Washington treaty making an attack on a NATO member an attack on all, the strongest guarantee of NATO member security. Furthermore, he maintained that

"The three new members of NATO will enjoy that guarantee; they will accept, too, the responsibility that it imposes on them. We will help to defend Poland, Hungary and the Czech Republic; they will help to defend us. The principle of collective defence will not be weakened by the expansion of NATO's numbers. On the contrary, the capability to deliver on that principle will be strengthened by the increase in numbers and the greater security of our present borders[40]."

Cook also described the process by which the applicant countries were narrowed down to three. He admitted that the UK would have supported Slovenia, but that consensus among the sixteen NATO nations was necessary and it was a difficult decision on which applicant countries to choose for membership:

"Critical to that judgment was the broad view that NATO enlargement should proceed at a pace that is consistent with NATO absorbing its expanded membership. We would do no service to the other countries that aspire to join NATO if we expanded so rapidly that NATO lost its effectiveness as the military guarantor of peace on our continent. As I have said, this will not be the last NATO enlargement. No one should be under any illusion about the magnitude of the current enlargement[41]."

Continuity in policy towards the extension of the NATO alliance to the east was welcome by the House. The Madrid summit, where Britain was represented two months after Labour's general election victory by the Prime Minister Tony Blair, brought to a successful conclusion the work begun at Brussels in 1994. The Opposition whole-heartedly supported the three former Warsaw pact nations seeking membership of NATO.

THE ALLIANCE PARTNER AND IRELAND PROBLEM

Until suspended in March 1972, Northern Ireland—with the British Government retaining ultimate responsibility—had its own parliament and prime minister. Then, in response to deteriorating security and political conditions in the province, direct rule from London was established through a Secretary of State for Northern Ireland. Northern Ireland is represented by 17 members in the House of Commons. The six counties of Northern Ireland comprise about 900,000 Protestants and 650,000 Catholics.

On November 15, 1985, the United Kingdom and the Republic of Ireland signed the Anglo-Irish agreement to diminish the divisions in Northern Ireland and to achieve peace and stability. In the agreement, both governments affirm that any change in Northern Ireland's status will come about only with the consent of a majority of its people. An intergovernmental conference was established to deal with political, security, legal and cross-border cooperation issues and provides for possible future devolution of responsibility for some matters within Northern Ireland.

In December 1993, the U.K. and Irish Governments adopted a joint declaration reiterating both governments' commitment that there would be no change in Northern Ireland's constitutional status unless a majority of the voters in the province so desired. All constitutional parties were invited to take part in a negotiation aimed at achieving a political solution to the conflict in the province. The U.K. and Irish Governments also cooperate in promoting economic and social development in the unstable areas and are seeking international support for this effort.

In February 1995, U.K. Prime Minister Major and Irish Prime Minister Burton announced a Joint Framework Document (JFD) outlining their governments' shared proposals for inclusive talks on Northern Ireland. The JFD lays the foundation for "all-party talks" among the political parties of Northern Ireland and the U.K. and Irish Governments. At the same time, the U.K. Government separately announced a Framework for Accountable Government—proposals for a new, devolved local assembly in Northern Ireland. These proposals are intended to form the basis for negotiations between the U.K. Government and Northern Ireland's political parties.

Resolving the Northern Ireland problem remains the leading political issue in the country. "Nationalists" in Northern Ireland want unification with Ireland, while "Unionists" want continued union with Great Britain.

Since the 1985 Anglo-Irish Agreement granting Ireland a formal voice in Northern Ireland affairs, there has been an extensive dialogue between the Governments of Ireland and the United Kingdom on how to bring about a peaceful, democratic resolution of the conflict. In December 1993, the "Downing Street Declaration," holding out the promise of inclusive political talks on the future of Northern Ireland, was issued. This led the Irish Republican Army (IRA) to call a "total cessation" of military operations on August 31, 1994. This was followed 6 weeks later by a similar cease-fire by the loyalist paramilitaries. Following up on the cease-fires, the two governments in February 1995 issued the Framework Document, which proposed a basis for negotiations. Generally welcomed by nationalists, it was rejected by unionists, who disparaged it as a "blueprint for a united Ireland." Despite the negative unionist reaction, the two governments tried to launch the negotiating process by announcing they would hold a series of bilateral with all the constitutional parties in the north. The process stalled in 1995, due to disagreements between the British Government and Sinn Fein, the political arm of the IRA, about the decommissioning of IRA weapons. After this stalemate the role of the United States becomes more important.

U.S. relations with Ireland are based on common ancestral ties and on similar values and political views. The United States seeks to maintain and strengthen the traditionally cordial relations between the peoples of the United States and Ireland. Economic and trade relations are an important element of the bilateral relationship. U.S. investment has been a major factor in the growth of the Irish economy, and Irish membership of the European Union means that discussion of EU trade and economic policies, as well as other aspects of EU policy, are a key element in exchanges between the two countries.

Emigration, long a vital element in the relationship, has declined significantly with Ireland's economic boom in the 1990s, and immigration to Ireland, especially of non-Europeans, is a growing phenomenon with political, economic, and social consequences. However, temporary residence overseas for work or study, mainly in the U.S., UK and elsewhere in Europe, remains common.

President Bill Clinton's policy on Northern Ireland marked a sharp break in a long-standing US policy of non-involvement in keeping with the sentiments of Britain. The issue became elevated to be an important item on Clinton administration's agenda. The responsibility for Northern Ireland was shifted from the US State Department to the White House in 1993 and the peace process witnessed Clinton's intervention at several stages. With the development of the peace process, the US role became considerably enhanced. Following the **Joint Declaration** of December, 1993 - and in order to encourage democratic politics in Ireland - President Clinton authorised the first US visa for Mr. Gerry Adams, the President of Irish Republican Party Sinn Fein. The US Administration also encouraged the political engagement of Sinn Fein in Northern Ireland. It also opened up a dialogue with Unionist Party leaders. The granting of visa issue strained Britain's relations with the United States during this period due to Clinton's decision to grant a 48-hour visa to the Sinn Fein leader Garry Adams in 1994 to visit the United States. The US decision was taken overriding intense efforts by Britain to persuade Clinton against it. The visit went ahead and attracted considerable publicity, discomforting Britain greatly. The visa issue once again became a bone of contention in 1995 when Adams applied for another US visa. Once again, Britain went through the painful process of lobbying hard to prevent Clinton from granting a visa only to taste defeat yet again. The open disagreements between the two countries on the Northern Ireland issue, compounded by Clinton's disregard for British sentiments on the issue constituted a low point where the vaunted "special relationship" was conspicuous by its absence.

In the aftermath of the August, 1994 IRA cease-fire, President Clinton appointed former Senator George Mitchell as his "economic envoy" to Ireland. The Senator's key role was subsequently extended when he later chaired the **International Body on Decommissioning**, which produced the "*Mitchell Report*[42]" in January, 1996 and then went on to be the outstanding co-Chairman of the **Multi-Party Talks**, which culminated in the Good Friday Agreement of April, 1998[43].

International intrigue, closed-door diplomacy, and a monumental struggle between two world powers; this is the true story of the Clinton administration's work to negotiate a new British-Irish accord. Much has been happened behind-the-scenes as the White House's secret negotiations with the Irish Republican Army (IRA), the furious diplomatic struggles between Britain and the U.S., and Clinton's controversial trip to Northern Ireland were the point which overshadowed the special relationship[44]. The Clinton administration had publicly addressed the issue of Irish peace, America's activist role in organizing the parties and mediating an agreement had been a matter of great concern for the John Major Government. On March 1997, the Irish Times correspondent Conor O'Clery writes on this issue which said,

"Four years ago no one could have foreseen the dramatic events that lay ahead, the bitter crises in the U.K.-U.S. relationship over Gerry Adams, the Kissinger-like use of informal diplomatic channels to shape major U.S. policy decisions, the throwing open of the doors of the White House to the Irish and the emergence of a new, dual set of special relationships - between the United States and both Britain and Ireland, and between Irish Americans and both peoples on the island of Ireland[45]".

Why would Clinton get involved in a situation like Ireland at the risk of special relationship? Apart from the routine diplomatic answers the answer to this question lies somewhere else. The relationship waned once John Major and Bill Clinton came into office. There were suspicions that the Tories had helped Clinton's Oxford files get into the hands of his political opponents. White House communications director Dan Bartlett, unable to refute these reports, has tried to dismiss them as "partisan politics." Perhaps the most imaginative response came from Republican pundit and operative Peter Roff, who suggested on MSNBC news that perhaps aides of Bill Clinton ransacked Bush's military records in the 1990s, which would account for the gaps in Bush's personnel file. In fact, during the 1992 campaign, Bush administration officials hunted through Clinton's records and even prompted the Conservative government of Prime Minister John Major in Britain to search its security files to find any damaging information about Clinton from the time when he was a Rhodes Scholar at Oxford.

The alleged act of transferring Clinton file into the hand of the Republican by the Major Government on the eve of 1992 election cast a shadow on the US foreign policy towards Northern Ireland once Bill Clinton came to power in 1993. Clinton was already a prejudiced man when he enters White House. Apart from this Clinton involved in Ireland because:

(1)   He made promises in the 1992 election campaign to do so;

(2)   He was asked to get involved by the Irish Government and powerful Irish-Americans;

(3)   He was told it would help bring peace; and

(4)   He has a personal interest - his mother was a Cassidy, descended from Irish immigrants.

President Bill Clinton in his autobiography "My Life", portrait himself candidly as a global leader who decided early in life to devote his intellectual and political gifts, and his capacity to pursue a vibrant foreign policy. Reports in the media revealed that the Oxford file of Bill Clinton has been provided to the Republicans by the John Major government before 1992 election campaign. But Clinton did not mention all this in his autobiography or anywhere else, while pursuing the Ireland policy. He mentioned his role as a peacemaker rather than any vendetta. Clinton admitted that he had a heated discussion with his foreign policy team over whether to grant a visa to Gerry Adams of IRA. Clinton cited that a number of Irish-American activists agreed including his friend Bruce Morrison (R-CT), US Ambassador to Ireland Jean Kennedy Smith, Senator Chris

Dodd (D,CT), Pat Moynihan (D-NY), and John Kerry (D-CT); and New York Congressmen Peter King (R-NY) and Tom Manton (D-NY). Clinton also tried to justify his stance with the fact that the National Security Council Staff who were working on the Irish issue had supported the visa[46].

On the US-UK special relationship issue the US President on March 8, 1993 made it clear that;

"The Prime Minister, as you know, has been in office a lot longer than I have. And I asked him for his advice about a number of things and his opinion about others. We had a very, very good meeting, and I'm looking forward to our dinner tonight.

A second point I would like to make reaffirms something that some of you asked me during the photo opportunity, and that is whether the United States will continue to have a very special relationship with Great Britain. The answer to that from my point of view is an unqualified yes. I think that only two presidents ever lived in England I think I'm one of only two; there may have been more somewhere in the past centuries. But this is a very important relationship to me, and I think it's off to a very good start. And I would like to say again how much I appreciate the candor with which the Prime Minister has approached the issues (and) with which we've discussed our mutual interests[47]."

The impact of the White House's involvement in Ireland on Anglo-American relations was quite glaring with John Major's aid for Bush in the 1992 election; Clinton's decision to get involved had been based on an urge to show-up the British Prime Minister his displeasure. The "special relationship" suffered a set-back when Clinton became the first U.S. President to defy Britain on an Irish issue and gave a temporary visa to Gerry Adams of Sinn Fein in January 1994. He certainly felt he owed nothing to John Major because of helping Bush in 1992. Clinton did not expect any big breakthrough until there is a new government in London in 1997.

With over 35 million Americans being of Irish descent, it is not surprising that the United States has abiding interest in the solution of the Northern Ireland conflict. Consequently, constructive US role has embraced a number of US Presidents, the US Congress and the wider Irish-American community. Its focus has included both political support for the evolving peace process and practical assistance in the areas of economic regeneration and cross-community reconciliation.

President Carter was the first President to commit the US to a constructive role in Northern Ireland. His 1977 statement promised that, should an overall agreement be secured, the US would provide financial support to assist its implementation. President Reagan further developed that policy by encouraging the negotiation of the *Anglo-Irish Agreement* in 1985 and facilitating US support for the creation of the **International Fund for Ireland**, which was established in 1986 by the Irish and British Governments to promote economic regeneration and reconciliation in those areas most affected by the violence.

The US Congress was also very helpful during this period in supporting the work of those democratic leaders in Ireland who were looking for a peaceful way forward in Northern Ireland. The so-called "Four Horsemen" (Speaker "Tip" O'Neill, Senator Edward Kennedy, Senator Daniel Patrick Moynihan and Governor Hugh Carey of New York) became powerful advocates for the achievement of peace, justice, human rights and political stability in Northern Ireland. The actions of the "Four Horsemen" were broadened and deepened by the formation of effective Congressional caucuses which were focused on Northern Ireland - the **Friends of Ireland** (which includes both members of the House and Senate) and the **Ad-Hoc Committee on Ireland** (comprising House members only). The UK's response to the US Ireland policy was not very cordial till John Major was in office that the 10, Downing Street. The resistance to the US' role as a mediating agent in solving

Ireland problem ended once Tony Blair became Prime Minister in May 1997. Since then the US administration did not face any adverse response from the UK while pursing the peace and developmental policies for Ireland.

The Irish-American leaders, in particular Speaker "Tip" O'Neill, played a critical role in the commitment of US support for *International Fund for Ireland*. Under the leadership of Speaker O'Neill, the US made an initial contribution of $85 million to the Fund. Its cumulative contribution to the Fund over the last 13 years amounts **to $327 million.** Along with the financial support provided by the European Union, Canada, New Zealand and Australia, the Fund has to date committed $730 million promoting some 4,850 projects, facilitating the creation of 32,000 jobs in largely disadvantaged areas. These projects have levered additional funds from private and public sources of some $950 million, so that total investment in Fund projects amounts to some $1.7 billion[48].

In May, 1995 the US hosted in Washington the **White House Conference on Trade and Investment** which focused on developing economic opportunities in Northern Ireland and the border counties in the South. A follow-up Trade and Investment Conference was organised by the US Department of Commerce in Pittsburgh in October, 1997. Moreover, under the leadership of the Department of Commerce and the President's "economic envoy" the US organised a number of trade and investment missions to Northern Ireland and the adjacent border counties in the south.

In November 1995, President and Mrs. Clinton paid a historic visit to both parts of Ireland. This was the first visit by a US President in office to Northern Ireland. The people of Northern Ireland have given a rapturous welcome to President Bill Clinton, the first serving US president to visit their country. At the end of an emotional day on November 2, 1995 that saw Bill and Hillary Clinton visit communities on both sides of the sectarian divide, the president lit Belfast's Christmas lights from behind a bulletproof screen. Standing in front of a giant Christmas Tree shipped over from Belfast's twin city, Nashville, Tennessee he told the thousands of Clinton fans that America and Northern Ireland were "partners for security, partners for prosperity, and most important, partners for peace".

The President visited Londonderry, Northern Ireland's predominantly nationalist second city where he was accompanied by SDLP leader John Hume. The president made his speech at the Joint House of Irish Parliament on 1st December 1995 urging both sides in Northern Ireland to maintain the 15-month-old ceasefire through continued dialogue.

The January 1996 "Mitchell Report" recommended decommissioning be addressed during a negotiating process. The report was widely praised. However, the British Government decision to hold elections for a negotiating body was seen as a step backwards, and in February 1996, the Ireland Republican Army officially ended its cease-fire with a bomb attack in London which killed two. At the end of February 1996, the two governments announced that all-party talks would begin in June and be open to all parties disavowing violence. In May 1996, elections were held to determine participation in the talks, with Sinn Fein gaining nearly 16% of the vote. However, the party turned away from the negotiations when they began on June 10 because of the IRA's continued campaign of violence. The negotiations were chaired by Senator Mitchell. Notwithstanding the collapse of the first IRA cease-fire in February, 1996, President Clinton and his Administration remained committed to the achievement of an inclusive political settlement. The President supported the *Multi-Party Talks* when they began in June, 1996 and encouraged the republican movement to reinstate the cease-fire[49].

Following the IRA cease-fire of July, 1997 and Sinn Fein's

inclusion in the Talks in September of that year, the US Administration - along with the Prime Ministers of Ireland and Britain, Bertie Ahern and Tony Blair - intensified their efforts to reach an overall agreement. Throughout the latter half of 1996 and early 1997, the negotiations made little progress. The May 1997 election of Tony Blair and the Labour Party government in the UK, however, re-energized the process and led to increasing pressure on the IRA to restore the cease-fire. After gaining assurances that the negotiations process would be time-limited and that decommissioning would not again become a stumbling block, the IRA did restore its cease-fire in July 1997, and Sinn Fein was admitted to the talk process in September 1997. The negotiations moved from process to substance in October 1997. In a final marathon push in April 1998, which included the personal intervention of President Clinton, all parties, on 10 April 1998, signed an agreement. The "Good Friday" (April 10 was Good Friday) agreement was put to a vote, and strong majorities in Northern Ireland and the Republic of Ireland approved it in simultaneous referendums on 22 May 1998.

With the target date for agreement of 9 April having been set by Senator Mitchell, the various party leaders traveled to Washington in March, 1998 for the St. Patrick Day's celebrations. President Clinton availed of the opportunity to encourage each of the party leaders to demonstrate courage, vision and generosity in the final stages of the negotiations. In the final hours of the Talks, the President's personal diplomacy by phone was crucial in securing the historic **Good Friday Agreement** of 10 April, 1998[50].

President George W. Bush has been a staunch supporter of the Good Friday Agreement and visited Northern Ireland in April 2003 for a two day summit with British Prime Minister, Tony Blair at Hillsborough Castle. In June 2004, while visiting Dromoland, Co Clare for an EU-US Summit, the President

3

MERE ANGLO-SAXON TIES OR AN ALLIANCE ON FIRM FOUNDATION

THE ALLIANCE IN APPROACHING 21ST CENTURY

Throughout the 1980s, the Soviet Union fought an increasingly frustrating war in Afghanistan. At the same time, the Soviet economy faced the continuously escalating costs of the arms race. Dissent at home grew while the stagnant economy faltered under the combined burden.

Western historians often argue that one major cause of death of the Soviet Union was the massive fiscal spending on military technology that the Soviets saw as necessary in response to NATO's increased armament of the 1980s. They insist that Soviet efforts to keep up with NATO military expenditures resulted in massive economic disruption and the effective bankruptcy of the Soviet economy, which had always labored to keep up with its western counterparts. It was estimated that the Soviets were a decade behind the West in computers and falling further behind every year. The critics of the USSR observed that computerized military technology was advancing at such a pace that the Soviets were simply incapable of keeping up, even by sacrificing more of the already weak civilian economy. According to the critics, the arms race, both nuclear and conventional, was too much for the underdeveloped Soviet economy of the time. In fact, Gorbachev himself states that defense spending was a major reason in forcing Soviet reforms, quote "I think we all lost the Cold War, particularly the Soviet Union. We each lost $10 trillion". For this reason, President Ronald Reagan is seen by many conservatives as the man who 'won' the Cold War indirectly through his escalation of the arms race and then diplomacy with Gorbachev.

The Soviet Union provided little infrastructure help for its Eastern European satellites, but they did receive substantial military assistance in the form of funds, material and system control. Their integration into the inefficient military-oriented economy of the Soviet Union caused severe readjustment problems after the fall of Communism. Research shows that the fall of the Soviet Union was accompanied by a sudden and dramatic decline in total warfare, interstate wars, ethnic wars, revolutionary wars, the number of refugees and displaced persons and an increase in the number of democratic states.

Thatcher's leadership at this time was under increasing pressure, and when she was challenged, John Major supported her in the leadership election of November 1990. When she stepped down, Major entered the contest himself, and with Thatcher's support he went on to beat Michael Heseltine and Douglas Hurd. Major appointed both colleagues to his new Cabinet. When elected, he was the youngest Prime Minister for over a century. Once installed in the post of PM, Major had immediately to deal with an international crisis when Kuwait was invaded by Iraq.

On 2 August 1990 Saddam Hussein invaded Kuwait. That day Mrs. Thatcher received a telephone call from the Presidents of the US who was at his home in Kennebunkport, Maine. They discussed the crisis, and Mrs. Thatcher argued for a strong response and she told the President, it was not the time 'to go wobbly'. The President armed with such a strong supporting statement from one of US' closest allies started thinking strong military action against the Iraq. Because of the wide international support, President Bush and his advisers, particularly Secretary of State James Baker and Secretary of Defense Richard Cheney, were able to line up financial and military support from many nations. There were 34 nations in the Coalition to support US' action in Iraq with United Kingdom prominent and most vital among all. Britain not only supported ground troops but also aircraft and pilots.

The Thatcher government's eagerness to re-establish the dormant 'special relationship' with the United States may have played a part; so did other factors, such as Britain's professional army and a modern history free from the experience of invasion and defeat. The restoration of the special relationship during the Thatcher era was symbolized by the Trident agreement of July 1980 and March 1982 and the close military (and intelligence) collaboration during the Falklands War. Despite her misgivings, the Prime Minister was also prepared to face considerable domestic political costs in supporting the deployment of Cruise missiles in Britain, not being too critical of American actions in Grenada, and allowing American F111 aircraft to use British bases to bomb Libya in 1986. In the last case, as Margaret Thatcher points out in her memoirs that, there were significant benefits from supporting the United States. Special weight, she says, was given to British views on arms control negotiations with the Russians and the administration promised to give extra support to the extradition treaty which the government regarded as vital in bringing IRA terrorists back to Britain. The fact that so few had stuck by America in her trial, she suggests, strengthened the 'special relationship[51]'.

Whatever the causes, the United Kingdom's unwavering hard-line attitude was at variance with the viewpoint prevailing among its main continental partners, though it was congruent with the strategic perspective of the Bush administration. Hence

Washington found it far easier to harmonize its diplomatic effects and military plans with London than with any other ally. The immediate consequence was to restore the deep sense of comity and mutual interest that had been the exclusive trademark of Anglo-American relations.

The cleavage between London and its EC partners complicated the task of forging a single, unified Community approach to the Gulf crisis. On 14 January 1991, on receiving reports of UN Secretary-General Javier Perez de Cuellar's failed visit to Iraq, the twelve foreign ministers meeting in Brussels decided to shelve earlier plans to send representatives to Baghdad. Unknown to his partners, including the new British Prime Minister, John Major, with whom he had just lunched at the Elyse'e, President Mitterrand launched his own last-gasp diplomatic effort. It was a two-pronged strategy. An emissary was sent on yet another mission to Saddam Hussein, while France submitted a six-point proposal at the Security Council that raised once again the idea of an international peace conference on the Arab-Israeli conflict while offering Iraq a guarantee of non-aggression if it complied with UN resolution. The French demand failed, as Saddam turned a blind eye to this latest initiative, denying Mitterrand the chance to present the Council with the ingredients for a last minute deal.

In the US, President George Bush aligned political support in the Congress for demanding the removal of troops from Kuwait by Saddam Hussein. By the time the war begins, Mrs. Thatcher had been replaced by John Major, but British policy remained unchanged and supportive of the USA. Upon becoming prime minister in 1990, Major followed in the footsteps of Margaret Thatcher and the legacy of her government. He moved into 10 Downing Street facing a war in the Persian Gulf. Continuing the United Kingdom's strong ties with the United States, Major gave full support to the United States in the Gulf War of 1991, and thereafter to the U.S. position on Iraq in the United Nations. By mid-January 1991 when the US began the air strike of Operation Desert Storm the British Government led by John Major was fully behind the United States' action in Iraq. The British commitment to the Gulf War was second in size only to the United States. Britain provided the largest European component of the military force that took on the Iraqi army and was the most outspoken and staunchest supporter of the US-led mission to liberate Kuwait. Bush was soon praising the British effort and the special relationship his country enjoyed with them. US and British forces carefully selected targets of military significance in Iraq and worked to avoid hitting civilian facilities, especially mosques, schools and hospitals. Knowing that the US and British forces sought to limit such collateral damage; the Iraqi military based their troops and weapons storage facilities in civilian residential neighborhoods. Even so, the fat that the British and Americans used guided munitions, which could follow a laser beam directly to a specific target, reduced the number of civilian casualties.

After the Gulf War the relation between Major and Bush was warm and cordial, but never any thing more than that and after Bill Clinton beat Bush in 1992 a man even cooler to the idea of close ties with Britain was at the helm of affairs in the USA. During the first two years of office from 1993 to 1995 there was hardly a single incident or even that one could point to as indicative of close relations. Indeed the years were peppered by minor, but no less worrying disputes and arguments to do with GATT trade talks, problems over the Anglo-American Air-service argument, and the visit of Gary Adams, the Sinn Fein leader, to the USA in 1994. Once the visit was over there was a public attempt to smooth Britain's ruffled feathers. Protestations were forthcoming from Clinton about the importance of good and close Anglo-American relations, and a number of friendly 'Photos' opportunities were arranged during the visit of John Major to Washington in 1996. But for the most part, neither of the administrations in Britain and the USA has done much to continue the kind of relationship Mrs. Thatcher and Reagan had in the 1980s. Both are preoccupied with domestic, economic and political problems, have shown little skill in foreign affairs, and seen content with the lower-key and less over relationship.

Anglo-American relations have gone through worst doldrums than the Clinton-Major era in the past without any permanent damage being done. Major's seven years as prime minister were not easy ones. Unlike Thatcher, his party only had slim parliamentary majorities. Nevertheless, on May 1, 1997, he handed over one of the strongest economies any incoming government had inherited, with The Daily Telegraph in London observing that "John Major leaves a richer legacy than any of his predecessors." So the resilience of the relationship was again on track once Major was replaced by Blair.

Major's style was radically different from his predecessor. His unassuming and down-to-earth manner was considered a breath of fresh air, and a contrast to Margaret Thatcher's forcefulness. Under Major the Conservatives went on to win the 1992 election with a workable majority, despite opinion polls which had predicted a hung parliament. However, over the next five years by-election losses and defections would whittle the government's majority down to single figures. Perhaps the lowest point of John Major's premiership came soon after the election: the sterling crisis of September 1992 forced the pound to leave the European Exchange Rate Mechanism (ERM). A new economic policy was swiftly devised and led to five successive years of growth between 1992 and 1997 with falling unemployment and inflation. In 1995 Major made a bold move to reassert his authority within the Conservative Party when he resigned as leader (but not as Prime Minister) and submitted himself for re-election. In the subsequent contest he was challenged by the Welsh Secretary, John Redwood, whom he defeated. However, the

Conservatives were defeated by Labour in the 1997 General Election, and John Major resigned as leader, having been PM for seven of the Conservatives eighteen consecutive years in power.

Both the United States and Britain provided forces for the coalition army which liberated Kuwait in the Persian Gulf War. The British Labour Party were elected to office in 1997 for the first time in twenty-three years. Blair used Clinton's expression 'Third Way' to describe the ideology of his own party. Forces from both countries were again used to impose a peace during the Kosovo War. This led to the 'mass graves' controversy, with claims that the Kosovar Albanians were facing genocide becoming disputed[52].

The United States became involved in negotiations over peace in Northern Ireland, and this may have helped to secure the eventual disarmament of the IRA. The United Kingdom is one of the United States' closest allies, and British foreign policy emphasizes close coordination with the United States. Bilateral cooperation reflects the common language, ideals, and democratic practices of the two nations. Relations were strengthened by the United Kingdom's alliance with the United States during both World Wars, and its role as a founding member of NATO, in the Korean conflict, and the Persian Gulf War. The United Kingdom and the United States continually consult on foreign policy issues and global problems and share major foreign and security policy objectives. In the United Nations, the United Kingdom is a permanent member of the Security Council.

The United Kingdom is a founding member of the North Atlantic Treaty Organization (NATO) and has been a member of the European Community (now European Union) since 1973. The United Kingdom is one of NATO's major European maritime, air, and land powers and ranks third among NATO countries in total defense expenditure.

It is to Tony Blair's credit that on becoming Prime Minister in 1997, when he had many more pressing domestic policy concerns, he put a very high priority on restoring a good relationship with Washington. Such restoration was certainly necessary. The replacement of George H. W. Bush by Bill Clinton in 1993 had ushered in a period of quite bad Anglo–American relations. John Major's closeness to Bush and the British Conservative Party's foolish involvement in an apparent campaign to discredit Clinton ensured that an atmosphere of personal mistrust prevailed.

The weakness of the Major government was also well-understood in Washington: Contempt thus supplemented dislike. But it was the insistence of the British—especially the two British Foreign Secretaries of the period, Douglas Hurd and Malcolm Rifkind—on sticking to a failed policy in the Balkans which led to a serious rift with Washington. Clinton, with support from leading Republicans including Senator Robert Dole, wanted to lift the arms embargo on Bosnia and launch air strikes against the Serbs to prevent further genocide. The British veto of these plans led to what the U.S. ambassador of the day described as "the worst moment in Anglo–American relations since Suez." Eventually, the U.S. insisted. The Croatian and Bosnian armies, supported by the U.S., shifted the balance of power against Serbia sufficiently to allow peace to be restored by the Dayton Agreement of November 1995[53].

The departure of Major after the Conservative Party's unprecedented severe defeat in 1997 thus permitted a new beginning for the Special Relationship. Blair had, in fact, closely studied Clinton's success and sought to emulate it. In the first few years, he was even prepared to be Clinton's junior partner, notably in the President's attempts to establish an international "Third Way," or "New Middle" (Neue Mitte) as Germany's Chancellor Gerhard Schröder preferred to term it.

In any case, as in the First Gulf War, Britain proved by far the best ally America could find in an international crisis.

Blair alone was prepared to collaborate in or even openly support American attempts to force Saddam Hussein into line or to punish the early manifestations of Islamic terrorism. In one instance, Britain actually took the lead in a major foreign policy initiative involving the U.S.: the NATO campaign of 1999 against Serb forces ethnically cleansing Kosovo. Blair was morally right, but he was also lucky that Yugoslav President Slobodan Miloševiæ buckled when he did and withdrew his forces.

The British Prime Minister was lucky in another respect as well. His prominence in the operation irritated Clinton exceedingly and soured relations. But Clinton was now approaching the end of his term, so the fallout for the Special Relationship was insignificant. Indeed, as it turned out, Blair's track record of liberal interventionism would prepare him well for cooperation with George W. Bush in the wake of the Islamist attacks of 9/11.

Yet while the Clinton–Blair years were more practically fruitful than the Bush–Major years that preceded them, they were also notable for the failure to address two issues of profound importance to the countries' strategic relationship. The first of these was the need to decide how far and in what respects national sovereignty should be yielded to international institutions in the light of what some argued was an unstoppable movement toward "globalization." Britain, for example, strongly supported the proposed International Criminal Court (ICC), which the U.S. eventually refused to accept. But this was merely the tip of the institutional iceberg of differences in attitude toward the wider question of universal jurisdiction, "global governance," and the role of the United Nations.

The second question concerned Britain's relationship with the European Union. One could argue, of course, that the doubts on this issue were not new, and one would be right, as these pages have already shown; but Blair's resolve to have

Britain play a central, perhaps leading role in Europe meant that, for the first time since the fall of Edward Heath in 1974, Washington was suddenly faced with the full strategic implications of its own long-term approach to European integration. Moreover, the now unmistakably federalist thrust of EU policy generally, and the way in which Britain under Blair had shifted its position on military integration with Europe, required proper analysis from Washington. This it never received. So the new millennium opened with two large but barely acknowledged problems facing the Special Relationship. They are still unresolved.

Tony Blair had determined to forge a close relationship with President George W. Bush right from the moment of the latter's election. In this he was not only following the advice of Bill Clinton; he was also pursuing a well-established strategy of "hug them close" (as his advisers described it), much like that which his successful predecessors adopted toward whoever was in the White House. Bill Clinton had been Blair's "friend," as the British Prime Minister declared at the height of Clinton's troubles in February 1998; but Blair's friendships are never exclusive and always flexible, and George W. Bush soon became his best friend too.

In these early days, Blair's considerable charm was much required. It allowed him to finesse his way out of several tricky situations. Thus, he persuaded Bush, quite against the actual contents of the EU agreement signed at Nice in December 2000 that European defense plans posed no threat to NATO. This somewhat shaky basis for his relationship with a conservative U.S. President might well have collapsed, however, were it not for al-Qaeda's attacks on New York and Washington.

Tony Blair's response rightly secured him the President's and the American people's gratitude and admiration. He palpably shared their outrage and immediately offered full support in punishing those responsible. He sat in the gallery as the President addressed Congress ten days after the attacks and heard the applause as Bush declared that America had "no truer friend than Great Britain."

It is fair to say that Britain never stood higher in American affections than at that time. British troops subsequently participated in the American-led campaign against the Taliban in Afghanistan despite various grumbles from the British military and foreign policy establishment. The President's "axis of evil" speech again tested Blair's mettle; but once more, despite criticism in the British media and snide remarks from his own Foreign Secretary, Jack Straw, Blair endorsed both the analysis of the danger and the strategy of "pre-emption" which lay behind it.

The period of the buildup to the war in Iraq was still more difficult for the Prime Minister, and it was now that his broader political approach began to founder. It is, indeed, from the consequences of Blair's actions during those months that many of his own and, more significantly, the Anglo–American Relationship's problems flow. It is important to understand why this is so (and just as important for supporters of the Iraq War as for its critics) because the Special Relationship cannot stand a repetition of what transpired. The trouble stemmed from the fact that although Blair appeared to subscribe to the "everything's changed" doctrine adopted by America.

President Bush had proclaimed in addressing Congress after 9/11: "Every nation, in every region, now has a decision to make. Either you are with us, or with you are with the terrorists[54]." But Blair, for all his zeal in supporting America, did not really see the world in these terms. He was and is the result of a sort of historic compromise between Left and Right. His considerable success in politics has been built upon an instinctive preference for "both...and" rather than "either...or." He is a creature of compromise, even if his bellicose language serves to disguise it. So, despite the clear message from Washington, he continued to regard Britain's supreme international role as that of a "bridge" between the U.S. and Europe[55].

This did not reflect reality, and so, as often happens when awkward realities are ignored in international affairs, the path of illusion proved the road to ruin. Of course, Blair could argue that Europe was not exactly (in the President's words) "with the terrorists." But most European countries and the governing bureaucracy of the European Union were certainly not "with" America in the sense of accepting American strategic goals in the war against terrorism. They were, indeed, shocked and appalled by the "axis of evil" speech. They did not see any reason to change their approach of putting commercial interests and political rivalry with the United States above any need to counter Islamic terrorism and the proliferation of weapons of mass destruction (WMD)[56].

Moreover, in this, the Europeans were far from alone. Despite their own problems with Islamic militants, neither China nor Russia would go along with America's analysis in any consistent manner. Blair particularly wanted good relations with Russia, where he had hoped to recreate with Vladimir Putin Mrs. Thatcher's relationship with Mikhail Gorbachev, and he was also keen to cultivate China; Britain had, after all, been at the forefront of those wishing to renew arms sales to the People's Republic. He had, above all, spent his first four years in office proclaiming the need to strengthen the United Nations. Even more important, because fundamental to Blair's ability to control events at home, was the fact that his whole approach to managing the Labour Party was thrown into doubt. Of course, most Labour MPs, like their electors, had the greatest sympathy with the American people after 9/11, but that did not remove Labour's deep suspicion of American policy. Labour MPs felt that they had already been drawn into too close an embrace of America because of Blair's "friendship" with first Clinton and then Bush.

They had some reason to be suspicious. Partly through

guile and partly because he simply preferred that way of doing things, Blair had led them along a foreign policy path that allowed him to be acclaimed as Washington's friend at the expense of concealing his true intentions from his colleagues. Each step had been solemnly proclaimed as the last: acceptance of U.S. plans for ballistic missile defense but not participation in it; action against Afghanistan but not Iraq; then action against Iraq but only with U.N. approval and as part of a wider coalition. But what then? What if there was no such approval, no wider coalition, and outright hostility from Europe? At this point, the famous "bridge" analogy seems all too appropriate, but more as the subject of a disaster movie and less as a reassuring metaphor. Bridges can tolerate much buffeting by the elements, but they cannot stand when the span they are bridging expands. Tectonic shifts, like that set off by 9/11, cause them to totter and fall[57].

Yet Blair hung on desperately to his bridge. He defended it by engaging in an extraordinary globe-trotting campaign of diplomacy, first to gain support for attacking Afghanistan and then, and much less successfully, for the war against Iraq. But he also indulged in and encouraged in others a large amount of wishful thinking. The height of this was perhaps his speech at the George H. W. Bush Presidential Library in Texas on April 7, 2002:

Forget the talk of Anti-Americanism in Europe. Yes, if you call a demonstration, you will get the slogans and the insults. But people know Europe needs America, and I believe America needs Europe too. This message was grossly misleading. Europe, at least in the Donald Rumsfeldian sense of "Old Europe," was already profoundly anti-American and would become ever more stridently so. For almost another year, the British Prime Minister squandered his capital in Washington in trying to persuade America to wait until it had a clear authorization from the U.N. Security Council to act against Saddam Hussein[58].

He could have used it otherwise. He might have tried to ensure that better preparation was made for the aftermath of the war. He could have reassured himself that a political strategy for post-war Iraq engaged as much of Washington's attention as the military or diplomatic strategies for fighting the war. He could have done what Thatcher always did with Reagan: ask those tricky practical questions which get overlooked by politicians, generals, and officials as they cope in Washington with the need to justify themselves to each other and to the media. Instead, Britain became furiously involved in intradepartmental squabbles within the Administration whose existence made successful planning more difficult, not less[59].

Paradoxically, during the same visit on which Blair airily assured Americans that anti-Americanism was no danger, the difference between America's and Britain's justification for war against Iraq had been nakedly exposed. At a joint press conference with the British Premier, President Bush said, apparently without intentional irony: "Maybe I should be a little less direct and be a little more nuanced, and say we support régime change (in Iraq)[60]."

This was, of course, far from nuanced in Blair's eyes. It was embarrassingly frank. He had been warned that a war undertaken for such a purpose was probably illegal. More important, without this legal cover, he would be unlikely to bring the Labour Party, or perhaps even a majority of his Cabinet, to support it. For Blair, the only sufficient justification for war was Saddam Hussein's continued possession of WMD. One can debate the extent to which Blair and his officials manipulated or glossed the evidence to suggest that Saddam had these weapons and that they posed a serious threat. The fact is that he had to put all his eggs in this one fragile basket. When it was clear that there were no WMD and that the supporting evidence was wrong, his credibility with the British public as a war leader was irrevocably destroyed, and with it his capacity to lead public opinion in support of America.

Could matters have been handled differently? The question is of more than academic interest because it goes to the heart of whether the Anglo–American Special Relationship is sustainable—and a relationship that inevitably crumbles when casualties mount is not. The answer is encouraging: It need not have turned out this way. Given the fact that there turned out to be no WMD, there was always bound to be anger among critics of the war in Britain. Given the failure to bring stability to Iraq and arrest the spiral of military and civilian casualties, that criticism was bound to spread further. But it was the sense of having been deceived, directly by Blair and indirectly by America that caused the approval ratings for the war to plunge. This was avoidable, but probably not by Blair or any other leader of the British Labour Party. Again, it is important for Americans to understand why this is so.

The Conservative Party leader, Michael Howard, came in for some strong criticism and even, it seems a severe political snub from the White House because of his attacks on Blair over the war. The Tories deserved what they got; opportunists in matters of war and peace always do. But the fact remains that a Conservative Prime Minister would have been better able to deliver America the sustained support of the British public than was Tony Blair. A direct and simple appeal to British national interest in the Atlantic alliance—and thus to supporting America, right or wrong (though preferably and probably right)—could have been made by a right-of-center politician as it was made, in more or less these terms, by John Howard in Australia. By contrast, Blair's and New Labour's liberal idealist and internationalist ideology precluded such an appeal. That is what prompted the Prime Minister to make exaggerated and subsequently discredited claims to the House of Commons.

The enduring lesson for the Special Relationship is stark: Personal good will—even personal courage of the sort Blair displayed during the crisis—is no substitute for getting the arguments right. And unless one can base one's arguments and subsequent explanations and, when necessary, excuses on the sure foundations of national interest, public support will crumble. This it has done, along with Blair's bridge of Euro-Atlanticism.

The brutal reality is that, as he reaches the end of his time in Downing Street, Tony Blair's legacy is a gravely weakened, not strengthened, Special Relationship. Of course, Blair is still popular in America, and he will be able to put that popularity to good use during lecture tours for years to come. Britain's Prime Minister also has the ear of the world's most powerful leader. Britain even seems, on occasion, to be able to influence American policy. Some instances of British influence on America are: the Administration's shift in favor of aid to Africa reflects one of Blair's private obsessions; the U.S. has taken a marginally more favorable view of the Palestinians, at least until the election of Hamas, because of British badgering; America, equally ill-advisedly, allows its policy toward volatile Southeast Europe to be set largely by the British Foreign Office. Above all, American attitudes toward the European project—very foolishly indeed, as will be explained— have become more favorable, in part to make Tony Blair's life more comfortable.

For these ambiguous triumphs, Blair may take a little personal credit; but what they all have in common is that they do not advance British national interest in the slightest degree, and they accordingly cut no ice with British public opinion. Blair has delivered nothing of substance to the country in exchange for sacrifices that have become highly unpopular. For example, Britain gained no preferential treatment when it came to handing out contracts for Iraqi construction over competitor countries that had spent years bankrolling Saddam and had ferociously opposed the war.

THE ALLIANCE ON CRITICAL ISSUES

Since the end of World War II, the Persian Gulf region

has always been a top priority in the US security policy. The most important US security concern in the region is an assured and uninterrupted supply of oil. Throughout the Cold War period, the US policy was primarily concentrated towards containing and countering the threats of growing Soviet political and military influence in the Gulf.

The most significant US policy goal in the Gulf is to maintain uninterrupted flow of oil at a reasonable price and in sufficient quantities to meet its requirements and those of its allies. US policy is also designed to preclude and counter any hostile foreign and regional power from gaining control and influence in the region. To achieve these goals, the US has evolved a series of alliances, security relationships, and arms transfer agreements essentially re-cycle petro-dollars with the Gulf States. In the post-Gulf War era, Washington has armed the Gulf Cooperation Council (GCC) states with sophisticated weapons, and trained them to effectively defend their territorial integrity and political interests against Iran and Iraq.

The huge reserves of oil and natural gas have made the Gulf a critically important region of the world. By current estimates, the Gulf region contains approximately 60 per cent of the world's total proven petroleum reserves. This oil is vital to the world economy and the geo-strategic location of this region adds to its importance. The Gulf is a major waterway for shipping between the East and West. The geographical proximity to Russia has enhanced its importance to the United States.

Since the end of the Cold War and the Gulf War, one of the main objectives of American foreign policy has been the containment of "rogue states" (Iran, Iraq and Syria). President Clinton has described the "rogue states" as the major challenge to the Cold War order that poses a serious danger to regional stability in many corners of the globe. President Clinton's National Security Advisor Anthony Lake, argued that "as sole superpower, the United States has a special responsibility for developing a strategy to neutralize, contain, and through selection of pressures, perhaps eventually transform the 'backlash states' into constructive members of the international community". Therefore, he advocated the doctrine of "dual containment" towards Iran and Iraq, because they are included in the list of "backlash states". The "backlash states" consist of Cuba, Libya, North Korea, Iran and Iraq. Anthony Lake blamed these regimes-their authoritarian ruling cliques, their aggressive and defiant behaviour, their chronic inability to engage constructively with the outside world; and their pursuit to acquire weapons of mass destruction (WMD) made clear "their commitment to remain on the wrong side of history." Thus, it was an effort by the Clinton Administration to articulate a containment doctrine to deal with the challenges posed by "rogue states". US Secretary of State Madeleine Albright expressed her concern to the members of the Council of Foreign Relations in September 1997: "Dealing with 'rogue states' is one of the great challenges of our time, because they are there with the sole purpose of destroying the system." She argued that the "rogue states" constitute one of the four distinct categories of countries in the post-Cold War international system.

Martin Indyk, the senior director for Near East and South Asian affairs, enunciated the policy of "dual containment" in a speech at the Washington Institute for Near East Policy on May 19, 1993. In his address, he stated: "The Clinton Administration's policy of 'dual containment' of Iran and Iraq derives in the first instance from an assessment that the current Iraqi and Iranian regimes are both hostile to American interests in the region. Accordingly, we do not accept the argument that we should continue the old balance of power game, building up one to balance the other. We reject that approach not only because its bankruptcy was demonstrated in Iraq's invasion of Kuwait. We reject it because of a clear headed assessment of the antagonism that both regimes harbour towards the United

States and its allies in the region. And we reject it because we do not need to rely on one to balance the other."

The Clinton Administration, during 1995-96, struggled to maintain its allies' support for comprehensive containment and isolation of Iraq through multilateral sanctions. Unlike Iran, although no one has advocated an engagement policy with Iraq, concerns have been raised about the dire impact of sanctions on the Iraqi people and the unexpected political durability of Saddam Hussein. Therefore, these concerns, in turn, have raised questions about the efficacy and effectiveness of the American strategy. Some US officials referred to this policy as the "endgame".

During the initial days of the Clinton Administration's second term, the strategy of "dual containment" came under strong criticism in regard to its coherence and efficacy. There was growing concern and the view in the policy-making community that "dual containment" was a strategic dead-end. By the year 1997, it was observed that the US policy towards the states of the Persian Gulf was at an impasse and stalemate. Maintenance of the policy of "dual containment" concerning Iran and Iraq has produced uneven results, not all of them positive from the point of view of either the US or those of its allies and friends among the Gulf States.

In 2001, George W. Bush inherited a stalled peace process in the Arab-Israeli dispute, as well as related renewed violence in the area. For several months, the new US president did not appear interested in getting involved in the perennial Middle East dispute. But, 11 September 2001 changed everything in US foreign policy, including the approach to the Arab-Israeli conflict. The priority of addressing global terror threats on the United States and its assets forced a renewed effort to win regional allies to aid in such a mission. Many of those allies in the Arab world sought movement on the peace process in order to give aid in the US agenda. Under such strategic circumstances, the United States has put the cause of a Palestinian state at the brink of reality – a phenomenal even in regional and world affairs, if it actually comes about.

But the same strategic circumstances prodding the United States toward this position of sympathy for the Palestinians also served as a constraint. The amount of Palestinian violence toward Israeli targets that can be defined as terrorism – for out purposes, *premeditated, politically motivated violence perpetrated against noncombatant targets by sub-national groups or clandestine agents, usually intended to influence a target* – has been quite high since the beginning of the latest cycle of conflict in September 2000. This fact makes it difficult for a President 'fighting terrorism' to get too close to those in the cause. Though Arafat has denied involvement or endorsement of the activities, he had been seen as either unable or unwilling to stop the terrorism and, thus, part of the problem. The distancing from Palestinian officials was coupled with renewed sympathy for Israel's own 'war on terror', which effectively stalled or slowed the momentum of the Bush plan for a Palestinian state. Such a position also played well domestically, as the US public and interest group community has largely favored Israel over the Palestinians.

President Bush has renewed the American foreign policy towards the Middle East by designating some states as "axis of evil" and must be contained. In his characteristic style he said:

"Our second goal is to prevent regimes that sponsor terror from threatening America or our friends and allies with weapons of mass destruction. Some of these regimes have been pretty quiet since September the 11th. But we know their true nature. North Korea is a regime arming with missiles and weapons of mass destruction, while starving its citizens.

Iran aggressively pursues these weapons and exports terror, while an unelected few repress the Iranian people's hope for freedom.

Iraq continues to flaunt its hostility toward America and to support terror. The Iraqi regime has plotted to develop anthrax, and nerve gas, and nuclear weapons for over a decade. This is a regime that has already used poison gas to murder thousands of its own citizens — leaving the bodies of mothers huddled over their dead children. This is a regime that agreed to international inspections — then kicked out the inspectors. This is a regime that has something to hide from the civilized world.

States like these, and their terrorist allies, constitute an axis of evil, arming to threaten the peace of the world. By seeking weapons of mass destruction, these regimes pose a grave and growing danger. They could provide these arms to terrorists, giving them the means to match their hatred. They could attack our allies or attempt to blackmail the United States. In any of these cases, the price of indifference would be catastrophic."

The Arab-Israeli conflict could be summarized in the way that 'at the heart of the problem is the Jews' sense of insecurity and the Arabs' feeling of injustice and dispossession'. There are several components to the Arab-Israeli conflict: that of the Zionist effort to establish statehood in friction against competing Arab interests in the area of Palestine; that of the subsequent conflict between the state of Israel and the Palestinian nationalist movement; and that of the conflict between Israel and its Arab and Muslim neighbors in the region. Since achieving statehood in 1948, Israel faced immediate and enduring hostility that, in conjunction with a history of persecution, has bred intense feelings of insecurity about its existence and safety in the years since. To the degree that insecurity brings occupation (for 'buffer zones' or 'strategic depth') of Palestinian filled lands in the West Bank and Gaza, the result is increased resentment by those under the permanent military rule of Israel: the Palestinian people. Each side feels the other 'started it'. And each side feels they are merely responding to aggression with resistance.

After 9/11 particularly, a second strategic priority has been the pursuit and disruption of terrorist networks with 'global reach', especially but not exclusively al-Qaeda. Confronting the capabilities and causes of terror in the region presents the United States with new motivation to bolster relationships in the region for intelligence, law enforcement and military action.

Sometime it is stated that the power of domestic politics explains US policy. The source of domestic political influence comes in many forms, but can be summarized by institutional and societal inputs: Congressional-Executive relations, interest groups, and broader electoral politics, as well as the decision-makers' perspectives and beliefs.

A running theme in the history of US policy in the Arab-Israeli conflict involves a pro-Zionist/pro-Israel Congress clashing with an Executive interested in balancing considerations. While Congress appears to be subordinate to the President in power and decision-making, all executives have to deal with the reaction their policies will have on the Hill. Most decisions relating to foreign relations are made in the Executive branch. Nonetheless, Congress has the will and ability to serve as a check on presidential power on this particular issue. In lock-step behind Israel by huge margins on most any issue, the US Congress does not hesitate to produce resolutions of support and appropriations and legislation aimed at publicly declaring support for Israel and cautioning the sitting president not to stray too far from this course.

How the US Congress came to be so pro-Israel may have a lot to do with interest groups. The most noted interest group related to US foreign policy is AIPAC, the American Israel Public Affairs Committee. Its electoral connections and financial and organizational strength are unparalleled by anything constituting an 'Arab' or 'Palestinian' lobby. From 1978-2000, one study concludes, Israeli Political Actions Committees (PACs) outspent Arab/Muslim PACs 99 to 1 in Congressional contributions. The Jewish' lobby includes other groups, such as the Conference of Presidents of Major American Jewish Organizations, composed of 38 groups that formulate and express the 'Jewish position' on foreign policy, including the Arab-Israeli conflict.

The pro-Israel domestic influence extends past the Jewish lobby. There is a coalition of conservative Christians and neo-conservative policy-makers siding strongly with Israel on most any issue. On the religious right, some 55 million evangelical Christians are claimed to support Israel due to a perceived 'powerful spiritual connection between Israel and the Christian faith' and belief that Palestine constituted 'covenant land' that God bestowed upon the Jews. In response to two attacks in Tel Aviv by Palestinian terrorists in early 2003, the Christian Coalition of America (the largest Christian grassroots organization in the United States) issued a statement: saying that 'the enemies of America and the enemies of Israel are one and the same and seek the wanton goal of killing Westerners for their twisted cause'. They vowed to urge Americans 'of all faiths to stand by Israel and urge our government to understand that the Palestinian Authority is devoted to the destruction of the State of Israel'.

No such parallel exists in the power of the Arab or Muslim voting community, where the vote is less potent or more diffuse. The four to six million estimated Muslims in the United States have not had a cohesive, single-issue record on the Arab-Israeli conflict, for example. Nonetheless, one study suggests that George W. Bush's narrow Presidential victory in 2000 could be attributed to the increasingly organized, bloc-voting constituency of Muslim-Americans. As a whole, however, the 'balance of power' in the domestic arena has tilted toward Israel, with public opinion, the media, and formal and informal aspects of the Israel lobby providing pressure and cover for elected officials.

The growing movement favoring democracy and human rights in the Middle East has not shared the remarkable successes of its counterparts in Eastern Europe, Latin America,

Africa and parts of Asia. Most Middle Eastern governments remain autocratic. Despite occasional rhetorical support for greater individual freedoms, the United States has generally not supported tentative Middle Eastern steps toward democratization. Indeed, the United States has reduced — or maintained at low levels — its economic, military and diplomatic support to Arab countries that have experienced substantial political liberalization in recent years while increasing support for autocratic regimes such as Saudi Arabia, Kuwait, Egypt and Morocco. Jordan, for example, received large-scale U.S. support in the 1970s and 1980s despite widespread repression and authoritarian rule; when it opened up its political system in the early 1990s, the U.S. substantially reduced — and, for a time, suspended — foreign aid. Aid to Yemen was cut off within months of the newly unified country's first democratic election in 1990.

In the meanwhile, the United States had largely pursued the first battle of the War on Terror, without much help from the Arab world. Operation Enduring Freedom, combining US air power and Special Forces with local armies in Afghanistan, ousted the Taliban from Kabul and set up an interim successor through a UN conference, all by the end of 2001. By the spring of 2002, the operation was one of 'mopping up' and pursuit of the still-elusive Osama bin Laden and associates.

Increasingly, emboldened by its success in Afghanistan, the United States turned to its next priority in its vision of a War on Terror: Iraq. The Bush administration had been careful to define the 'war' more broadly than merely al-Qaeda and the events of 9/11. Some in the US Administration were convinced that Saddam Hussein, as a sympathizer to some terrorism while allegedly possessing weapons of mass destruction, was an unacceptable combination. As early as February 2002, the Bush Administration made the decision to 'oust Saddam Hussein'. The discussion of just when and how divided the administration between unilateralist hawks – Cheney and

Rumsfeld – and internationalist Powell, who made the case for going to the UN for the legitimacy of the mission. The latter joined a chorus of domestic and international voices concerned with the 'day after implications' of a unilateral, preemptive war on Iraq.

The internationalist won for a time, with the United States taking the case to the UN demanding Hussein is held accountable for his material breach of Security Council Resolutions pertaining to weapons of mass destruction. The Council passed Resolution 1441 ordering inspections back in Iraq, and threatening 'serious consequences' if Iraq did not fully comply.

The United States was skeptical that this process would yield disarmament, and spent the fall of 2002 and winter of 2003 building forces in the Persian Gulf and courting support for the eventual use of force. They had little success. As it has happened with his father before him, Bush sought to wage war against Iraq in midst of a jittery region. Unlike his father, the junior Bush appeared to be hurtling toward confrontation with or without the region, the UN, or the world – all this with less legal justification than the elder Bush, who at least was responding to an Iraqi act of aggression. Middle East states were reluctant to participate or endorse a war started by a Western superpower against an Arab or Muslim fellow state. Jordan's King Abdullah said that a US attack on Iraq would be catastrophic for the Middle East. Thousands of people took to the streets in Arab capitals to protest against a possible US war on Iraq, labeling President Bush a 'butcher'. Most Arab countries opposed war against Iraq fearing it would further destabilize the Middle East, and advocated instead a peaceful solution to the crisis over Iraq's alleged weapons of mass destruction.

Vice President Dick Cheney visited the Middle East in early 2002 to solicit support for US plans to oust Saddam Hussein from power. The Bush Administration already offered a major missile sale to Egypt and an increase in foreign assistance to Jordan, but the concern for the Palestinian issue would not go away, nor was an Arab state politically able to side with the United States in a war on an Arab country while the 'other war' (Palestinian) continued to be ignored by the United States. Bush did as his father have done, promising action on the Arab-Israeli problem after dealing with Iraq.

Britain shares broadly the same interests as other Western countries regarding the Middle East: maintaining the flow of oil, combating radical forces and preventing them from threatening regional stability or Britain itself with a lethal combination of terrorism and WMD. Britain also has extensive commercial interests in the region, though arms sales, which were very important in the past, are likely to become much less important in the future. Within British policy there are two long-standing orientations as to how to advance these interests that can be termed 'Strategic' and 'Diplomatic'.

The Diplomatic orientation emphasizes maintaining the best possible relations with existing regimes or those forces that seem likely to take power. It recommends that Britain try to meet the demands of such forces as much as possible and to avoid confrontation. Often, a major demand of such regimes is the adoption of a pro-Arab stance on the Arab-Israel conflict. Against this background, Israel tends to be viewed as a cause of instability and anti-Western feeling in the Arab world. The Diplomatic orientation is associated with a mutually reinforcing combination of ideological sympathy for the Palestinians, the Foreign and Commonwealth Office, a pro-European orientation and, to a decreasing extent, commercial interests. (Israel was actually the UK's biggest bilateral trading partner in the Middle East in the first years of the new millennium.) In contemporary domestic politics, the Diplomatic approach is strongest on the left, within the Labour party and the Liberal-Democrat party. It also has increasing domestic political value, due to the improved political effectiveness of Britain's Muslim community, which greatly outnumbers the Jewish community.

The Strategic orientation focuses on threats - military, political and ideological, and on countering them. It perceives aggressive anti-Western governments and belief systems as the principle threats, which must be contained and sometimes actively challenged. Against this background, Israel is viewed positively due to its Western orientation, its military strength and by virtue of common enemies: Islamist Iran, Iraq under Saddam Hussein, Ba'athist Syria, Hamas and Hezbollah. The Strategic approach is associated with a mutually reinforcing combination of ideological sympathy for Israel, a pro-US orientation and the office of the Prime Minister. It is well represented in the contemporary Conservative party and among moderate Labour leaders.

Of the factors underpinning the two orientations, the most important is the tension between an 'Atlantic' (pro-US) orientation and a 'European' orientation. Since its decline from Great Power status in 1945, Britain has sought to retain influence by working more closely with these partners. Rather than choose between them it has generally sort to act as a 'bridge' between the two. Yet it has proven much easier for Britain to enunciate such ideas that to actually implement them, as is clear regarding recent British policy in the Middle East.

From the beginning of the post-Cold War era when Saddam invaded Kuwait, Britain has been the most loyal ally of the US. During the 1991 Gulf War, Britain deployed an armoured division, putting it in a clear number two position to the US within the coalition. In the 1990s Britain supported the US against French and Russian attempts to lift the oil embargo on Iraq and to dilute the weapons inspections system. Britain was also America's only ally to be actively involved in the military strikes in the late 1990s against Saddam. While backing the US against its critics in Europe, Britain's attempts at bridging were apparent in its consistent efforts to encourage the US to gain wider legitimacy for its actions by working through international institutions. The most obvious example of this was Blair's success in persuading a reluctant Bush administration to try and gain prior UN backing for the 2003 war in Iraq. Ultimately however, this bridging tactic failed, forcing Blair to side with the US against France and Germany. The fallout seems to have damaged Blair's position within the Labour party more than Britain's standing within the EU, due to the support the US received from new members of the EU such as Poland and the Czech Republic.

Sympathetic observers might point to recent policy on Libya as example of British success. During the Thatcher era, the 'Strategic' orientation dominated British policy towards Libya, as was most obviously apparent in British support for the US bombing of Libya in April 1986. In the 1990s, lacking a clear lead from the US, UK policy drifted towards the European position. In 2003, as a byproduct of the Iraq War, the Libyan President, Col. Gaddafi, announced that he would dismantle all of Libya's nuclear, chemical and biological weapons programs. Britain played a central diplomatic role in making this happen. Britain's successful 'engagement' of Libya was quite closely coordinated with the US, however the Europeans were far less involved.

In the 1990s, while the US pursued a policy of 'dual containment' towards Iran and Iraq, opposing diplomatic and economic contacts, the EU, including Britain, pursued a 'critical dialogue'. The most powerful force behind Britain's drive to normalize relations with Iran was commercial advantage. As a result, Britain accepted verbal, as opposed to written, assurances that Tehran would not continue to proffer the bounty on Salman Rushdie's head. As late as 2003, Foreign Secretary Jack Straw, who made four visits to Teheran in 2002-2003, described Iran as an 'emerging democracy' and stressed the 'good cooperation' that Britain has enjoyed from the regime in Teheran. Nevertheless, British engagement of Iran has so far failed to yield solid gains regarding the most important strategic issue - Iran's nuclear program in which US was greatly involved. In the latter part of 2003, following a concerted effort led by Britain in cooperation with France and Germany, the Iranians announced the cessation of efforts at enriching uranium, and re-admission of nuclear inspectors into their country. However, Iran quickly reneged on that agreement and despite continued negotiations; Britain has become extremely disillusioned with Iran and is leading efforts to bring the Iranian nuclear question to the Security Council, much to the satisfaction of the US. The US and UK expressed their disagreement on India's intension of strategic cooperation with Iran. Recently, Britain has also begun to publicly criticize Iranian support for Hizbullah and Islamic Jihad terrorism. In tandem, a far more critical line towards the Syrian regime has been pursued, as part of an emerging consensus that includes both France and the US.

The issue of 'bridging' has been most acute in the Arab-Israeli arena. On the one hand, Britain accepts and supports substantive US diplomatic leadership in this arena, while seeking to coordinate EU and US positions. Unlike France, it does not generally want the EU to 'balance against' the US in this arena. On the other hand, Britain has demonstrated a consistent willingness to adopt formal European positions that differ from the US stance. This was evident after the International Court of Justice ruled against Israel on the issue of the separation barrier in 2004. Britain was initially inclined to oppose a UN General Assembly resolution condemning Israel. However, following intra-European negotiations, Britain gave way to France and voted with the EU bloc in favour of the resolution.

In the 1990s it was relatively easy for Britain to pursue a policy of 'balance' due to the existence of the peace process. Thus, in 1995 Prime Minister John Major became the first Western leader to hold talks with Yasir Arafat, inside Palestine Authority (PA) territory, while the first official royal visit to Israel took place in 1998. In addition, following the ending of the

British arms embargo on Israel in 1994, the defence relationship grew significantly until the collapse of the peace process in 2000.

The first consequence of the collapse of the peace process was the re-emergence of the diplomatic orientation evident in comments by the Foreign Secretary Jack Straw, on alleged 'double standards' at the UN regarding Security Council resolutions dealing with Iraq and those dealing with Israel. Such statements were designed to 'cover' Britain's support for the Iraq war. More generally, this orientation was bolstered by the Left's outrage at Israeli policy and domestic political calculations aimed at appeasing the Muslim community. This 'red-green' alliance played the leading role in the campaign to boycott Israeli universities and delegitimize Israel as the new version of South African Apartheid. Though the 2005 British Association of University Teachers (AUT) boycott was reversed almost immediately, support among trade union activists (and many Church leaders) for a wider boycott is widespread, despite the opposition of both the government and the Conservative opposition. Israel is also extremely unpopular with middle-class, educated, public opinion.

In terms of British-Israeli relations, this transnational dimension is far more problematic than official state-to-state relations, which are currently quite positive since Prime Minister Blair is sympathetic to Israel and has pushed British policy in a more Strategic direction. Thus, Britain opposed calls within the EU for the freezing or rescinding of trade agreements with Israel. Moreover, Blair was among the European statesmen most critical of Arafat's failure to act against terror. He also recently took a lead in Europe proposing that Hizbullah be defined as a terrorist organization. Nonetheless, Blair has consistently sought to encourage the US to be more active in advancing the Road Map, with some success. While Blair supports Bush's plan for reform of the Arab world, he argued that it required a resolution of the Arab-Israeli conflict, since

Arab regimes used the conflict as an excuse for blocking domestic reform, while Al Qaida used it to garner support. However, Britain has sought to advance the peace process, while taking seriously Israeli concerns regarding security. In this vein, Britain has been the leading international power trying to facilitate reform of the Palestinian security services, the first chronological step of the Road Map. Britain has also taken the lead on Palestinian reform more generally, hosting an international conference on the subject in London in March 2005.

In the wake of the 2003 Iraq War, there has been an enormous amount of criticism directed at British policy, mainly by those opposed to the war who advocate Britain adopting a more wholehearted European orientation (though in the wake of the 7/7 terrorist attacks on London, criticism has become more muted). Yet it is doubtful that such a change would actually increase British influence (or indeed prevent terror attacks on London). In fact, it would probably diminish British influence.

Britain's standing in Europe has not declined as a result of its support for the US in Iraq. Meanwhile, alone in Europe, only Britain has played any serious diplomatic role in the Israeli-Palestinian arena, due to its consistent support for the US and its acceptability to Israel - which in turn is due both to the US factor and to the fact that it has adopted a more balanced approach to the conflict that the EU as a whole. However, while 'bridging' probably remains the best strategy open to Britain, one that can provide it with a constructive role, it does not necessarily make Britain a central player. In this vein, Blair's grandiose Churchillian vision of Britain as a 'pivotal power, a power that is at the crux of alliances and international politics which shape the world' is completely unrealistic. Ultimately, British diplomatic efforts depend on the good will of other parties, not on British power. Consequently, while 'bridging' gives Britain a satisfying sense of 'punching above its weight', it often produces only a semblance of substantive influence, rather than the real thing.

DEFENCE AND NUCLEAR COOPERATION

In the 19th century, there was no particular warmth in interstate relations between Britain and the United States. There was one, albeit short, war between them and periodic tensions. The United States continued to follow the advice of the founding fathers and avoided "entangling alliances," concentrating on western hemispheric concerns. The United Kingdom devoted its energies to the empire and the maintenance of a balance of power in Europe. Even World War I, when both countries fought a common foe, did not bring the two noticeably closer together. Indeed, American hostility to colonialism and the British exploitation of victory to expand their empire left relations decidedly cool. Naval rivalry exacerbated this coolness. The British soon realized they could not afford a naval race and had to reach an accommodation on American terms. However the growing threat of fascism failed to shift the United States away from a disapproving isolationism born of disillusionment with the Versailles settlement.

The US-UK "special relationship" was a product of the combined endeavor to defeat Nazi Germany and Imperial Japan. In origin, it was thus a relatively recent phenomenon. Moreover, the close wartime relationship, often stormy as a result of disagreements over strategy, masked continuing differences over the desired nature of the postwar world. Initially, as if little had changed, the UK reverted to the pursuit of national interest—a Mediterranean strategy and the maintenance of empire.

As British power and influence steadily became more threadbare and the retreat from empire accelerated, Britain clung ever more closely to the United States. It argued, to itself as much as to other powers, that its influence over America, stemming from the special relationship, still gave it the status of a great power—a status underscored by its possession of a nuclear deterrent (even though the independent nature of its force soon became illusory as it became dependent on the United States for its delivery system). The special relationship thus assumed a central place in London's worldview and strategy. It was not mirrored in Washington. The United States was a genuine world power, pursuing a global mission and interests. In doing so, it would cooperate with the UK where that was advantageous, for example in NATO and over the Falklands dispute. But where national interest dictated, it would cheerfully ignore Britain. Actually it was apparently a close call whether or not it would side with Argentina in 1982, and in the next year America trumped up an excuse to invade a Commonwealth country, Grenada, without so much as a word to its closest ally.

Nevertheless, the special relationship had substance during the Cold War as both parties shared a common, and overriding, strategic goal. While differing over some issues, for instance the desirability of closer European integration (favored by Washington, resisted in London), the two countries were happy to work together to give leadership and coherence to a sometimes wavering NATO. Of course, the United States gave the direction and Britain gave it loyal support. However, the end of the Cold War revealed important latent differences in national interests and in attitudes to problems.

It is clear that the 60-year-old Anglo-American special relationship was a product of specific Cold War circumstances and based on a common need. The ending of those circumstances and needs is progressively revealing major differences in policy. The United States has global interests and aspirations that are not always shared by Britain. It could also be added that the relationship was never based on mutual admiration; for cultural and historical reasons, each partner traditionally has felt a measure of indifference, even condescension and disdain, for the other.

DEFENSE RELATIONSHIP

This British approach to defense reflects the conviction of Prime Minister Tony Blair that Britain must conduct an active foreign policy, when necessary reinforcing it with armed intervention, to make the world a safer and better place. As the UK can do relatively little on its own, this will require close cooperation with a similarly activist United States. This, in turn, reflects—and dovetails effectively with—the primary aim of foreign policy as set out by Blair in his definitive address to British ambassadors in January 2003—that Britain should remain America's closest ally (in the hope and expectation that the United States would reciprocate). In June 2003, then Defence Secretary Geoffrey Hoon echoed his master's words, setting out the assumptions that guide his department's work:

- there is a moral requirement for Britain's armed forces to be a force for good in the world;

- the reality is that, in all but minor affairs, little can be accomplished without help from the Americans, who will participate only if they lead;

- the special relationship is the bedrock of British foreign policy, and, to sustain it, the country must be prepared to pay a price, including blood, to prove that it is the most dependable U.S. ally;

- UK defense gains much from close association with America; and,

- loyalty and reliability gain Britain significant influence in Washington.

Britain also profits from intelligence cooperation. The intelligence relationship goes back over 60 years (and cooperation continued even during periods of wider policy disagreements). Until the explosion of American investment in intelligence collection during the Cold War, especially in outer space (which the UK could not match), Britain led the field. Even today, its expertise in analysis in the areas of imagery intelligence (IMINT), signals intelligence (SIGINT), and technical intelligence (TECHINT) makes a significant contribution to the joint endeavor. But there can be no doubt that, deprived of uniquely privileged access to the fruits of American collection efforts, Britain would be critically lacking in situational awareness.

But despite the wishful thinking, indeed boasting, of most politicians and journalists and some military men, the harsh reality appears to be that British participation is not highly valued in purely military terms. In a few niche areas, such as intelligence, mine clearance, photo reconnaissance, and special operations, the contributions are indeed important. However, the Royal Navy and Air Force as a whole are seen to be perilously close to critical mass and add little of significance to American strength. Similarly, in the realm of ground forces, any British contribution is somewhat marginal; numbers often still matter, as the Iraqi insurgency is demonstrating anew, and the Army lacks them.

Consequently, British influence on American military doctrinal development is marginal—at least unless and until events prove the formers ideas to be superior. Similarly, in both the 1991 and 2003 attacks on Iraq, while the British had an impact on tactical planning, their say in defining the end state and in campaign planning was minimal. There was no reestablishment of the wartime Combined Chiefs of Staff committee. British involvement was not critical to American success.

Very often the USA laid to take UK for granted. Thus, for instance, President Bill Clinton undermined British policy over the wars of Yugoslav succession and interfered in the internal affairs of the UK over the Northern Ireland problem. President George W. Bush has conceded little or nothing to Prime Minister Blair over issues dear to the latter's heart, such as involvement of the United Nations (UN) in the invasion of Iraq, combating climate change, the International Criminal Court, and the way in which the Israeli-Palestinian problem should be approached. These examples rather suggest that the special relationship has not survived the end of the Cold War in a fashion palatable to a UK that seeks to promote its own national interests.

Europeans can be forgiven for occasionally asking if Americans *really* support the EU's European Security and Defense Policy (ESDP). Since NATO's creation in 1949, Washington has alternately encouraged and hectored its allies to assume a larger share of the responsibilities and burdens of collective defense and—beginning with NATO's involvement in Bosnia in 1995—crisis response. At the same time, Republican and Democratic administrations alike have looked to NATO as the anchor of U.S. engagement in European security affairs and the primary multilateral venue for shaping allies' defense policies and capabilities. Hence, when Prime Minister Blair and President Jacques Chirac agreed at St. Malo, France, in December 1998 that the EU "must have the capacity for autonomous action, backed up by credible military forces, the means to decide to use them and a readiness to do so, in order to respond to international crises," Washington's initial response was polite but distinctly chilly.

The European Union did not make its own internal boundaries irrelevant after World War II which has reinforced by the 1975 Helsinki Conference. Moreover, the presence of US military power in Cold War Europe guaranteed the survival and economic development of the European peoples separately within the territorial boundaries of Europe's nation-states.

The politics in the Balkans had always been Euro-Centric. During the two World Wars and after that the crisis in the region was always viewed as a European crisis. However, the scale of "ethnic cleansing" after the disintegration of Yugoslavia and failure on the part of European countries to manage the crisis and its spillover effect, brought US engagement into forefront in Balkan politics.

After the end of the cold war the danger of domination over the European continent by an expansionist power has vanished for the foreseeable future, as have the related political and economic dangers. At the same time, the danger of the United States becoming embroiled European conflict remains needlessly high. Indeed, this danger has at least three sources in the post-Cold War period.

First, US forces could become involved in European conflicts simply because fighting breaks out in countries where they are stationed. Such forces could even be attacked directly – especially by terrorist or irregular forces. Second, US forces could become involved because they are stationed close enough to the fighting to make use a tempting option for interventionist presidents. Finally, American forces could be involved in post-Cold War European conflicts out of a perceived need to strengthen NATO's credibility. Significantly, that rationale figured prominently in America's Bosnia and Kosovo interventions.

The United States with the support of the UK deals with the Balkans on terms its inhabitants understand and respect: power politics and fair agreements. All of the peoples who live on the territory of the former Yugoslavia deserve to survive and prosper within a just framework. But to create such a framework, the US dispensation understands that European themselves, rather than Americans far removed from the context, shape the path to regional stability. But due to the inadequacy of diplomatic maneuvering and military firepower of the Europeans including the UK the US intervention was inevitable.

In 1995 the Clinton administration concluded that American military intervention was indispensable to any resolution of the Balkan crisis. European reluctance to intervene militarily to stop the Yugoslav conflict reinforced this attitude.

After the shelling of a Sarajevo market place killed scores of innocent civilians on 28 August 1995, Clinton seized the opportunity to employ American and allied air power on the side of the Croat and Bosniac armies. In early September 1995 the Bosnian Serb leaders, confronting seemingly unstoppable ground forces and a ferocious allied bombing campaign, signaled a readiness to talk peace. Clinton then suspended the bombing and left resolution of the dispute to the diplomats gathered a Dayton, Ohio. The result was an uneasy truce that ended the fighting before either side could win or lose the war.

Fresh memories of intra-European wrangling over the former Yugoslavia in the early 1990s, combined with growing worries about the situation in Kosovo, no doubt played a role here. Some Americans worried whether, to use then French Defense Minister Alain Richard's analogy, the EU would be capable of "taking care of fires in its own backyard." Or would the EU, to be blunt, produce "all talk no action"? More broadly, some U.S. officials wondered whether key consultations and decisions on security matters might migrate over time from NATO, where America's unique political and military strengths ensure it has a preponderant role in shaping Alliance policies and operations, to the EU, where there is no U.S. seat at the table.

The wars in Yugoslavia began in the summer of 1991, when Slovenia broke away from the Federal Republic of Yugoslavia and gained its independence in a ten-day war. These events triggered a Croatian independence movement, which was followed closely by secessionist claims from Bosnia and Croatia in 1992. From 1992 to 1995, Croatia and nearly all of Bosnia remained engulfed in conflict, as Yugoslavian President Slobodan Milosevic actively supported Bosnian-Serb factions who operated across the region.

In 1992 and much of 1993, it can fairly be summarized that NATO's major allies preferred limited intervention into the region. US President Bush and his administration favored little more than UN-sponsored humanitarian assistance, and viewed the problem and solutions as essentially 'European'. Although Bill Clinton criticized President Bush's handling of the Bosnia crisis during the 1992 presidential campaign and called for a more assertive American military presence, once in office he too resisted meaningful military engagement in 1993.

Officially or through its former statesmen and diplomats Britain was involved in drawing up all the international community plans for a peaceful solution of the conflict in Bosnia and Herzegovina. Britain participated in the signing of the General Framework Agreement for peace in Bosnia and Herzegovina and was one of the first countries to have placed its military forces at the disposal of the United Nations in Bosnia and Herzegovina.

One of the controversial issues where the Conservative Government of Britain changed position is the issue of the territorial integrity of Yugoslavia and the recognition of Slovenia, Croatia and, in particular, Bosnia and Herzegovina. In the early phase of disagreements between individual republics with respect to the possibility of resolving the Yugoslav constitutional crisis the then Conservative Government firmly supported the territorial integrity of Yugoslavia. In keeping with this position, Britain stressed explicitly on a number of occasion that the republics wishing to secede from Yugoslavia would not get support. The British Government Gradually changed this position. Some doubts were first expressed (June-July 1999) "that it is perhaps not possible to keep the whole country together". In October 1991, it was finally uttered that "Yugoslavia could neither be kept together by force, not could old Yugoslavia be renewed". Contrary to its own warning to its European Commission partners' that early recognition of the seceded republics without a political solution could lead to violence and even to the outbreak of war, especially in Bosnia and Herzegovina, and contrary to the recommendations of the Bandinter Arbitration Commission, Britain recognized Slovenia and Croatia on January 15, 1992, and Bosnia and Herzegovina on April 7, 1992.

Britain was one of the chief advocates of political and economic pressure on the actors in conflict but was, at the same time, highly skeptical about any form of military intervention as a method of pressure, or resolution of the Yugoslav crisis. It was considered that military intervention could not enforce a solution for the problems in Yugoslavia. Britain was especially against the sending of troops to Bosnia and Herzegovina with such assignments, but also against air strikes. The British Conservative Government also excluded a third form of military intervention – bombing of Serb targets; it was against lifting the arms supply embargo for any warring party in Bosnia. While opposing the idea that the problems could be resolved and peace imposed by the use of troops, Britain however, joined the countries that placed their military forces at the United Nations' disposal, always stressing that these forces would not be used to intervene in the fighting between the rival groups in the former Yugoslavia. Still, the then British Government did not entirely rule out the possibility of selective strikes in which its forces would not participate. It reluctantly agreed to the UN and NATO decisions to launch missiles on April 1994 and bomb in August and September 1995 the positions of Bosnian Serbs, considering that such strikes could help to end armed conflicts and accelerate the negotiation process.

Throughout the summer of 1992, as the UN adopted a more assertive role in Bosnia and the possibility of military intervention was discussed, EC peacemaking efforts continued; however, little headway was made. When progress did come about, trans-Atlantic misunderstandings at times proved costly. The London Conference, co-chaired by British Prime Minister John Major and the UN Secretary-General, was attended from 26-28 August 1992 by delegates from the UN, the EC and the CSCE, as well as representatives of the main Yugoslav factions.

A special working group on Bosnia was established "to promote a cessation of hostilities and a constitutional settlement" in the republic, as well as a Geneva-based negotiating forum sponsored jointly by the UN and the EC. The UN representative remained Cyrus Vance, while Lord David Owen, a former British foreign secretary, replaced the recently retired Lord Carrington as the EC envoy. The Geneva Conference was to become the driving force behind all subsequent peace initiatives.

All parties to the conflict were urged "immediately and without preconditions to resume negotiations on future constitutional arrangements." Vance and Owen were to conduct these negotiations according to strict guidelines.

The London Conference provided new hopes for an end to the fighting; however, those hopes were short-lived. While the international community may have finally shown some degree of consensus in its handling of the war in Bosnia, the combatants showed no more willingness to settle their differences. Peace negotiations between the three ethnic communities in September yielded no results, while agreements reached at London to allow the UN to monitor heavy weapons around Sarajevo and other Muslim-held towns were ignored. Serb bombardment of Muslim territory continued unabated and by October 1992 the promise had largely been forgotten. Since the London Conference contained no real hint of punitive measures or the threat of outside force, Vance and Owen possessed limited leverage. As John Major remarked, "we cannot rely on the good will of the parties. We need pressure."

UN Resolution 781, approved by the Security Council on 9 October 1992, imposed a ban on flights by warplanes in Bosnian air space; however, UNPROFOR could only monitor compliance, not enforce it. Although Serbian warplanes were eventually persuaded to stay on the ground, it made little difference – air power had played a negligible role in the conflict. Finally, on 23 November warships of NATO and the

WEU began to stop and search any ships entering or leaving Yugoslav waters suspected of ignoring UN sanctions against Serbia.

As the early promise of the London Conference began to fade and the Serbs continued their success on the ground, popular pressure for military action again mounted. The Islamic Conference Organization hinted at possible intervention but in Geneva Cyrus Vance and David Owen made a strong plea to avoid any military action that would imperil either their negotiations or the 7,000 peacekeepers in Bosnia. Senior UN military officials in the region agreed.

On 2 January 1993, the leaders of the three ethnic groups sat down in Geneva to hold direct talks for the first time. Under the terms of the Vance-Owen plan, Bosnia would become a decentralized state with most governmental functions carried out by its provinces, although the latter would possess no "international legal personality" or authority to sign agreements with foreign states. The Vance-Owen plan was a desperate attempt to do the impossible. The Serbian president may have begun to feel the sting of sanctions or understood that although the Vance-Owen plan was not perfect, the possible alternatives – isolation, foreign intervention, substantial loss of Serb territory – might be worse. However, the Bosnian Serbs would not accept the map, even after 14 January 1993, when EC foreign ministers gave them a six-day ultimatum to accept the plan in its entirety.

By the end of January 1993 the two sides were deadlocked. The talks were moved from Geneva to New York at the beginning of February in the hope that the Security Council and the United States would endorse the plan. Although the EC had approved the package on 1 February 1993, the US remained skeptical. The American press made references to Munich and appeasement, while Warren Christopher, the Secretary of State, believed that the plan was impractical and rewarded Serb aggression. President Clinton reportedly wanted the map redrawn to give more territory to the Muslims. But the Americans offered no real alternatives. Clinton had chided President Bush during the election campaign for his timid stance on Bosnia and had even suggested possible military intervention. Now the American president was being criticized for his own indecision and lack of vision. Washington's policy on Bosnia, the critics were shouting, was adrift.

On 10 February 1993, Clinton's administration spoke out. The American government finally endorsed, somewhat reluctantly, the Vance-Owen plan, although it stipulated that in no circumstances should it be imposed on any one party. The president also promised to become "actively and directly engaged" in the peace process and made a number of proposals aimed at breaking the deadlock. These included tightening the sanctions against Serbia; enforcing the no-fly zone through a Security Council resolution; establishing a war crimes tribunal to try those suspected of committing atrocities; lending American support, in cooperation with the UN and NATO, to the enforcement of a "viable agreement" on Bosnia, using force if necessary; and encouraging the greater involvement of Russia in the peace process. Clinton also appointed Reginald Bartholomew, US ambassador to NATO, as special American envoy to the international peace talks on the former Yugoslavia.

With the American government's decision to become more involved in the peace process and to support the Vance-Owen plan, there was hope once again that a turning point in the Bosnian conflict had been reached. But the fighting continued through the winter and early spring of 1993, especially in the east, where Serb forces attempted to consolidate those regions designated Muslim under the Vance-Owen plan. On the negotiating front, progress remained slow. After moving the talks to New York at the beginning of February 1993, little headway was made over the next month. In early

March 1993, Izetbegovic finally accepted the cease-fire provisions, after having been assured by UNPROFOR that it would take possession of the Serbs' heavy weapons.

Throughout this period of frenzied negotiation, the logistics of implementing the Vance-Owen plan were being discussed within UN and NATO circles. Although Boutros-Ghali was insistent that the UN should have ultimate political and strategic control of the operation (it would after all be financed collectively by UN member-states), he realized from the start that the agreement would exceed the planning capability of the UN Secretariat and UNPROFOR. Since NATO was the only body with an adequate organization to manage such a large operation, it agreed to lay the groundwork. NATO experts estimated that 60 - 75,000 troops would be required to carry out the various military tasks; the bulk of the force would be provided by the United States, with Great Britain and France supplying large contingents as well.

By the time the Serbs had rejected the Vance-Owen plan on 5 May 1993, however, talk had shifted away from the logistics of peacekeeping to the prospect of immediate military intervention. Never had such discussion been taken so seriously, especially in the United States. The American military remained opposed on both tactical and strategic grounds to any large-scale military action. Although some military experts suggested that the Serbs could be defeated within a week by two or three well-trained divisions, most were arguing that it would now require hundreds of thousands of troops over an indefinite period. Clinton took this advice to heart; he continued to insist that the Unites States would not deploy ground troops in Bosnia unless a viable peace agreement had been signed. However, his administration was running out of patience with Serb recalcitrance. Warren Christopher, Vice-President Al Gore and National Security Adviser Anthony Lake were in favour of air strikes; Defense Secretary Les Aspin was non-committal, while Chairman of the Joint Chiefs of Staff General Colin

Powell opposed such action. Finally, at the end of April Clinton chose the so-called "lift-and-strike" option: suspending the UN arms embargo and launching air strikes against the Bosnian Serbs to keep them at bay while the Muslims learned to operate the new sophisticated weaponry that was flooding in. It was soon revealed that Washington had already deployed 100 military-intelligence troops in Bosnia to locate possible targets, especially supply routes across the Serbian border.

Christopher was dispatched to Europe to sound out Washington's NATO allies but it quickly became apparent that, with the exception of Germany, no country in the EC would support "lift-and- strike." Both new and old arguments were employed. Britain and France once again expressed the fear, as did UN officials on the ground, that any military action ran the risk of precipitating Serb reprisal attacks against their peacekeeping troops in Bosnia. Moreover, as the EC Foreign Ministers pointed out in Denmark on 25 April 1993, lifting the arms embargo might escalate the conflict and perhaps allow it to spread outside Bosnia's borders. There were other questions, some basic, some not: Where would the arms come from? How would they be delivered? What were the political and military objectives of air strikes? Field Marshal Sir Richard Vincent, the British Chairman of NATO's Military Committee, advised Western governments in late April 1993 that they should decide what they wanted to achieve in Bosnia before advocating any kind of enforcement.

The Europeans would compromise very little, as they remained committed to the idea of peacekeeping and the delivery of humanitarian aid. At the very least, they hoped to avoid any serious talk of military action until Milosevic's pledge to seal the border with Bosnia had been tested. The British government hinted that they might agree at a later date to limited air strikes against Serb supply and communications lines (Lord Owen had even suggested that this might be necessary) but only as a last resort. The Russians suggested that an easing of sanctions against Belgrade might produce results, while the French once again recommended creating safe areas to protect besieged Muslims in eastern Bosnia and elsewhere.

The Americans were not prepared to act on their own. Attending a meeting of senior NATO military officials in Brussels on 27 April 1993, General Colin Powell made it clear that the American government would not consider any military action without specific authority from the UN. Since there was a possibility that Russia or France might veto any Security Council resolution advocating the lift-and-strike option, Washington had effectively reached a dead end. The Bosnian Serb gambles that a lack of consensus in the west would prevent any possibility of direct military intervention continued to pay dividends.

The growing rift between the US and Europe was soon being labeled by some observers as the greatest crisis in trans-Atlantic relations since the Suez debacle of 1956. The language was not always diplomatic. Joseph Biden, senior Democrat on the Senate Foreign Relations Committee and a firm supporter of "lift-and- strike," characterized European policy as a "discouraging mosaic of indifference, timidity, self-delusion and hypocrisy." Perhaps more important, the split revealed different concepts of what the conflict was about. The Europeans saw Bosnia as being consumed by civil war, while the Americans viewed it as an independent state being victimized by externally directed aggression.

The tide of war and diplomacy turned fully against the Bosnian Serbs, who suffered military defeats at the hands of the Federation forces and US-led NATO air strikes in August, 1995. The Serbs had little choice but to accept the US-peace plan, in the face of military defeat and international sanctions. The Dayton Peace Agreement divided Bosnia between two separate entities, the Muslim-Croat Federation, which held 51 percent of the territory, and the Serb-held region, Republika Srpska (RS), which held 49 percent. A settlement little different to the Lisbon proposals rejected by the US, prior to the war, back in 1992. There has been little critical consideration of the international community's facilitation of the disintegration of Yugoslavia and the role that over-extended international regulation has had in institutionalizing ethnic divisions and weakening political structures across the region.

As one of the leading European and world powers, with special interests and a prominent position in the European Community (Union) and NATO, as one of the five permanent UN security Council members, Britain has been playing a key role in the complex combination of influences exerted by the international community on the course of the Yugoslav crisis in its entirety. Either directly, by expressing its views, acting on its own and through European and world institutions, or by providing "good offices", Britain was among the countries most actively engaged in the resolution of the Yugoslav syndrome. As one of the initiators, it hosted the first International Conference on the Former Yugoslavia held in London in August 26-17, 1992. It proposed and co-sponsored a great number of UN Security Council Resolutions dealing with the Yugoslav crisis. As one of the five members of the Contact Group, Britain participated in the Dayton negotiations. It was one of the principal initiators of the Rambouillet and Paris meetings dedicated to Kosovo and Metohija.

In the early stage of the Yugoslavia crisis (1991), Britain formulated a number of general points of its stand towards the former Yugoslavia, and the crisis it was faced with. At the beginning, the British Government strongly supported the territorial integrity of Yugoslavia. It supported the democratic processes in individual republics and in the country as a whole. The then Conservative British Government claimed that it had no intention of interfering with internal affairs or taking anybody's side; it pointed out its willingness to offer "good offices" to the parties in conflict in order to find a peaceful way for settling their differences. Its basic motto, according to British officials, was "impartiality and an actively neural attitude" towards the crisis and all parties in conflict.

Some of these stands have remained the general points of Britain's policy. It renounced or changed some others due to the changed policies of the major international community factors towards the crisis, due to the necessary adjustment to the dramatic changes in Yugoslavia.

At the early stage of the Yugoslav crisis, Britain proclaimed as one of its basic principles the "offering of good offices," "non-interference in internal affairs", "impartiality and an actively neutral attitude" towards the crisis and all parties in conflict. In practice, however, there were considerable departures from these principles. In accordance with the proclaimed "pressure and talks" principle, expressed for the first time on the eve of the International Conference on Yugoslavia which took place in London in August 1992, this pressure on "non-cooperative actors" was mainly directed at the Serbian side, "the authorities in Belgrade and representatives of the Serbs in Bosnia and Herzegovina", because it deemed them to be the main and most responsible culprits for the outbreak of the crisis and the horrors of war.

In principle the policy of the British Government regarding the Kosovo problem incorporated three elements. Firstly, Kosovo and Metohija had to remain an integral part of Serbia, and/or Yugoslavia. Britain officially took this stand as early as mid-1992. Secondly, all Kosovo and Ketohija citizens should be guaranteed all human rights, including the corresponding rights for the Albanian national minority, in keeping with international standards. Thirdly, in view of the existing large Albanian ethnic group in Kosovo and Metohija, this province should have "an adequate autonomous or special status within the Yugoslav Federation". As an integral part of the Western Alliance, and consistent with the EU Common Foreign and Security Policy, Britain was in some situations ready to renounce some of its positions for the sake of "common European interests". At the same time, there is a number of examples proving that Britain acted fully independently, often contrary to the positions of the majority of EU member countries, even the United States. These differences, particularly in relation to Germany and the United States, reached sometimes a degree of undisguised dissatisfaction, and even confrontation, but they never exceeded the limits that would endanger "the Union unity" or "special relationship" between Britain and the United States.

The newly-formed Labour Government inherited the process of implementation of the Dayton Accords for Peace in Bosnia and Herzegovia, and the overall set of issues relating to the numerous problems of a peaceful resolution of the relationship within and between the newly-formed states in the territory of the former Yugoslavia. The Labour Government however was confronted with the most serious challenges, when the crisis in Kosovo and Metohija flared up again. This basic feature of the Labor Government's approach to this challenge is a large gap between the positions and principle regarding the crisis solution, and the specific actions in all stages of the Kosovo drama. Also, many aspects of the British Labour Government's policy show a pronounced change in its foreign policy strategy compared to that of the preceding Conservative Government.

Tony Blair in his first appearance in the international arena after the May 1997 election sought to achieve two complementary goals. The first was to have Britain impose itself as one of the leading players in Europe. The Government endeavored to achieve this goal by articulated initiatives for further build-up of the European Union, by seeking to strengthen efforts for the creation of the common EU foreign security policy, the creation of a separate European defense identity within NATO and through the Western European Union, by attempts to achieve a more important role in hotbeds of crisis, particularly in the territory of the former Yugoslavia and in Kosovo and Metohija, primarily with the Contact Group. The second objective within the traditional "special relations" between Britain and the United States, was to establish the closest possible links with the Clinton administration, to express the "Anglo-Saxon" solidarity and the unshakable loyalty to the single super-power, the United States and to build up a dual axis where Britain would occupy a special place in the new post-bipolar constellation of forces. It is symptomatic that in his attempts to establish the special relationship with the United States and President Bill Clinton, Tony Blair also launched the ideas, such as the creation of a "new centre-left politics" where the leading role would be played by the British Labour and American Democrats.

At the beginning of the acute crisis in Kosovo and Metohija in late 1998 and early 1999, the new Labour Government generally advocated some principles already supported by the previous Conservative Government. The Labour Government also expressed in view on the need of maintaining the territorial integrity of the Federal Republic of Yugoslavia and of complying with the principle of the inviolability of borders. It also supported the view that Kosovo and Metohija should remain an integral part of Serbia and Yugoslavia, and that the issue of its autonomous or special status should be solved peacefully "in a dialogue between the two sides".

The escalation of violence in Kosovo and Metohija and the conflicts between the security forces and the so-called "Kosovo Liberation Army" intensified the engagement of the Contact Group in connection with the crisis, where Britain played a prominent role. Foreign Minister of the Contact Group member states met in London on January 29, 1999 and adopted the conclusions containing the general principles for the resolution of the conflict and elements of the future structure of "high-degree autonomy" of Kosovo and Metohija. In this document, the Minister invited the representatives of the FR of Yugoslavia and the Serbian Government, and the representatives of Kosovo Albanians to meet at Rambouillet (France) to start discussions with direct participation of the Contact Group. The meeting was to be co-chaired by the French and British Foreign Ministers Hubert Vedrine and Robin Cook.

The two phase meeting devoted to the issue of self-administration in Kosovo and Metohija, was held in February and March 1999, first at Rambouillet and then in Paris. In fact, there were no direct talks between delegation designated by the Government of Republic of Serbia nd the representatives of Kosovo Albanians. The British co-chairman, foreign minister Robin Cook, played a special role at those meetings. He pressed Kosovo Albanians who had first rejected and then, precisely upon his insistence, signed the draft document offered during the final stage of the meeting held in Rambouillet. The signature of the Albanian side was necessary in order to ensure the "basis" for military intervention and bombing of the FR of Yugoslavia. The British participants in Paris were familiar with the contents of the so-called "military annex", which was submitted by the US administration.

The decision of the NATO Secretary General, Javier Solana, of March 23, 1999 that NATO forces, without consultations with and approval by the UN Security Council, should carry out an armed attack on the FR of Yugoslavia, was taken with the consent of all the Member States of the Alliance. It turned out that the chief advocates of armed intervention were the American administration and the British Government.

Although immediately before the NATO military intervention against Yugoslavia the nineteen NATO members expressed, at least in their public pronouncements, their common position, while the decision about the aggression was taken unanimously, it turned out that there were later some disagreements and even open differences of view among certain alliance members. This was manifested in the approaches of a number of countries to the bombing of Yugoslavia, in discussing the issue of a possible sending in of ground troops, and in particular with regard to the taking of some initiatives for the suspension of the aggression and resumption of negotiations. The United States and Great Britain, as the principal initiators of military intervention and belligerent approach to the resolving of the Kosovo crisis were on one side. On the other were small NATO member countries that did not participate in air strikes, or that withdraw from them (Norway), then Greece, Spain, and partly Italy, all of them having certain reservations with respect to the NATO action. Although among the main advocates of military option, France and Germany were among the countries that encouraged initiatives for finding a compromise way out of NATO war in the Balkans. Also, within the governments of these two countries there were differences of view of some coalition partners.

In December 1992 the Bush administration leveled a stiff threat: "in the event of conflict in Kosovo caused by Serbian action, the US will be prepared to employ military force against Serbians in Kosovo and in Serbia". In February and July 1993, the Clinton administration repeated the threat. Then political meltdown in Albania in spring 1997 sent a flood of small arms into Kosovo, and the Kosovo Liberation Army (KLA) began a bona fide insurgency, vowing to liberate ethnic Albanians in Kosovo and Macedonia and unite them in a "Greater Albania." On 23 February 1998 after meeting with Milosevic in Belgrade, U.S. Special Envoy to the Balkans Robert Gelbard stated in Pristina that the KLA was "without any question a terrorist group" and that the United States "very strongly" condemned terrorism in Kosovo. Gelbard's statements have been sometimes recast as an unwitting "green light" to the Serbian crackdown that followed." But Gelbard was speaking policy, not off the cuff." The Clinton administration saw that the KLA threatened Balkan stability, and it was sending a warning.

THE ESCALATION OF REBELLION AND REPRESSION

Within days, the situation exploded. Four Serb policemen were assassinated on 28 February 1998, and Belgrade responded with heavy reprisals against KLA strongholds. On 5 March 1998, Gelbard condemned the overreaction and restated the threat to use force against Serbia. The Serb attacks on the KLA aroused massive protests in Pristina, which Serb police in turn brutally suppressed. That month, the Kosovo shadow government held new elections, and Rugova's Democratic League of Kosovo (LDK) took more than 90 percent of the vote. The KLA, however, boycotted the election and condemned Rugova's policy of nonviolence.

The Contact Group (The Contact Group was composed of Britain, France, Germany, Italy, Russia, and the United States to establish interim political settlement and to enforce NATO's plan) tried to "isolate the terrorists" and edge the LDK and Belgrade into negotiations "without preconditions." "What we are calling for," said British Foreign Secretary Robin Cook "is a political solution that enables the moderate, peaceful, non-terrorist leadership of the (Kosovars) the opportunity to explore their legitimate political objectives." The Contact Group vowed to use "all appropriate elements of pressure and influence with both sides to ensure that violence does not escalate and that. . . Kosovo's status. . . is resolved strictly through peaceful means."" Next came a UN Security Council Chapter VII resolution (1160), which condemned the violent excesses of Serbian forces and "all acts of terrorism" and imposed an embargo on arms to Serbia and "terrorists" in Kosovo. It demanded a political solution "based on the territorial integrity" of the Federal Republic of Yugoslavia (FRY) that gave "a substantially greater degree of autonomy and meaningful self-administration" to Kosovo."

As the LDK fragmented over the issue of nonviolence, Rugova recruited a Group of 15 to engage in the Contact

Group's negotiations. NATO scrambled to shore him up, even though, as a European Union report noted, his "precondition" demand for Kosovo independence now directly conflicted with Security Council resolution 1160." The North Atlantic Council's (NAC) statement of 30 April condemning "the excessive use of force by the Yugoslav army" thus also reiterated that NATO was "firmly opposed to independence for Kosovo" and to "all use of violence . . . by terrorist groups."?

Richard Holbrooke orchestrated a 15 May 1998 meeting in Belgrade between Rugova and Milosevic, which he and Gelbard mediated. It backfired. Nothing was accomplished, and just a few days later Serbia launched a new campaign against the KLA. Rugova's stock among Kosovars plummeted. On 29 May hewent to Washington to meet Clinton and then to New York to meet UN Secretary General Kofi Annan." Rugova's team informed Clinton that they were pulling out of negotiations with Belgrade and that after the recent offensive, nothing less than a quick transition to full independence was acceptable. Thus, the Kosovo moderates now set out an agenda deeply at odds with NATO's.

On 23 June, Richard Holbrooke, acting as President Bill Clinton's special envoy, met with Milosevic to follow up. Between 4 and 6 July, Holbrooke and the Russian deputy foreign minister shuttled between Milosevic and the LDK, pushing for an agreement. They failed, according to Holbrooke, because the Kosovars did not "get their act together." Rugova's spokesman blamed their disunity on the lack of a coherent Contact Group strategy, saying that the "biggest problem for us is that there's no international agenda." There was, however, a clear international agenda. As Christopher Hill, the Contact Group's chief negotiator, put it, Kosovo could not "shoot its way out of Serbia."

On 23 September 1998, the Security Council passed Resolution 1199 (UNSCR), which condemned "all acts" of violence in Kosovo, especially the "indiscriminate use of force by Serb security forces" and commanded the two sides to cease fire and seek a political solution. Significantly, Russia did not veto this Chapter VII resolution. On 30 September 1998, the British foreign secretary warned Belgrade to comply quickly with UNSCR 1199, and the next day Hill pitched a revised settlement plan. On 1 October 1998, Secretary of Defense William Cohen announced that the United States was ready to begin air strikes in two weeks. Three days later, Milosevic cracked and announced that Serb forces would be pulled back. On 5 October 1998, Holbrooke went back to Belgrade to pin him down.

On 13 October 1998, the NAC ordered air-strikes in ninety-six hours if Belgrade did not comply with UNSCR 1199." That day Milosevic and Holbrooke announced what is known as the Holbrooke Agreement. It affirmed that any Kosovo settlement must respect the territorial integrity and sovereignty of the FRY and unilaterally committed Serbia to completing by 2 November 1997 an agreement on the "core elements" of a settlement based on Hill's 2 October proposal. Most importantly, Milosevic agreed to withdraw Serb forces deployed in Kosovo after February 1998.

Holbrooke, acting as Clinton's special envoy, had negotiated the general contours. Now it was up to NATO officials-namely SACEUR Clark and Klaus Naumann, chairman of NATO's military committee-to meet with Milosevic and turn the broad language of UNSCR 1199 into fine print with specific benchmark. By the 27 October 1997 deadline, Belgrade had complied. In return, Naumann and Clark had assured him that NATO would "try to control" the KLA.' The KLA lambasted the Holbrooke Agreement. "All solutions but independence," they insisted, were "not acceptable." Said Albright: "We have . . . delivered a clear message to the leadership of the Kosovo Liberation Army: there should be no attempt to take military advantage of the Serb pull-back. Neither side can achieve military victory in Kosovo."

Rambouillet was an offer the KLA could not refuse, a negotiation they could not sit out. For the KLA, Rambouillet carried with it for once a powerful threat of abandonment. Moreover, while the Contact Group was demanding that the two sides reach a political settlement, NATO was demanding on a separate track that the implementation of the settlement include the deployment of NATO peacekeepers. This then was the political bargain: if the Kosovars would agree to the Contact Group's plan, they would get their international protectorate for the length of the interim period. Hashim Thaci, the political spokesman for the KLA and the head of the Kosovo delegation at Rambouillet, had blocked immediate endorsement of the plan on 23 February. Consequently, U.S. private assurances, which were contingent on immediate acceptance, lapsed. That was apparently forced to do this by KLA hard-liners. The Contact Group then announced that a "signing" conference would be held in Paris on 15 March 1999.

Throughout the Kosovo crisis, the British Government and its Prime Minister Tony Blair manifested a particular militant attitude. In the informally created axis USA-Britain the latter was given the role of the leader of aggressiveness. At the outset, Britain was one of the principal initiators along with the United States of NATO military operation against Yugoslavia. Britain opposed the initiatives to suspend bombings all along. Britain was the chief advocate of the option in NATO plans that, in the case of failure of air strikes, the Alliance should start a land invasion of Yugoslavia. Britain insisted on the continuance of intensive air raids and on undertaking ground operations "to the final victory" of NATO, without compromise and a "half-way agreement". It was persistent even at the time when, in late May and early June, some positive signs were on the horizon suggesting that the then launched diplomatic initiatives could be transformed into an agreement. By such an attitude Britain remained isolated among its allies within NATO. At the summit meeting in Washington celebrating the 50th anniversary of NATO in late April 1999, the United States and Britain were the chief advocates of imposing an oil and gas supply embargo on Yugoslavia. also, at the Foreign Ministers' meeting of EU member countries held on September 13, 1999, the decision announced already in July concerning the lifting of the embargo on air traffic with Yugoslavia was not adopted due to the opposition of the foreign minister of Britain and Denmark; the "alleviation" of part of the sanctions against Yugoslavia banning sports events.

NUCLEAR COOPERATION

The *National Defense Strategy* and *National Military Strategy* developed in parallel and released in early 2005 barely mention the role of U.S. nuclear weapons. This is understandable for few reasons: the changed relationship with Russia; the priority given to capabilities needed to confront the "irregular" threats from insurgencies and international terrorism; and, perhaps, a desire to avoid any perceived brandishing of nuclear capabilities at a time when the United States is relying heavily on diplomatic tools to resolve concerns with North Korean and Iranian nuclear developments. An additional explanation might be that little of substance has changed since the *Nuclear Posture Review* was completed in late 2001. To briefly recap some of the main findings of this review were:

- Reliance on nuclear weapons should be reduced by developing non-nuclear offensive and defensive capabilities that allow the United States to raise the nuclear threshold.

- In keeping with the President's guidance to reduce the number of operationally deployed nuclear weapons to the lowest possible level, and to do so without some of the drawbacks of Cold War-style arms control negotiations and treaties, the United States will look toward unilateral reductions. In terms of force sizing, the *Nuclear Posture Review* set a goal of 1,700-2,200 operationally deployed warheads by 2012 (which represents a reduction of approximately 3,800 warheads from the level permitted by START I, which remains in force).

• Given the existing and emerging threat to the United States and its allies and friends from WMD and missile proliferation, U.S. nuclear planning needs to become more capable against a range of contingencies and less country-specific. The President needs a "more diverse portfolio of capabilities"—to include nuclear forces, non-nuclear strike forces, and missile defenses—to assure allies and friends, and dissuade, deter, and, if necessary, defeat adversaries.

• So-called "life extension programs" would keep the current types of delivery systems in service until 2020 or longer. This represents an important budgetary and technical effort, as the average ages of U.S. delivery systems (when the review was completed) were 26 years for the *Minuteman III* intercontinental ballistic missile, 9 years for the *Trident II* D- 5 submarine-launched ballistic missile, 40 years for the B-52 bomber, and 5 years for the B-2 bomber. Four of the 18 *Trident* strategic ballistic missile submarines (SSBNs) would be taken out of strategic service, and the remaining 14 SSBNs would be fitted with *Trident II* D-5 missiles. In addition, the *Peacekeeper* land-based intercontinental ballistic missiles (ICBMs) would be retired, and the B-1 bomber force would no longer be maintained for a nuclear weapon role.

• The United States would rely on its "stockpile stewardship" program designed to ensure the safety and reliability of the nuclear weapons stockpile without nuclear testing, but it would not ratify the Comprehensive Test Ban Treaty (CTBT). It also would study options to reduce the preparatory time needed—currently somewhere between 2 to 3 years—if the President were to determine that a resumption of nuclear testing was necessary to rectify a stockpile problem. The special relationship as related to nuclear weapon systems has had a long and enviable history. "Indeed, there exists no other program where the United States has worked so intimately with another country for such an extended period of time on the gravest matters of national security. This aspect of our special relationship remains very much alive. One could posit that this relationship grows even more important as the size of our respective nuclear arsenals has shrunk over the past decade. It perhaps is worth recalling that a relationship that many take for granted today has not always been problem-free".

The main concern driving this goal is not the ballistic missile force of major powers such as Russia; rather, it is the proliferation of WMD and ballistic missile capabilities of states such as North Korea and Iran. Indeed, for the most part, the administration has been careful not to oversell the initial U.S. defensive capabilities, characterizing the first deployments as "very basic" and a "nascent defensive system."

The original decision to acquire a nuclear capability was made in response to a perceived growth of anti-British and isolationist sentiment in the United States. The acquisition of an atomic bomb in 1952 and of a hydrogen bomb in 1958 was seen as restoring the country fully to the ranks of the great powers. However, the UK possessed a genuinely independent nuclear deterrent for only 10 years. With the purchase, on very favorable terms, of the *Polaris* system in 1962, Britain became dependent on the United States to keep its deterrent functioning. However, as then Prime Minister Harold Macmillan put it, *Polaris* solved the "problem of being poor and powerful at the same time." The same rationale underlay the acquisition of *Trident* in the early 1980s, the British *Chevaline* warhead having proved both too expensive and not good enough as an upgrade to the existing system.

In the mid-1980s, when the nuclear freeze movement was active in the United States, Europeans were protesting the deployment of U.S. cruise and Pershing missiles on their territories. People throughout Europe feared that with the emplacement of these nuclear-armed missiles on their soil, Europe would become the primary battleground for a nuclear war between the U.S. and Soviet Union.

While the United States had succeeded in stationing a few of its new weapons in Britain and West Germany, the issue of whether they should be there and whether others should follow was as divisive as ever, both within those countries and within the Alliance as a whole; and while the Administration had beaten back a number of congressional challenges to its strategic modernization program, support for the MX was still extremely shaky. In response to the American deployments, the U.S.S.R. escalated its side of the military competition, complicating the arms race and arms control alike.

In 1977, the Soviet Union began deploying the SS-20, an intermediate-range missile fitted with three accurate, independently retargetable warheads aimed at Western Europe. In December 1979, the North Atlantic Treaty Organization (NATO) countered with plans to deploy 108 Pershing II missiles and 464 Ground Lunch Cruise Missiles in Belgium, Britain, Italy, the Netherlands, and West Germany.

In the end, the Intermediate-Range Nuclear Forces Treaty that General Secretary Mikhail Gorbachev and President Ronald Reagan signed in December 1987 eliminated intermediate-range nuclear missiles in Europe. All SS-20, Pershing II, and GLCM missiles were removed and dismantled and turned into expensive scrap.

Dependence on America to keep the nuclear "show on the road" was not seen to be a major weakness. Solidarity in the face of the Soviet threat made that vulnerability mainly theoretical. And if war were to come, the Union of Soviet Socialist Republics (USSR) might calculate that, when the chips were down, the United States might hesitate to risk nuclear immolation in retaliation for attacks on Europe. But it would be far less certain about the actions of a Britain that was more or less in the front line.

The U.S.-UK relationship has "hung together" in the face of threats to national survival. Initially, the partners opposed imperial Germany, then confronted Hitlerian fascism, and finally faced down the threat posed by the Soviet Union and communism, acting in all three cases within the context of a broader alliance. During this time, the United States accepted the basic grand strategic principle that despite overwhelming American power, it needed allies for the capabilities they provided as well as the legitimacy gained from collective action. The two countries might have periodic severe disagreements over such issues as Suez, Vietnam, the Falklands, and Grenada, but both knew that the common threat was so great that reconciliation was likely, if not certain, in each case.

This common threat ended with the collapse of the Berlin Wall and demise of the Soviet Union. But in terms of defense links, the experience of 75 years established certain cooperative arrangements that are now routine and indeed taken for granted. These include unparalleled sharing of intelligence, regular consultations on military doctrine, American support for the UK nuclear deterrent, robust liaison teams in both the Pentagon and Ministry of Defence, and now British representation at several American regional combatant commands. Furthermore, American and British officers regularly cooperated on a host of issues at North Atlantic Treaty Organization (NATO) headquarters and during conflicts in Iraq, Bosnia, and Kosovo over the past 20 years.

To date, U.S.-UK cooperation related to missile defense has been limited but important. In February 2003, the UK gave the United States permission to upgrade the U.S.-owned; RAF operated *Fylingdales* early warning radar, which is important to track potential threats from the Middle East region. Later that year, the sides signed a new memorandum of understanding on missile defense cooperation covering arrangements for joint work on system research, development, testing, and evaluation. These arrangements currently include British participation within DoD's Missile Defense Agency in Washington and Colorado Springs. In addition, reflecting the high level of U.S. transparency with regard to the UK on missile defense operational issues, British officers are "embedded" in the U.S. Strategic Command.

In the aftermath of September 11, 2001, many in continental Europe, however, did not share the view that 9/11 changed the way in which America should perceive the world and evaluate threats. In spite of the attacks on Spain, Greece, Turkey, and now even London, it appears, from the American side of the Atlantic at least, that many Europeans still view 9/11 as fundamentally a U.S. problem that somehow Europe can avoid if it chooses. In terms of the special relationship, however, President George W. Bush observed following the attacks in London in July 2005, "Just as America and Great Britain stood together to defeat totalitarian ideologies of the 20th century, we now stand together against the murderous ideologies of the 21st century."

COMMUNICATIONS INTELLIGENCE

The intelligence community gathers intelligence from various sources. These are typically classified as:

* Interception of communications and other signals (SIGINT)
* Satellite photography or imagery (IMINT)
* Reports from human sources (HUMINT)
* Measurement and signature (MASINT)

One of the most important intelligence sources comes

from the interception of communications. The more communications one can intercept the more accurate and unclouded the messages will be. This is the task of project echelon.

Throughout World War II, the U.S. and Britain cooperated to intercept any communication that would aid them in their war effort. This cooperation was formalized in 1948 as the UKUSA agreement. Though initially aimed at the Soviet Union, currently it links the largest intelligence gathering agencies in five countries: United States, United Kingdom, Canada, Australia, and New Zealand. These agencies help collect, decrypt, and analyze practically all communications sent throughout the world. These communications include fax, e-mail, phone, and broadcast transmissions. The majority of intelligence dollars go to collecting, selecting, and examining these communications.

The UKUSA agreement of 1948 is also known as the UK-USA Security Agreement or the Secret Treaty. This highly-classified agreement, involving 15 countries but more importantly the United States and five partners of the British Commonwealth, is mainly about the sharing of signals intelligence with the parties to the treaty, each of them being responsible for a specific area of the world to cover.

By the beginning of 1946, the four main parties – Australia, Canada, United States and United Kingdom – had all agreed on their willingness to negotiate a future postwar SIGINT alliance. Ottawa and Canberra gave authority to the British to negotiate on their behalf. A conference to settle the details of collaboration met in London for most of February and March 1946 and produced a still-classified agreement of about 25 pages, which seemed at the time to have settled all outstanding details of SIGINT collaboration between the United States and the British Commonwealth. That document was not, in fact, the final text of the accord. Further negotiations, all still classified, followed at intervals for the next two years to deal with problems which included commonwealth reorganization after Indian independence and the start of the Cold War. The alliance was already firmly in place in March 1946 but the final text, the UKUSA agreement, was not signed until June 1948.

Today, the UKUSA agreement involves 15 states. The United States is the First Party. The Second Parties are Australia, Canada, New Zealand and the United Kingdom. And the Third Parties, which seem to play a very minor role in the global network of collaboration, include Austria, Denmark, Germany, Greece, Italy, Japan, Norway, South Korea, Thailand, and Turkey.

The primary emphasis of the agreement was to provide a division of SIGINT collection responsibilities between the parties. Under the present division of responsibilities the United States is responsible for signals intelligence in Latin America, most of Asia, Russia, and northern China. The UK is responsible for the former Soviet Union west of the Urals, and Africa. Australia's area of responsibility includes its neighbors – such as Indonesia –southern China, and the nations of Indochina. The polar regions of Russia are the responsibility of Canada, and New Zealand's area of responsibility is the western Pacific.

Very little is known about the UKUSA agreement. Officials of the governments involved have always refused to confirm or deny its existence. However, its technological aspect, involving supercomputers and an impressive network of satellites, has got the attention of plenty of organizations worldwide, many of which are concerned by the tremendous interception capabilities of the UKUSA parties and the virtual absence of legal framework or independent supervision. And less than three months ago, the European Parliament adopted a report that says the global electronic-surveillance network known as 'ECHELON' does exist. That report, dated 7 September 2001, is called 'Report on the existence of a global system for the interception of private and commercial communications (ECHELON interception system)'.

That 194-page report simply puts on paper what most people already knew. The European Parliament officially declares that the ECHELON network really exists but fails to present any strong and reliable evidence on the usage of intercepted communications by the American NSA for unlawful purposes. And although it implicitly recognizes the existence of the UKUSA alliance, it does not provide more details about the content or the depth of the 1948 agreement. As a matter of fact, the UKUSA agreement has been signed in secret 58 years ago, is still secret today, and is clearly intended to stay secret for as long as possible.

The UKUSA agreement naturally leads to improvements in data collection techniques. A major networked system for this data collection is code named project *echelon*. The Echelon system, hinted at in a description of the Menwith Hill receiving station in a July 18, 1980 *New Statesman* article by Duncan Campbell and first described by Nicky Hager in his 1996 book *Secret Power*, consists of a worldwide network of intercept stations. These stations capture satellite, microwave, fax, telex, cellular, cable and fiber optic (primarily as it emerges to microwave towers) communications traffic.

Designed during the Cold War, Echelon primarily intercepts worldwide non-millitary communications including those from governments, organizations, businesses, and individuals. It could intercept practically any communication between, and often within, countries anywhere in the world. The project echelon receiving system feeds these streams of millions of communications every hour to massive arrays of computers. These computers decrypt messages when necessary, then when required, utilize optical character recognition (OCR) or advanced voice recognition techniques to extract words from each message. Every message captured is analyzed for keywords or phrases found in the Echelon "dictionary." Keywords include all the names, places, codewords, or subjects that might be of interest. There are separate search lists for each member country.

Messages acquired at any of the listening posts containing requested keywords are then automatically passed on to the intelligence organization requesting those keywords. Those messages are flagged for further analysis. There are three broad components of Echelon.

A) Receiving International Telecommunications Satellites (Intelsats): An array of receiving stations collect all international communications carried by approximately 20 Intelsat satellites. The Intelsats are used by the telephone companies of most countries. Though they carry primarily civilian traffic, they also carry diplomatic and governmental communications. These Intelsats are positioned in stationary orbit around the equator and carry tens of thousands of simultaneous phone calls, faxes, and e-mails. Echelon's Intelsat receiving stations include:

- **Morwenstow, England** - Atlantic and Indian Oceans satellites transmitting to Europe,   Africa and western Asia

- **Sugar Grove, near Washington, D.C.** - Atlantic satellites beamed to North and South America

- **Yakima Firing Center, near Seattle, Washington** - Pacific and Far East satellites

- **Waihopai, New Zealand** - Pacific and Indian Ocean satellites covering Asia and the South Pacific

- **Geraldton, Australia** - Pacific and Indian Ocean satellites covering Asia and the South Pacific

- **Ascension Island** - Atlantic satellites covering the southern hemisphere.

B) Receiving Non-Intelsat Satellites: Numerous satellites carry domestic communications. These regional communications are monitored by the above stations as well as the following additional monitoring stations.

- **Menwith Hill, England**
- **Shoal Bay, Australia** - targets Indonesian satellites
- **Leitrim, Canada** - targets Latin American satellites
- **Bad Aibling, Germany**
- **Misawa, Japan**[61]

Scores of other reception locations are maintained by UKUSA members. These are located primarily at military bases and embassies throughout the world. These listening posts were especially critical before the advent of satellite communications. Interception of communications flowing through underground or under water cables is easy once the cables surface and connect to microwave towers. Microwave transmissions move communications in a line of site fashion from tower to tower. Placing an antenna in the "beam" of these microwave transmissions gives access to international as well as domestic communications.

Microwave communications frequently converge at most of the large cities, typically a capital city. Embassy buildings in major cities, protected by diplomatic privilege, are ideal sites to intercept these communications. In addition to ground-based observation centers, spy satellites and airplanes are also used. They are capable of receiving high frequency radio broadcasts as well as cellular transmissions[62].

The following are various intelligence gathering stations of US intelligence agencies and armed forces or their allies.

- Alert (Ellesmere Island, Nunavut, Canada)
- Agios Nikolaos (Cyprus - UK)
- Bremerhaven (Germany - UK)
- Buckley Air Force Base (Colorado, US)
- RAF Chicksands (Bedfordshire, UK)
- Diego Garcia (Indian Ocean - US-UK)

- Digby (Lincolnshire, UK)
- Elmendorf Air Force Base (Alaska - US)
- Feltwell (Norfolk, UK)
- Fort Gordon (Georgia, US)
- Gander (Newfoundland and Labrador, Canada)
- Gibraltar (UK)
- Griesheim (near Darmstadt, Germany - US)
- Guam (Pacific Ocean, US)
- Karamursel (Turkey - US)
- Kunia (Hawaii, US)
- Leitrim (south of Ottawa, Canada)
- Malta (Malta - UK)
- Masset (British Columbia, Canada)
- Medina Annex (Texas, US)
- Osan Air Base (South Korea, US)
- Rota, Spain (Spain - US)
- Scampton (Lincolnshire, UK)

FORMER GROUND STATIONS

- Augsburg (Germany - US) - closed in 1993
- Bad Aibling (Germany - US) - moved to Griesheim in 2004
- Clark Air Base (Philippines - US) - closed in 1997
- Edzell (Scotland, UK) - closed in 1997
- Kabkan (Iran - US) - closed in 1979
- Little Sai Wan (Hong Kong - UK) - closed in 1984
- Nurrungar (South Australia, Australia - south of Woomera, South Australia) closed in 1999
- San Vito dei Normanni (Italy - US) - closed in 1994
- Teufelsberg (West Berlin, Germany - US) - closed in 1989
- Silvermine (near Cape Town, South Africa - US)

Over the years several major overhauls of the Echelon system have taken place. Several recent projects, the details of which are concealed, have been detected. One was codenamed "Platform" and was intended to bring 52 separate computer systems together as a massive network feeding the main computers at NSA headquarters at Fort Meade.

Another major project is identified as P415. This enhancement is intended to allow NSA to track civilian communications well into the 21st century. This project involves the traditional members of UKUSA as well as Germany, Japan, and the People's Republic of China.

Echelon has been successful in monitoring international and domestic communications for some time. A number of international criminals have been detected. Among the known or suspected uses are:

- Discovery of missile sites in Cuba
- Capture of the Achille Lauro terrorists
- Discovery of Libyan involvement in the Berlin discotheque bombing

In addition to rooting out those who commit crimes, the systems have been used to detect the planning of crimes. This allows police action to prevent these crimes. But, this power has often been used for less noble purposes. It has also been used for political and economic purposes to spy on individuals who are not involved in international terrorism or plots against a national government. Some suspected uses are:

- Target calls from U.S. Senator Strom Thurmond.
- Monitor anti-Viewnam war leaders such as Jane Fonda and Dr. Benjamin   Spock.
- Monitor Black Panther leader Eldridge Cleaver
- Monitor Amnesty International organization
- Monitor Greenpeace organization
- Monitor Christian Aid organization

- Margaret Thatcher requested to have two government ministers monitored
- Margaret Thatcher ordered observation of the parent company of the London *Observer* after publication of negative articles
- Kissinger used NSA to intercept messages from rival Secretary of State William Rogers
- Monitor phone calls of Maryland Congressman, Michael Barnes
- Menwith Hill station received the 1991 "Station of the Year" prize for its role in the Gulf War.
- Monitoring delegates of the five-day Asia-Pacific Economic Cooperation conference
- Monitoring Mexican trade representatives during the NAFTA trade negotiations

Echelon represents a powerful force that can be used for good. Echelon has been used to detect plans for sabotage and espionage; events that were thwarted before they came to fruition and were therefore never reported. It has been used to locate and capture international criminals.

The power of the system also lends itself to corrupting influences. Those whose goal is power have used the system to enhance their positions and diminish the power of others. As the system is further enhanced, its capabilities will improve. It will likely be used increasingly for police, political, and economic purposes.

Supporters stress that echelon is simply a method of sorting captured signals and is just one of the many arrows in the intelligence community's quiver, along with increasingly sophisticated bugging and communications interception techniques, satellite tracking, through-clothing scanning, automated biometric recognition systems that can recognize faces, fingerprints & retina patterns.discussed Northern Ireland with the Taoiseach during their bilateral meeting. In December 2004, President Bush made separate telephone calls to the leader of Sinn Féin, Gerry Adams, and to the leader of the Democratic Unionist Party, Ian Paisley, to encourage them to reach agreement on their remaining difficulties. He has continued to make clear his intention to assist the two governments in their attempts to secure the full implementation of the agreement.

Early in his Administration, President Bush appointed Mr. Richard Haass, Director of Policy Planning at the State Department, as his Special Envoy to Northern Ireland. After a successful period as Envoy during which he worked very closely with both Governments and the parties, Haass left the administration in 2004 and was replaced by Mr. Mitchell Reiss. Mr. Reiss has continued his predecessor's good work.

4

IDENTIFIED CORE COMMONALITIES BEYOND LINGUISTIC ONENESS

ECONOMIC, POLITICAL AND LEGAL RELATIONSHIP OF THE ALLIANCE

Viewed from the economic/business perspective, the relationship is, in many respects, distinctive and, in some respects, unique. In that context America and Britain have the existence of such a special relationship. To what extent does promoting the existence of and drawing attention to this special relationship promote national interests? While any such relationship is necessarily complex, and thus generalization can be misleading, the United Kingdom, as the smaller of the two partners, often compete for U.S. attention to enhance its influence over U.S. economic policies, particularly foreign economic policy, and promote its trade and investment objectives. Thus, there are clear advantages to the United Kingdom in propagating the idea that a special relationship exists, which is presumably why special relationship rhetoric is more prevalent there than in the United States. Of course, it is also important for the United States to obtain support for its foreign economic policies and to achieve its trade and investment goals. However, the United Kingdom plays a less important role relatively for the United States than the other way around. In any event, there is a downside for the United States in touting a special relationship—for it implies that other bilateral relationships are less "special."

Two essential constituents distinguish economic interaction between the United States and United Kingdom. In one respect, the economic relationship is distinctive and important to both sides, while in the other, it is less so. The key of the U.S.-UK economic special relationship is the shared belief in and practice of what is often called the "Anglo-Saxon economic model" (while one can debate the appropriateness of this term, the intended distinction is between it and the more regulated form of capitalism prevailing in much of continental Europe). It refers to a web of laws, practices, and attitudes that reflect acceptance of a business culture and system that facilitate entrepreneurial activity (and permits failure), encourages wealth accumulation, promotes competition, and provides flexibility in the use of labor and other inputs.

The "model" contains many elements. One is a relatively reduced role of government as a participant in and, especially, regulator of the economy. Another is the preponderant role played by the stock and bond markets as a source for investment capital—compared to the Continent, where the banking system is more heavily involved—and, related to that, the high percentage of shareholding by the general public, which thus has a direct stake in the economy. A third is the similarities of the two countries' legal and accounting systems. Fourth is the strength of the financial services sector, consisting of a vast array of market participants ranging from financial intermediaries and accountants to insurance and pension funds. And, finally, the economies operate in a relatively transparent manner. This is perhaps more so in the United States than the United Kingdom in regard to the government and, increasingly, the private sector, as corporate governance issues assume ever greater prominence.

For the United States, these elements represent an essentially continuous pattern of policy and practice, whereas in the United Kingdom, they are the result of a significant measure of policies promoted by and adopted under the Prime Ministership of Margaret Thatcher in the 1980s, and, after their success became apparent, continued by the Labour government under Tony Blair. The net result of the mutual embrace of this economic model is a strong tendency to look at economic issues—domestic and international— from a similar point of view.

However—and this is the second constituent—this similarity of system and outlook is to some extent counterbalanced by UK membership in the European Union (EU). The United Kingdom is thus not a free agent in terms of economic policies and actions. EU economic integration has progressed to a remarkable degree. The EU single market, while clearly deficient in many areas, is nonetheless a reality over a wide range of economic activities. The EU has competence in major areas, notably competition policy and trade policy. Thus, the United Kingdom is but one of 25 member states making an input to those policies. Similarly, the voluminous corpus of EU law and regulation, the *acquis communautaire*, covers economic subjects, and the United Kingdom, like all member states, is bound by them. Thus, the freedom of action of the United Kingdom is, in many respects, limited.

Nonetheless, there is an important exception; that is the British "opt-out," i.e., nonparticipation, in the EU's Economic and Monetary Union, whose central feature is the single currency. This sets the United Kingdom apart—and enables it to play an independent role—in a major area of economic activity, one where the U.S.-UK bilateral relationship is unique. With that exception, however, the economic counterpart of the United States is, in large measure, the EU rather than the United Kingdom, or, indeed, any of the other EU member states. Thus, the United States cannot interact in the economic area with the United Kingdom in isolation from the EU, which means dealing with the European Commission and many or all of the member states.

The simplest measure of bilateral economic interaction is trade— a significant, though not special, relationship. The United Kingdom consistently has been an important trading partner of the United States. In terms of trade in goods, the United Kingdom is currently the fourth ranking overseas U.S. partner—not counting its contiguous neighbors, Canada and Mexico—after Japan, China, and Germany. It accounts for 3.6 percent of total U.S. goods trade, about the same level as Korea, amounting to just over $80 billion per year. However, the composition of U.S.-UK trade has changed dramatically from goods to services, a trend that is likely to continue. In this sector, the United Kingdom accounts for 12 percent of world trade in services, ranks as the biggest U.S. trading partner. Regarding total trade flows in the two directions, the United Kingdom was the destination for 4.3 percent of U.S. exports in 2004, while imports from the United Kingdom were a smaller share of the total—3.1 percent. Interestingly, these shares are lower than those achieved in recent years: export share peaked at 5.3-5.7 percent in 1997-2001, while imports fell within the 3.4-3.8 percent range during the period 1991-2002.

Trade is, however, a much narrower indicator of economic interaction than investment. Intra-company trade accounts for a significant share of total trade, and sales by foreign affiliates dwarf trade volumes. In addition, of course, investment relations are deeper and more lasting than trade. Looked at in terms of both investment flows and stock of investment, the United Kingdom is the top destination for U.S. direct investment. In 2004, over $23 billion was invested in the United Kingdom, amounting to 10 percent of U.S. worldwide investment and 28 percent of its investment in Western Europe. The total stock of U.S. investment in the United Kingdom is almost $300 billion, a figure approximately 30 percent greater than that in the next most important destination, Canada. Over one million people in the United Kingdom work for U.S.-owned companies. Small and medium-sized U.S. enterprises participate very actively in this investment.

By the same token, the United Kingdom predominates as a destination for U.S. investment in the EU. Except for one "bad" year (2001), the United Kingdom accounted for between 28 percent and 49 percent of annual U.S. foreign direct investment (FDI) that flowed into the EU during the 10-year period from 1994 to 2003. Similarly, when measuring the stock of U.S. FDI in the same period (without excluding 2001), the United Kingdom has accounted for a range of 32-41 percent in the EU. Of possible significance, both shares (the United Kingdom as a destination of U.S. FDI in the EU and in the world) peaked in the late 1990s; nevertheless, the United Kingdom easily maintained its number one position.

The attractions of the United Kingdom as a destination for U.S. investment are many—some tangible, others less so. A common language and a somewhat lesser extent common culture rank high on the list. The business environment is clearly favorable: the United Kingdom offers a well-developed infrastructure, receptivity to inward investment (and more generally to "outsiders" doing business in the United Kingdom), a political and legal system that offers confidence to investors that they will be equitably treated, ease of entry (and departure), low taxes, a skilled and well-educated workforce, labor flexibility, a strong research and development (R&D) sector, and, finally, an intangible but significant factor of comfort level.

In the early stages of the EU, the United Kingdom was viewed by many U.S. companies as a gateway or staging area into what began as a customs union and then developed into an increasingly integrated economic area. However, over time the attraction of the United Kingdom was reduced by rising costs, competition from other destinations (notably Ireland, which featured low taxes, a common language, and a plentiful and well-educated workforce), and American firms' increasing comfort with locating elsewhere in the EU. Thus, there has been some increase in investment in the rest of the EU. Reflecting the decline in manufacturing in the United Kingdom, the share of that sector in U.S. investment in the United Kingdom has fallen from 39 percent to 15 percent. However, the decline was offset by other attractive areas, with most of that money moving into the finance, information technology, and property sectors.

One factor potentially affecting investment in the United Kingdom is the British opt-out of the single currency, and its continued reluctance to join. The "drying up" of inward investment predicted by some when the Euro was introduced, without UK participation, has not taken place. However, the further away British entry into the Economic and Monetary Union seems, the more likely investment in the United Kingdom—not only by U.S. firms—will be adversely affected. That will be particularly so if the UK economy ceases to outperform that of the Eurozone. Observers in the United Kingdom report that Britain's opt-out has not been a major factor in inward investment decisions thus far, as most investors have assumed that the United Kingdom will eventually join the Eurozone. However, firms that operate on small margins and are currency sensitive are concerned about the situation.

Another potentially negative factor in U.S. investment decisions is the further development of EU social legislation—regulating many of the conditions of employment and the rights of workers—and its extension to the United Kingdom. Although the United Kingdom received an opt-out from this legislation, there are pressures within the EU to terminate this exemption. Were the exemption to be rescinded, the attractiveness of the United Kingdom as a destination for U.S. investment would be diminished. Still, developments in these two areas—the future of the single currency and social legislation— may be affected by the crisis within the EU as a result of the French and Dutch rejection of the draft EU Constitution.

On the other side of the ledger, the United Kingdom remains a popular site for U.S. companies. An estimated 7,500 U.S. firms have offices in the United Kingdom. Of these, 500 are corporate headquarters, often of regional operations. It is estimated that one-half of U.S. companies with corporate offices in Europe have located those offices in the United Kingdom.

The United Kingdom is the most important U.S. partner in two way tourism. Although U.S. residents travel more frequently to Canada and Mexico, expenditures on travel and transportation are highest for visits to the United Kingdom. In 2000, more than four million Americans spent over $11 billion traveling to the United Kingdom, compared with $7.5 billion (the second highest sum) in Mexico. In the other direction, British visitors to the United States number annually just under five million and spend almost $13 billion, figures that place it only slightly below Japan[63].

Here is perhaps where the "special economic relationship" is most evident—indeed, the word "unique" is not out of place. The historical ties between American and British capital date back to the 19th century, when British investment played an important role in the economic development of the United States. Banking relationships have a long history; many banks were well-established in the other's country in the period between the two world wars, if not before. One can speak of a single financial market, located in London and New York. Each is a financial powerhouse, and each is an undisputed financial center—London in Europe and New York in the United States. The New York Stock Exchange is the biggest stock exchange in the world, and it, together with New York-based Nasdaq, gives the United States its preeminent position for stock trading. London manages almost half of Europe's institutional equity capital, and 70 percent of Eurobonds are traded in London. It is also the world's largest international insurance and foreign exchange market. American and British financial institutions are major players in the world, accustomed to working globally. The U.S. investment banking community has acquired a preeminent position in London, while UK commercial banks are very competitive and present globally. Of the world's top 15 "tier one capital" banks, over one-half are American or British (four banks each). There are more American banks in London than in New York (a reflection of the prevalence of U.S. regional—not New York—banks that have international operations). These developments were facilitated by the similarity of economic and legal systems and the role of stock and bond markets in the two countries. It also has spurred the expansion of American-British ties in other related sectors, notably insurance and law firms. In one manifestation of this relationship, U.S. bank claims on and liabilities to the United Kingdom are vast, second only to the Cayman Islands. U.S. claims on the United Kingdom and Cayman Islands at the end of 2004 were both about half a trillion dollars, with the next country, the Bahamas, accounting for only about one-fifth of that amount. U.S. liabilities to the British were about $430 billion (for the Cayman Islands, it was double that figure). The total U.S. banking relationship (claims and liabilities) with the United Kingdom has grown from the equivalent of 10 percent of world trade in 1978 to 19 percent in 2004.

Although close relationships exist in a number of industrial sectors, probably none is closer than in the defense industry. However, unlike the other sectors, government policies and actions largely determine the nature and extent of the relationship. Closely held and subject to government control, U.S. defense technology sharing takes place at a higher level with the United Kingdom than with virtually any other country (Australia and Canada also vie for that position). Trade in defense equipment is significant, and it flows in both directions. American firms are routinely invited to bid on British defense tenders, and they have registered many successes. The United

Kingdom is by far the largest overseas buyer of American products. Major British purchases have included the Apache helicopter, Airborne Warning and Control System (AWACS), and Airborne Stand-off Radar (ASTOR). Moreover, the United Kingdom is the launch customer for the C-130J aircraft.

By the same token, UK companies are among the most active participants in the "special security arrangement," under which U.S.-based subsidiaries of foreign companies can be certified to bid as subcontractors on U.S. tenders. The most notable recent instance was the U.S. Navy's decision in early 2005 to accept the Lockheed Martin-led bid for the new Presidential helicopter fleet, which includes a British component. Significant shares of the U.S. market are held by such British firms as Rolls Royce, Martin Baker, and Smith Industries. However, the leading British player is British Aerospace and Marconi Electronic (BAE), the fifth largest supplier of hardware to the U.S. military (and the largest foreign supplier). Like other British firms, BAE has been looking to increase its business opportunities in the United States. Its recent multibillion dollar purchases include Lockheed-Martin's electronic assets and United Defense Industries, the latter ($3.5 billion) being the largest foreign takeover of an American defense company. By any measure, BAE is a significant player in the U.S. defense industry sector, employing over 25,000 in its U.S. operations.

A further example of close cooperation is the Joint Strike Fighter project, in which the United Kingdom is a major partner. BAE is an associate prime contractor, participating in the work and technology on the new aircraft, which will be purchased by both governments. The dispute that erupted in 2004 between the United States and the EU over the possible lifting of the latter's embargo on arms sales to China placed the British defense industry in a delicate position. While it did not want to forgo business opportunities in China, at the same time it did not want to jeopardize existing and potential business and the transfer of technology with the United States. On balance, the latter consideration prevailed, and BAE, for one, announced publicly it would not participate in trade with China. The British government generally reflected industry's position, at first going along with the French and German-led initiative to lift the embargo, but backing away quickly when vociferous U.S. opposition surfaced.

The world's multilateral economic agenda is vast, and so is the range of multilateral institutions that deal with it. Both the U.S. and UK governments interact on these many issues as they operate in a multilateral context. In general, the two governments convey similar messages on issues relating to the world economy—what policies national governments should follow to enhance economic growth, operation of the international monetary system, trade policy, operation of the international financial institutions, and the like—in the course of what might be called normal international discourse, including more specifically the G-7/G-8 and the Organization for Economic Cooperation and Development (OECD). On the whole, the United States and United Kingdom work together in these forums to promote their mutual interests.

In some areas, however, there is a significant difference in policy. The most notable example is the environment, particularly in attitudes toward the Kyoto Convention. The United Kingdom has agreed with the consensus view within the EU—and indeed virtually the rest of the world—and worked toward the adoption of the Convention, while the United States has firmly refused to accede to it. Nonetheless, the United Kingdom accepts that the United States will not accede to Kyoto, and thus seeks to find common ground in other aspects of environmental policy.

On the other hand, the two governments have traditionally seen eye-to-eye on trade, where they have been leaders in efforts to build and maintain a liberal trading system, including the current work on the Doha multilateral trading round. However, on trade, the United Kingdom cannot carry out an independent policy because competence for trade lies with the EU. Thus, the United Kingdom remains one voice out of 25—albeit a strong and influential one—on all trade issues. Nonetheless, that has not prevented U.S. and UK negotiators on the Doha round from working closely together.

The United States and EU have grappled with a host of trade disputes over the years, while at the same time enjoying an unprecedented and flourishing economic relationship (a sometime so overlooked, but critical, fact). Looking through the list of recent issues, one finds some concordance of position, but also many instances where the United States and the United Kingdom are on opposite sides of the argument.

EU regulation of chemical substances : With similar industrial interests and views on regulation (less is better than more), the two governments have fought for an extensive watering down of the proposal of the European Commission for registering, evaluating, and authorizing chemicals (REACH).

U.S. foreign sales corporation : In the long struggle over U.S. legislation, the United Kingdom played a constructive· role in the ultimately successful effort to keep the issue from getting out of control, giving the United States leeway in terms of time and modalities for settlement. Following the adoption of new tax provisions in the United States, the British government sought to prevent a return of the issue to the World Trade Organization (WTO) and the reimposition of sanctions by the EU.

EU banana regime : The United Kingdom historically protected the banana exports of its former colonies in the Caribbean at the expense of Latin American producers, and thus it was not particularly sympathetic to U.S. efforts to prevent a restrictive EU regime from replacing the various national regimes. However, it believed the EU should comply with the WTO ruling in favor of the United States, a view that was reinforced by U.S. retaliation against imported cashmere sweaters.

Biotechnology/genetically-modified organisms : In the long-running U.S.-EU battles over a number of issues in this area, the United Kingdom generally has supported the U.S. view that decisions should be based on scientific evidence, despite strong opposition from the British public that is very "proenvironmentalist."

U.S. safeguard action against steel imports : Like the rest of the EU, the United Kingdom, which exports significant quantities of specialty steel to the United States, sharply criticized President Bush's first-term action (subsequently rescinded). It pressed for, and received, exemptions from the increased tariffs.

Airbus subsidies : As a major participant in the Airbus consortium, the United Kingdom has stoutly defended Airbus against U.S. allegations of unfair subsidization and criticized what it considers to be comparable subsidies by the U.S. military to U.S. commercial aircraft manufacturers. Nonetheless, it favors a negotiated settlement rather than seeking recourse to the WTO.

EU's Common Agricultural Policy (CAP) : Because of the nature of its agriculture and its domestic agricultural policy, the United Kingdom has been among the sharpest internal critics of the CAP, thus lending support to the United States in its long-standing efforts to reduce the distortions it has caused to world agricultural trade. Prime Minister Blair made this clear in the EU budgetary dispute in June 2005[64].

Regulatory convergence : This is a major undertaking designed to reduce the impediments arising from differences in regulatory regimes in the United States and EU. While American and British regulators generally share a similar regulatory philosophy, some problems have arisen from differences between the regulatory structures in the two countries. The United Kingdom has been bothered by the reluctance of the U.S. Securities and Exchange Commission to recognize decisions of British regulators and the problems caused by regulation of insurance at the state, rather than national, level. On the other side, U.S. regulators occasionally have felt that the UK Financial Services Authority has not adopted sufficiently tough positions in the EU, where it plays an influential role. Whether in agreement or not, there is intense, extensive, and positive interaction between the two governments. U.S. government officials have found their British counterparts to be open and helpful. The British are good sources of information on the inner workings of the EU for their American colleagues. However, this occurs primarily when the two governments are on the same side of an issue.

Not surprisingly, when they are not, the United Kingdom is considerably less helpful. Traditionally, there has been a tendency for some parts of the U.S. government to assume that the United Kingdom is on its side on issues under consideration at the EU, and that the British can, or should, be counted on to promote U.S. views. As seen above, the first premise is by no means universally correct. While overall the British outlook and objectives are in accord with those of the United States, on many specific issues that simply is not the case. With regard to the British role inside the EU, the United Kingdom is an active and influential player in the EU deliberations. Suspect in the eyes of many other members for Britain's "outsider" status—i.e., opt-out of the Euro and generally weak support for further integration and market regulation—British officials have to take care not to be perceived by other member states as carrying water for the United States as they pursue UK policy objectives.

Significant bilateral economic differences are rare. The major exception is the civil aviation relationship. This relationship is governed by a long-standing bilateral agreement, Bermuda II, which specifies the conditions under which

American and British carriers can operate between the two countries. It has long been a bone of contention, with the United States chafing under what it considers to be unduly restrictive provisions, particularly as regards access of its carriers to Heathrow Airport; and the United Kingdom complaining about U.S. restrictions on foreign ownership of U.S. airlines and the ban on foreign carriers flying between points inside the United States. The United Kingdom has stoutly resisted U.S. efforts to bring the bilateral agreement more closely into accord with the series of "open skies" regimes it has negotiated with almost all European countries in recent years. However, after an unsuccessful 2-plus year effort to renegotiate Bermuda II bilaterally, the issue will move from the bilateral to the EU sphere. The European Court of Justice has confirmed that civil aviation agreements fall within the competence of the EU, rather than the individual member states, and thus this issue will be added to the U.S.-EU portfolio.

The great British Prime Minister Lord Salisbury is said to have remarked to Her Majesty Queen Victoria, "Change, change, why do we need more change? Aren't things bad enough already?"

As one of the architects of the Anglo-American rapprochement at the end of the 19th century, Lord Salisbury would be delighted by the revitalization of the British economy and the strengthening of the Anglo-American economic relationship over the past 25 years, and especially over the last 8 years. The United Kingdom (UK) was sinking into increasing poverty because of its declining productivity and competitiveness.

In broader strategic terms, therefore, Britain was counting for less and less, and its ability to function as an effective strategic partner for the United States was almost at an end. What a difference the consistent and rigorous application of sound fiscal, micro, and macro economic and monetary policies make. Britain is experiencing the longest period of continuous economic growth and increased living standards seen in the past half a century. As Chancellor of Exchequer said, "Britain begins the 21st century from a firm foundation of the lowest inflation for 30 years, the lowest interest rates for 40 years, and the highest level of employment in our history. Unlike the United States, the Eurozone, and Japan, the British economy has grown uninterrupted every quarter over the past 6 years."

Despite the world economic downturn of 2001-02, Britain has overtaken France as the world's fourth largest economy and, if current economic trends continue, some experts believe the UK could overtake Germany as the world's third largest economy by about 2012. Perhaps the most telling statistics are that British unemployment is approximately half that in the Euro zone; that unlike the United States, the UK actually gained jobs during the slowdown of 2001-02; that the UK's productivity per capita has overtaken Japan and is poised to overtake Germany. Britain still lags far behind the United States in productivity, but continues to learn from American innovation, competition, and enterprise. There are two main reasons for this dramatic transformation: the first is the supply-side reforms of the Thatcher years, supplemented by those of Gordon Brown since 1997; the second is the new monetary and fiscal framework introduced in 1997 which has helped create a stronger, more flexible, more enterprising Britain. UK monetary and fiscal policy has responded successfully to the recent world economic downturn and kept the British economy stable and growing. This economically resurgent Britain is a more important economic partner for the United States than at any time since the beginning of the 20th century.

The first key feature of the U.S.-UK economic special relationship is the remarkable interpenetration of the two economies. Today, more than half of the total earnings of U.S. overseas investors are accounted for by Europe. And, within Europe, the UK is overwhelmingly the most important single national market for corporate America. On average, about 40 percent of all U.S. investment in Europe goes to the UK. British officials estimate that over 60 percent of American companies doing business in the European Union (EU) have their European headquarters in the UK. During the 1990s, U.S. investment in the United Kingdom (at $175 billion) was nearly 50 percent larger than the total invested by American firms in the whole Asia-Pacific region.

U.S. firms are also investing very large sums in China, India, and Brazil, but what is little noticed is that America's stock of assets in the UK alone is almost equal to the combined overseas affiliate base of U.S. firms in Asia, Latin America, Africa, and the Middle East. In an average year, total sales by U.S. firms in the UK alone, at over $400 billion, are greater than aggregate U.S. sales in the whole of Latin America and almost double those in Germany. The U.S. firms at present employ about 1.3 million workers in Britain. That is more than the entire U.S. affiliate work force in all developing Asia and five times greater than those working for American firms in China. Moreover, the British return the compliment. Over 1.2 million Americans go to work each day in British-owned companies in the United States. And just as the United States is Britain's largest investor, so the UK by far is America's largest foreign investor, with total foreign direct investment (FDI) of over $280 billion.

If the investment relationship is special, the links between the London and New York financial markets are truly unique. The historical relationship between British and American capital dates back to the 18th century when British investment played an important role in the economic development of the original 13 colonies and in stabilizing U.S. public finances after the Revolutionary War. Later, British investment bankers provided much of the capital that financed America's phenomenal economic growth in the 19th century. As Michael Calingaert writes in his contribution to this book, it is now possible to "speak of a single financial market located in London and New

York. Each is a financial powerhouse," and all the evidence is that they will continue to dominate global financial markets for the rest of 21st century. Together, London and New York account for just over 50 percent of global foreign exchange dealing, 92 percent of foreign equity trading, and 28 percent of cross-border bank lending. London is the world leader in fund management, New York a close second. New York is the global leader in mergers and acquisitions, London second. Their shared dominance is underpinned by the shared Anglo-American legal systems that govern such a large portion of international mergers and acquisitions and public stock offerings. Their shared dominance is reinforced by the UK-U.S.-led surge in international mergers and acquisitions throughout the 1990s and by the UK-led move to privatization of publicly-owned services and utilities.

Above all, the London-New York link has been reinforced by globalization and, ironically, the introduction of the Euro. Globalization has done three things to reinforce the unique New York-London partnership. The first is that it has encouraged the major players — Goldman Sachs, Citigroup, Merrill Lynch, HSBC — to have operations in both cities. The second is that globalization has compelled the big American investment houses to increase their operations in London because it is the best way to win more business in global markets. The third way globalization has reinforced the New York-London dominance is that it gives investors and issuers of stock what they both want: access to the widest range of global securities and investment products and a worldwide pool of global investors.

The introduction of the Euro has also strengthened the New York-London link because it has encouraged more U.S. investment houses to see London as their base for European mergers and acquisitions work and to increase their presence there accordingly.

The second special feature of Anglo-American economic relations is the remarkable breadth of agreement between contemporary U.S. administrations (Democrat or Republican) and contemporary British governments (Conservative or New Labour) over so many fundamental areas of economic policy. This level of agreement is the product of more than 20 years of convergence in thinking about economic policy and in results achieved. Britain has shaped U.S. thinking on deregulation, privatization of public services, and enterprise zones. The United States taught Britain the importance of flexible labor markets, welfare reform, and having an independent central bank responsible for monetary policy. Overall, the Anglo-American "model" aims to reduce the role of government as a regulator of economic activity and to change it from a provider to an enabler of services; to create flexible labor markets and entrepreneurship, promote competition, and encourage wealth accumulation through ownership of property and stocks, thereby creating an "ownership society." There are areas where they differ —the financing of health care being the most obvious. But what unites them is far more powerful than what divides them. What the Anglo-American model boils down to is: (1) the abandonment of the old-style socialist or Great Society welfare state in favor of free market capitalism; and (2) the belief that government should be an enabling force empowering, encouraging, and equipping its citizens to meet the challenges of globalization. These aspects are basic essence of President George W. Bush's compassionate conservatism with that of Prime Minister Tony Blair's Third Way.

President Bush's campaign for Social Security reform "is part of the large and coherent worldview that has evolved out of compassionate conservatism. What has made America exceptional is limitless opportunity for everyone, at all levels — the chance to find a job, to advance up the ladder as you prove yourself, and to prosper. A giant welfare state hampers the job creation that makes all this opportunity possible. Bush is determined to keep the dynamism vibrant and to encourage and empower the poor to take part in it, rather than suggest that they are unequal to the task." And Tony Blair view on the same topic: "The challenge of modern employment is about extending welfare to work, making work pay, and investing in the skills individuals need. In a more insecure and demanding labor market, it recognizes that people will change jobs more often, and believes government has a vital role in equipping individuals to prosper."

And it is no accident that the two major economies which have performed best over the period from 1990 to 2000 are the two that have put this philosophy into practice: Britain and the United States. And because Britain and the United States have created this model, the two governments generally approach most domestic and international economic policy issues from a shared perspective.

This is true, but understates the closeness and intensity of the policy collaboration between London and Washington today in all the key multilateral forums, including the EU. The UK and United States not only share a common business model, but also a belief that they must lead the process of labor, capital, and product reform in Europe so that they can create a more open market across the Atlantic which will benefit the EU as well as the United States. The total annual two way flow of foreign direct investment of goods and services between the United States and the EU is over $2.5 trillion, but it could be even higher.

The British and U.S. treasuries believe that if the United States and EU break down more of the remaining transatlantic barriers and create a more open market across the Atlantic, then this could bring about $350 billion in benefits for both the United States and the EU.

Not surprisingly, elements of this reform agenda are key priorities for the British Presidency of the EU, including initiatives to reassess and, if necessary, roll back unnecessary regulation now damaging competitiveness; and strengthening systems used to monitor whether the benefits of proposed regulations outweigh the costs, etc. That Britain will be able to achieve any of these much needed reforms is highly questionable.

The United States and Britain disagree on several legal issues with a political dimension, or political issues with a legal dimension, ranging from landmines to climate change. But unlike disagreements over the Ottawa Convention and the Kyoto Protocol, given both nations' shared cultural, historical, and constitutional commitments to the rule of law and judicial independence as a means of securing fundamental values and governmental accountability, the disagreement between Britain and the United States over the International Criminal Court (ICC) seems especially unexpected. The nations' divergent positions toward the ICC perhaps are not as surprising as they first appear. Given the international political and military mobilization against agents of terrorism around the world, the presence of an international criminal tribunal provides a legal mechanism for prosecuting those who commit terrorist acts (as well as, perhaps, those who might resort to untoward methods while pursuing otherwise legitimate military operations on foreign soil).

The ICC traces its antecedents back, ultimately, to the Nuremberg Trials. British leaders had grave doubts about the efficacy of an international tribunal; the official British position toward the punishment of identified war criminals from 1943 until the end of the war was summary execution. Nevertheless, Nuremberg and the aftermath of World War II generated international awareness of and momentum for the creation of an international legal tribunal responsible for the prosecution and punishment of those responsible for war crimes. After Nuremberg, and in light of persistent questions about the legal legitimacy of those proceedings, the UN General Assembly appointed a body of experts to organize and codify international legal principles. In particular, this International Law Commission (ILC) was asked to draft a statute instituting an international criminal court along with an international criminal code, the so-called "Nuremberg Principles," which would be enforced by the international criminal tribunal.

These efforts culminated in the ILC's draft statute for the creation of an international criminal court in 1994. Two years later, the ILC completed its draft international criminal code. As background to the ILC's work, international pressure was building for the creation of tribunals to try individuals in connection with the human rights atrocities in the former Yugoslavia. In 1994 the UN Security Council passed a resolution to create a second ad hoc tribunal as a result of the genocidal activities in Rwanda. Building on the ILC's draft statute and referencing the two ad hoc tribunals as prototypes, the UN General Assembly issued resolutions that led to the Diplomatic Conference of Plenipotentiaries on the Establishment of an International Criminal Court, which met in Rome beginning on June 15, 1998. On July 17, the Rome Statute of the International Criminal Court was signed by 120 states, with 21 abstentions and over the objections of seven states, including the United States. The ICC was formally created upon the ratification of the Rome Statute by 60 states and entered into force on July 1, 2002[65].

Four crimes may be prosecuted before the ICC: genocide, crimes against humanity, war crimes, and aggression. These crimes are understood to possess an intrinsic international dimension as a result of their scope and extraordinary inhumanity, which raise a concern for all nations. The jurisdictional limitation of the ICC to these four crimes is tied to its historical predecessor at Nuremberg, because all four of these crimes also were prosecuted in some form at the Nuremberg Trials. Also, like Nuremberg, the ICC was created to provide a forum for prosecution of leaders and organizers most responsible for these crimes, not lower-level functionaries. Indeed, the Rome Statute specifically rejects official capacity as a bar to prosecution and highlights the potential criminal responsibility of commanders and other superiors. At the same time, the ICC hearkens back to Nuremberg by expressly precluding exculpation for core crimes through the defense that those responsible were "just following orders." Finally, the ICC contains explicit provisions that preclude the legal and theoretical challenges raised concerning the legitimacy of Nuremberg. By specific, separate articles, the ICC incorporates the principles of *nullum crimen sine lege, nulla poena sine lege*, and a prohibition against *ex post facto* criminalization[66]. The ICC is most sharply distinguished from its predecessor tribunals by its jurisdictional mandate. Unlike the Nuremberg tribunal and the Yugoslav and Rwandan ad hoc tribunals, the ICC's jurisdiction is consensual and complementary. In other words, the states that consented to the jurisdiction of the ICC also consented to permit prosecutions in a supranational court of crimes committed on their soil or by their citizens. However, the ICC's jurisdiction only complements or supplements the authority of a state's national courts. The ICC assumes jurisdiction over trials for the four core crimes when the national judiciary of the state in question is unwilling or unable to proceed.

Britain's support was pivotal to the creation of the ICC, beginning with the formative discussions in 1997 of the Preparatory Committee on the Creation of an International Criminal Court (PrepCom). At the December 1997 PrepCom meeting, Britain agreed to withdraw the demand that ICC proceedings would depend upon prior Security Council approval. This "dramatic shift" altered the course of the negotiations and was a departure from the American position, although the issue of prior referral by suitable authority would return and remain contentious in Rome. In addition, in contrast to other Security Council members, Britain joined the so-called "like-minded group" (LMG) of smaller and mid-level states that wished the ICC to be a strong, influential court. Britain signed the Rome Statute on November 30, 1998, and ratified the

Statute on October 4, 2001. As the varying and contradictory U.S. formal postures indicate, American attitudes toward the ICC have been decidedly ambivalent. This ambivalence is further demonstrated by the U.S. decision to vote against the Rome Statute when it was initially adopted in Rome on July 17, 1998. The United States then chose to sign the Rome Statute on the final day it remained open for signature, December 31, 2000.

The United States then reversed its position again and "unsigned" the Rome Statute on May 6, 2002. The United States followed its repudiation of the ICC with the enactment by Congress of the American Servicemembers' Protection Act (ASPA), which ensures (so far as U.S. domestic law and policy are concerned) that no American soldier or government official will be subject to ICC jurisdiction. In fact, Section 7423 of ASPA specifically precludes any American court, state entity, or agency from supporting or assisting the ICC, and prevents any agent of the ICC from conducting any investigative activity on American territory. Where American and allied forces conduct joint operations in which an American is under the command of a state party national, ASPA authorizes the President to attempt to reduce the risk of American exposure to ICC jurisdiction. As a preemptive tactic, the United States has entered into bilateral agreements with dozens of nations in an effort to guarantee that these nations will never refer any American for prosecution before the ICC and has conditioned American participation in multinational military operations upon international immunization from ICC prosecution[67].

American reluctance to join the ICC might seem peculiar, given that the ICC was originally an American idea. The ICC has been accepted by the other allied nations and Security Council members that formed the Nuremberg tribunal (Britain, France, and Russia), every NATO nation (except Turkey), and Mexico. Nevertheless, the ICC was perceived by certain influential government officials as a "threat to American sovereignty and international freedom of action." This perceived threat related, at least according to these officials, to the prospect of the ICC restricting the United States (regardless of whether the United States subjected itself to ICC jurisdiction) from pursuing certain forceful responses to acts of aggression out of fear of prosecution before the ICC. As these officials put it, "The last thing America's leaders need is an additional reason not to respond when our nation's interests are threatened." American objections to the ICC all stem, in one form or another, from perceived threats to United States sovereignty. At hearings on the ICC held one week after the Rome Conference, Senator Rod Grams, Republican, Minnesota stated to the Senate Foreign Relations Committee that "the United States will not cede its sovereignty to an institution which claims to have the power to override the U.S. legal system and pass judgment on our foreign policy actions," and Senator Larry Craig, Republican, Idaho claimed that the ICC represented "a fundamental threat to American sovereignty." Such rhetoric demands, but sometimes overwhelms, careful examination of the concerns the ICC raises for the United States.

Institutionally, the ICC is viewed by some as supplanting the UN Security Council. According to the UN Charter, the Security Council has "primary responsibility for the maintenance of international peace and security . . ." and provides the Council with power to "determine the existence of any threat to the peace, breach of the peace, or act of aggression and . . . [to] decide what measures shall be taken. . . ."[68] The ICC, at least arguably, frustrates the UN Charter by usurping this role from the Security Council and by depriving the United States of its veto of Security Council measures. Accordingly, the United States (and others) sought prior review by the Security Council as a precondition for ICC proceedings. Absent a prior Security Council *imprimatur*, action by the ICC strikes some as displacing the role of the Security Council and nullifying the effect of the UN Charter. Of course, the response to this point is that the requirement of Security Council permission prior to ICC action effectively would negate any authority the ICC could have as an independent tribunal, particularly where an investigation or prosecution of a Security Council member or its allies was deemed necessary.

The ICC does not offer criminal procedures and protections that coincide completely with those offered under the U.S. Constitution. Most obviously, the ICC trial of an American need not (and would not) take place in "the State and district wherein the crime shall have been committed." Moreover, the ICC has no jury trial provision and does not protect against unreasonable searches and seizures, although it does acknowledge a modified form of exclusionary rule for improperly obtained evidence. Despite the presence of many familiar, fundamental constitutional protections afforded to criminal defendants under the U.S. Constitution and traditional American criminal procedure—such as *Miranda* warnings, presumption of innocence, notice of charges, assistance of counsel, prompt and public trial, modified confrontation and compulsory process, privilege against self-incrimination, and double jeopardy—the ICC does not protect Americans to the same degree that the U.S. Constitution does.

Another constitutional objection to the ICC concerns the legal source of its judicial authority. If we imagine that the U.S. Senate ratified the Rome Statute, it might seem that the ICC is just another court, which Congress has chosen to accept through its Article II advice and consent power rather than to create through its Article III power[69]. The problem is that Article III of the Constitution vests U.S. judicial power "in one supreme Court" and grants Congress the power to ordain and establish "inferior Courts." Joining the Rome Statute would give the ICC jurisdiction over American citizens for acts committed on American soil. Given the theoretical possibility that the ICC could prosecute an American for a crime committed in the United States and that the ICC's decision could not be reviewed by the U.S. Supreme Court, the ICC would be exercising U.S. judicial authority in a manner not contemplated or tolerated by the Constitution. Under these circumstances, the ICC genuinely could not be considered an "inferior court" and the ICC's recognition as a judicial authority over American citizens by the U.S. government would seem to conflict with the constitutional mandate that there be "one Supreme Court." Granting the ICC judicial authority over American nationals in a manner consistent with the U.S. Constitution would seem to require a constitutional amendment rather than a treaty. The need for a constitutional amendment prior to American acceptance of the ICC underscores the advantage (or the disadvantage) of having a written constitution.

A central U.S. concern involves the ICC provision granting it jurisdiction over nationals of nonparty states who are accused of crimes committed on the territory of party states. According to settled and fundamental doctrines of international law, a treaty is binding only upon the parties that sign and ratify it (unless the treaty codifies general customary international law principles). The subjection of nonparties to ICC jurisdiction seems to conflict with this fundamental doctrine.

There are three related responses to this objection. First, American resistance to the existence of the ICC or to American participation in the ICC could not prevent Americans from being tried by a foreign tribunal if, for example, members of the American military carrying out operations on foreign soil were accused of one of the crimes within the jurisdiction of the ICC (i.e., genocide, crimes against humanity, war crimes, or aggression). On the contrary, American military personnel who found themselves in this situation would, according to principles of international law, be subject to the jurisdiction of the courts of the state in which the operations were conducted. Second, and related to the previous point, the ICC's jurisdictional mandate simply incorporates the traditional jurisdictional foundations of nationality and territoriality. In other words,

Article 12 of the Rome Statute merely allows the ICC to do what national judiciaries commonly do, *viz.*, exercise jurisdiction over their own nationals for crimes committed outside state borders and exercise jurisdiction over nationals from other states who commit crimes within the subject state's territory. Third, the United States has ratified several treaties that require prosecution by state parties of any individual suspected of defined criminal activity, even if the accused's home country has not ratified the treaty. These treaties apparently conflict with the notion that a treaty cannot authorize jurisdiction over nonparties. Certainly this notion has not prevented the United States from executing these treaties. Such inconsistency raises doubts about the gravity of American objections to the ICC grounded on its purported violation of fundamental principles of international law.

In a manner related to ICC jurisdiction over nonparties, the United States argued in Rome and subsequently maintained that this unprecedented extension of international jurisdiction could restrict significantly military operations necessary to preserve American national security or to restore or maintain peace in politically volatile regions. For example, the United States maintains a wide-ranging commitment to employ its forces in peacekeeping missions around the world. This, it is argued, raises a not unlikely possibility:

American servicemen on duty in the 1990-91 Persian Gulf conflict or in the operations in Somalia would be subject to frivolous charges raised in the (International Criminal) Court by Iraqi President Saddam Hussein or Somali leader General Mohammad Farrah Aidid solely to deflect international criticism from their own capricious behavior. Then, in order to avoid the possibility of "malicious prosecution" of this nature, the U.S. reduces its commitment to participate in crucial international peacekeeping missions, thereby increasing the risk of global instability and war. In particular, this jurisdictional element has led to the United States seeking and securing immunization from ICC prosecution prior to committing troops for international peacekeeping missions.

These concerns are raised not only by politicians and others who oppose any form of international influence on U.S. policymaking. The concern about the threat of malicious prosecutions inhibiting U.S. participation in international peacekeeping missions is considered significant even by Ambassador David Scheffer, who headed the American delegation at the Rome conference.

A concern closely related to the previous discussion addresses the possibility that the ICC might be used to pursue political agendas rather than war criminals. The United States sees itself as a likely target for politically-motivated prosecutions before the ICC and therefore is reluctant to support the creation of a tribunal that might be manipulated pursuant to such political motivations. Additionally, America objects to the authority of the ICC prosecutor to initiate an investigation even in the absence of any state party or Security Council complaint or referral. For many U.S. military members, this is the insurmountable obstacle to America signing the Rome Statute or complying with the ICC.

The final, and in some ways the most fundamental, U.S. objection to the ICC is captured by the imagined spectacle of an American president or high-ranking military or political official standing trial before a non-American tribunal. The ICC does not recognize claims of official immunity, and it is unclear whether the ICC would honor a national grant of amnesty that shielded individuals from ICC prosecution. Accordingly, the concern about the spectacle and its symbolic and practical effects on American position, prestige, and power is not merely hypothetical. Its very possibility is intolerable to the sensibilities of many Americans. Of course, the response to this objection is that the prospective national embarrassment of a leader being prosecuted before the ICC would itself be a salutary deterrent effect of the tribunal's existence. This is hardly a basis for American objections to the ICC.

One plausible explanation for the disparate British and U.S. reactions toward the ICC might be found in their reactions to the perceived sovereignty threats posed by the EU and the UN, respectively. Britain has, after some constitutional indigestion, accepted the supremacy of EU law in two judicially relevant ways. First, Britain accepts—as all EU members ultimately must—the supranational jurisdiction of the European Court of Justice (ECJ) and the European Court of Human Rights (ECHR). Given that British citizens and the British government may appear as parties before the ECJ and the ECHR, and that the decisions of those courts are binding upon Britain's national judiciary, Britain has acknowledged the judicial authority over its citizens of courts outside its borders.

Second, EU law is directly enforceable by the national courts of Britain. British courts therefore apply external legal doctrine that has been incorporated into British law through, for example, the Human Rights Act of 1998. As a result of these two factors, by virtue of which Britain has made its (sometimes uneasy) peace with its presence within the EU, it likely does not view the ICC as a radical challenge to the authority or autonomy of its governmental structure. Unlike Britain and the EU, influential elements of the U.S. government continue to view the UN with measured circumspection. The United States tends to be most supportive of UN action when that action has no direct repercussions on U.S. foreign policy. Moreover, Americans tend to view their courts and their law as entirely sufficient for the expression and maintenance of legal doctrine and government accountability. Indeed, Supreme Court justices still have serious reservations about citing, to say nothing of following, decisions of foreign courts such as the ECHR. In other words, there is a constitutional dimension to sovereignty itself, which some would say American subjection to the ICC would contravene.

The unwritten British constitution is generally understood to grant Parliament the unfettered authority to bind Britain and its suojects to supranational jurisdiction as a condition of its constitutional authority. As with the EU, the power of Parliament to submit Britain to the ICC is a demonstration of Parliament's constitutional sovereignty. Unlike the case of the British Parliament, however, the very act of subjecting an American citizen to ICC jurisdiction might be a violation of America's constitutional authority in the absence of a constitutional amendment. Without amending the Constitution, some Americans would claim that deference to the ICC is tantamount to the abandonment of republican self government. According to this view, the mere existence of the ICC (should the United States ever join it) would constitute a challenge to American constitutional democracy, because for the first time in U.S. history, an institution outside the U.S. government would have "the ultimate authority to judge the policies adopted and implemented by the elected officials of the United States—the core attribute of sovereignty and the *sine qua non* of democratic self-government." Nevertheless, it seems entirely plausible that American republican government permits Congress to commit the United States, on behalf of the people, to an international or supranational institution with genuine influence over U.S. policy. There is nothing inherently undemocratic about giving governmental representatives the authority to bind their constituencies in ways that the constituents find surprising or objectionable. To borrow a phrase from the British context, so long as this congressional authority is not viewed as "self-embracing," there is no threat to American sovereignty or democracy, because not all delegations of sovereignty are derogations of sovereignty. Indeed, some would say it is the essence of constitutional democracy that the majority's representatives may take certain actions to preserve and promote constitutional values, fundamental rights, and the rule of law, despite the majority's disapproval.

Notwithstanding these differing perceptions of their place in the international community, the Anglo-American commitment to the rule of law both within and beyond national borders offers a meaningful incentive to support an international court of criminal justice. Britain and the United States are two of these few liberal governments. Britain's preference for summary execution of war criminals rather than legalism after World War II was the sole aberration in the commitment of liberal states to legalism when confronting war crimes. The rejection of the ICC by the United States is now, arguably, the second. The Anglo-American commitment to the rule of law and the historical contribution of both nations to the development of due process and norms of justice enforced by an independent judiciary has, in the past, anchored a shared commitment to legalism in the pursuit of international justice.

Britain and America have supported international war crimes tribunals largely out of a belief in the fundamental fairness of their own tradition of constitutional protection of criminal defendants and the intrinsic value of their principles and process as a means of achieving justice domestically and internationally. At Nuremberg, the United States had to persuade (or remind) Britain that trials alone were the only means of achieving justice for war crimes consistent with Anglo-American legalism. Perhaps Britain needs to return the favor with respect to the ICC. Though, to be fair, the United States strongly supports an international court of criminal justice (but not one that would try Americans without American consent). Inasmuch as Anglo-American dedication to international norms of justice enforced by international tribunals derives, at least in part, from the recognition and reinforcement of domestic rule of law values in those international norms and tribunals, it is reasonable to see Anglo-American legalism itself as a manifestation of national sovereignty. After all, "sovereignty does not arise in a vacuum, but is constituted by the recognition of the international community, which makes its recognition conditional on certain standards."

Just as American democracy theoretically is predicated upon a relinquishment of a measure of liberty in exchange for security and individual autonomy in a larger social context, so too can support for the ICC be viewed as the relinquishment of a measure of sovereignty in exchange for security and international respect in a global context. Put differently, supporting the ICC does not just mean sacrificing sovereignty, it also enhances sovereignty. To be sure, this view of sovereignty depends upon a particular view of the nature of political power. Power, in this view, is more than the ability of one state to bend other states to its will through coercion; it is also the ability of one state to persuade other states that their interests align. In other words, soft power can, in certain circumstances, be more effective than hard power. If the United States will achieve more, including the achievement of more of its own political goals, in a world that respects American leadership, then its ongoing opposition to the ICC may engender a very real loss of American influence and, ultimately, of American sovereignty and security. The international perception that U.S. opposition to the ICC tarnishes the long-standing American commitment to the rule of law inside and outside its borders could limit America's ability to influence international affairs and thus ultimately detract from America's sovereignty.Supporters stress that echelon is simply a method of sorting captured signals and is just one of the many arrows in the intelligence community's quiver, along with increasingly sophisticated bugging and communications interception techniques, satellite tracking, through-clothing scanning, automated biometric recognition systems that can recognize faces, fingerprints & retina patterns.discussed Northern Ireland with the Taoiseach during their bilateral meeting. In December 2004, President Bush made separate telephone calls to the leader of Sinn Féin, Gerry Adams, and to the leader of the Democratic Unionist Party, Ian

Paisley, to encourage them to reach agreement on their remaining difficulties. He has continued to make clear his intention to assist the two governments in their attempts to secure the full implementation of the agreement.

Early in his Administration, President Bush appointed Mr. Richard Haass, Director of Policy Planning at the State Department, as his Special Envoy to Northern Ireland. After a successful period as Envoy during which he worked very closely with both Governments and the parties, Haass left the administration in 2004 and was replaced by Mr. Mitchell Reiss. Mr. Reiss has continued his predecessor's good work.

5

THE BEST BONDING

SEPTEMBER 11 CRISIS AND IRAQ WAR: THE ESSENCE OF ANGLO-AMERICAN ALLIANCE

The repeated footage of the terrifying act in television, where two civilian aircraft crashed into the Great Towers of World Trade Center was unbelievable truth for the American and the rest of the world in the month of September 2001. The third plane roared into Pentagon, the hub of US security system, killed almost 800 officials in a single stroke. However, the most intriguing and appalling warning coming through television was "a fourth plane which couldn't be traced, could be heading towards the United Kingdom".

British intelligence had presumed that Canary Warf Tower, the tallest building in the United Kingdom, was the next target. After all, the Bank of New York was housed in this 50-storey skyscraper and it had already demonstrated or revealed that it was on the radar screen of terrorists after the IRA planted bombs in it six years ago in 1996. The building also houses the offices of several newspapers, including The Daily Telegraph.

Apart from Canary Warf Tower, the London Stock Exchange also has been a threat prone building due to its financial inevitability. The London Stock Exchange considered as the most prosperous only after the New York Stock Exchange in matter of transaction. It is also termed as the central nervous system of the flamboyant economic health of United Kingdom and Europe since its inception. Due to importance to the financial lifeline of UK and the fragile post-colonial policies of British around the world in general and in the Middle East in particular London has been receiving constant terrorist onslaught or threat through overt and covert means. It is worthwhile to takes a retrospective note on the chronology of this great city so far as terrorism is concerned. The city of London, a semi-autonomous square mile in the heart of the capital, is Britain's main financial center. Home of the largest number of financial institutions and foreign banks in Europe, the city was a target for the Provisional Irish Republican Army (IRA) during its mainland bombing campaign in the 1990s. The city responded with the most extraordinary security measures ever seen in Britain, with the exception of Northern Ireland itself.

In mid-1993s, the city ratified a series of measures to reassure residents and prevent another bomb attack. A Traffic Management Scheme monitored all traffic entering the square mile. Officially designed to meet traffic and environmental needs, the plan dramatically reduced the number of entry points into the city by sealing off streets and establishing police checkpoints. All vehicles entering the city passed police cordons where random searches took place, mainly of larger commercial vehicles. Closed-circuit television cameras were placed at strategic sites around the city. Private companies were encouraged to join a Camera Watch plan, whereby existing security cameras were positioned to cover the streets. Backing up the static security measures were mobile, armed city of London police units, which established checkpoints at random, checking vehicles and occasionally pedestrians.

The British Prime Tony Blair flew to US after the September 11 attacks to show solidarity and attended the Joint Session of Congress on 20th of September. Prime Minister Tony

Blair led the American cause in emphasizing special relation and spontaneous support for the war on terrorism. Other European leaders also expressed their solidarity with different style, intensity and concern. Leaders were keen to be seen to be engaging in bilateralism with George Bush. Jacques Chirac, Tony Blair and Gerhard Schroeder practically raced one another to the Oval Office. Although most European leaders, with the notable exception of Blair, were careful to insist that the emerging campaign against Al-Quaeda and the Taliban was not a "war against the Muslims" and upheld that their evaluation of the root causes rested in terrorism. Some countries stressed those tough questions needed to be asked about US policy across the globe; while others insisted that nothing could ever justify the events of 11 September. Most leaders, with the notable exception of Silvio Berlusconi, were careful to express their respect for and solidarity with Islam and with Muslim nations, but there was cacophony between those insisting that US military retaliation should be tightly "targeted" and those who offered "unlimited" support to the US military effort. Some leaders managed to articulate both propositions. Countries eager to incarcerate Islamic terrorists engaged in bitter recriminations with others prioritizing habeas corpus and the protection of asylum-seekers.

This heterogeneity of response was symbolized by two highly mediatised events. The first was the 19 October 2001 European Council meeting in Ghent, controversially preceded by a tripartite conclave between Chirac/Jospin, Blair and Schroeder to discuss the military involvement of their respective national forces in Afghanistan. This attempt to organize a widely represented Directory overshadowed the substantive decisions of the Council itself. The triumvirate planned to meet again on 5 November in London; Tony Blair made every possible effort to get the useful support of the European leaders. The European leaders committed their support with all the relevant precautions.

Above all, it was Tony Blair's crusading leadership style which, while commanding respect, also fostered divisiveness. Seemingly abandoning the precariously balanced structures of European Union, Blair threw himself into personal shuttle diplomacy on behalf of the US administration. He reverted overnight to a brand of unconditional Atlanticism which many in Europe (and even in Britain) had assumed to be anachronistic after Kosovo, the missile defense controversy and the Bush administration's generalized penchant for unilateralism. NATO's 12 September invocation of article V emanated from a telephone conversation between Blair and the Alliance's secretary-general Lord Robertson, is very significant.

Paradoxically, NATO's invocation of article V was high political symbolism. It also helps to explain why, despite the short-term disordered cacophony of European responses to 11 September, the longer-term dynamics of European Security alliances are likely to be reinforced. Although in mid-September NATO adopted a series of measures to enhance intelligence sharing, to increase security of Alliance and US facilities, to guarantee blanket over-flight for US and allied aircraft and to re-deploy certain naval assets to the Eastern Mediterranean, these must be regarded as the bare minimum given the gravity of the crisis. The US preferred to discuss military cooperation via multiple bilateralisms rather than through the framework of the Alliance itself. The response from Washington to article 5, as well as to national offers of military assets, was: "Don't call us, we'll call you."

The long standing and deep-mutual understanding of Anglo-US relationship which often referred to "special relation" again showed its true color at the aftermath of WTC attack. The post World War II scenario had been changed the relationship of US-UK in matter of both range and depth. Due to its heavy loss in the post colonial era Britain not only lost her super power status but also reduced to the position a subordinate like ally of the United States. Nevertheless, with the passing of time the leadership of United Kingdom converted this tie of both the country to a trust worthy and flamboyant one.

Britain provided to the United States with much needed moral support in the immediate aftermath of the terrorist attacks, and this helped to cement the very strong relationship that has persisted between the British and US governments since September 11. The Prime Minister Tony Blair privately and publicly pronounced the solidarity through the playing of the US National Anthem by the band of the Goldstream Guards at Buckingham Place. This was followed by the almost universally-observed 3 minute period of silence, to the cancellation of sporting fixtures and the thousands of expressions of solidarity by the British people at large, the United Kingdom's reaction to the acts of terror was seen as being both genuine and appropriate. The very spontaneity of the reaction illustrated perfectly the instinctive nature of the relationship. The importance of these symbols of support should not be underestimated. However, it was the actions taken by the government, which ensured Britain's immediate and deep involvement in shaping coalition policy.

At the beginning of the campaign, the British Government set out a series of objectives, which it made public through speeches and through two published documents. These clearly articulated objectives appear to have shaped to a significant degree the early stages of the war against terrorism. They also contributed to ensuring that the widespread support for the US in the aftermath of the attacks was translated quickly into global action against the terrorist threat.

In his speech to the House of Commons on 14 September, the Prime Minister emphasized three objectives; which, first, he argued, "we must bring to justice those responsible." Second, he called for the establishment of an international coalition: "this is a moment when every difference between nations should be put to one side in one common endeavor." Thirdly, he argued that "we need to rethink dramatically the scale and nature of the action the world takes to combat terrorism[70]."

The same objectives were set out in more detail in the Governments "Campaign Objectives" document, which was published on 4 October 2001. The "Overall Objectives" was to eliminate terrorism as a force in international affairs. The documents described immediate objectives relating to Osama bin Laden, his network, and the Taliban regime. Wider objectives were also described: the coalition would "do everything possible to eliminate the threat posed by international terrorism and deter states from supporting, harboring or acting complicitly with international terrorist groups. The coalition would also aim to reinvigorate Afghanistan as a responsible member of the international community." These publications went some way towards reassuring parliament, the British public and Britain's coalition partners of why military action against Afghanistan was necessary.

When Prime Minister Tony Blair addressed the Parliament of the United Kingdom October 4, 2001 on the subject of the terrorist attacks in the United States, he said that he would "put in the Library of the House of Commons a document detailing the basis for our conclusions." The document, Blair said, "covers the history of Osama Bin Laden, his relations with the Taliban, what we know of the acts of terror he has committed; and some of what we know in respect of 11 September. I enter a major caveat, much of the evidence we have is intelligence and highly sensitive. It is not possible without compromising people or security to release precise details and fresh information is daily coming in."

This document does not purport to provide a prosecutable case against Osama Bin Laden in a court of law. Intelligence often cannot be used evidentially, due both to the strict rules of admissibility and to the need to protect the safety of sources. But on the basis of all the information available Her Majesty's Government is confident of its conclusions as expressed in this document.

Responsibility for the terrorist atrocities in the United States, 11 September 2001, included;

•   Osama Bin Laden and Al Qaida, the terrorist network which he heads, planned and carried out the atrocities on 11 September 2001;

•   Osama Bin Laden and Al Qaida retain the will and resources to carry out further atrocities;

•   the United Kingdom, and United Kingdom nationals are potential targets; and

•   Osama Bin Laden and Al Qaida were able to commit these atrocities because of their close alliance with the Taliban regime, which allowed them to operate with impunity in pursuing their terrorist activity.

The material in respect of 1998 and the USS Cole comes from indictments and intelligence sources. The material in respect of 11 September comes from intelligence and the criminal investigation to date. The details of some aspects cannot be given, but the facts are clear from the intelligence. The document does not contain the totality of the material known to HMG, given the continuing and absolute need to protect intelligence sources.

The televised September 11, did make a difference to the rest of the world and the American mainland itself. May be it would have different if 4,000 people perished in an explosion in a crowded Delhi bazaar. There has never been enough justice to go round the world. But this was New York, the citadel of world capitalism and showcase of the world's greatest power. The outrage here changed the rules of the game.

"Every nation in every region now has a decision to make, either you are with us or with the terrorists", US President George W. Bush told the congress on 23 September 2001[71]. It was forthrightness that struck a chord in all the countries that had suffered the depredation of terrorists masquerading as freedom fighters. However, unwittingly, bin Laden made victim hood the basis of the global coalition against him. "We have to drain the swamp they live in", said the US Defense Secretary Donald Rumsfeld when preparing for the onslaught on terrorism. This new found zero tolerance made all terrorism unacceptable, whether Palestinian or Pakistani. New York Mayer Rudi Giuliani gauged the pulse and turned down a donation by a Saudi Prince because it was prefaced by gratuitous advice on the need for a "balanced" US policy on Palestine. Anti-terrorism had to be unconditional[72].

Within month after the September 11 attack, President Bush has met with leaders from at least 51 different countries to help build support for the war against terrorism. 136 countries have offered a range of military assistance to the United States and 46 multilateral declarations of support came from different organizations. The UN General Assembly and Security Council condemned the attacks on September 12, 2001. On the initiative of the Secretary General of NATO, Lord Robertson the North Atlantic Council reacted to the attacks by declaring on 12 September 2001 that: "if it is determined that this attack was directed from abroad against the United States, it shall be regarded as an action covered by Article V of the Washington Treaty, which states that an armed attack against one or more of the allies in Europe or North America shall be considered an attack against them all[73]".

This was the first time in NATO's history that its member invoked Article V. It may be recalled that during the formulation of the North Atlantic Treaty in 1949 and subsequent approval by the US Congress there emerged a major debate about the article V of the North Atlantic Treaty. The American Congressmen felt adhering to this class of the treaty would result in Congress lose the power to declare war. Article V of the North Atlantic Treaty formulated as- "The Parties agree that an armed attack against one or more of them in Europe or North America shall be considered an attack against them all and consequently they agree that, if such an armed attack occurs, each of them, in exercise of the right of individual or collective self-defense recognized by Article 51 of the Charter of the United Nations, will assist the party or parties to attacked by taking forthwith, individually and in concert with the other Parties, such action as it deems necessary, including the use of armed force, to restore and maintain the security of the North Atlantic area".

Any such armed attack and all measures taken as a result thereof shall immediately reported to the Security Council. Such measures shall be terminated when the Security Council has taken the measures necessary to restore and maintain international peace and security.

This article automatically calls on the signatories to take military action on the aggressor as the article proclaimed that any attack on ones would considered as attack against all. Therefore the members of the Congress felt that in approving the North Atlantic Treaty they would forfeit the power of declaration of war to the President as he would as the Commander in Chief would pursue military campaign against the identified aggressor. Yet the Congress passed the North Atlantic Treaty because the threat posed by then the Communist state Soviet Union was formidable. Strangely the clause V was never invoked by any member of North Atlantic Treaty during the cold war period. It was only after the collapse of the Soviet Union for which the North Atlantic Treaty was originally formed that article V was invoked by the US in September 2001. OAS (Organization of American States) and ANZUS (Australia, New Zealand and US) quickly invoked their treaty obligations to support the US.142 countries have issued orders freezing the assets of suspected terrorists and organizations. 89 countries and 76 countries have granted over flight authority and landing rights for US military aircraft respectively. Twenty-three countries have agreed to host US forces involved in offensive operations.

Through intelligence cooperation with a number of nations, the US government acquired evidence against those responsible for the attacks of September 11. By December 11, 2001 more than 120 nations around the world answered President Bush's call to reject terrorism and commemorate the victims of the attacks by holding remembrance ceremonies.

The European Union acted after September 11 with what the International Crisis Group described as "a pace of response almost unprecedented with in the EU". To ensure coordinated responses to the attacks, an emergency meeting of foreign ministers was convened in Brussels on 12 September 2001. EU heads of state met on 21 September and agreed to the introduction of a counter terrorism plan of action. This included a proposal for a European arrest warrant and the adoption of an EU-wide definition of terrorism; a Framework Agreement on freezing assets and evidence; increased cooperation between services responsible for terrorism; the early ratification of all member states of the UN Convention for the Suppression of the Financing of Terrorism; implementation by member states of the UN Security Council resolutions on countering terrorism; the review of relations with third countries in light of their performance in combating terrorism and the approval by the commission of improvement to air transport security. Over all, the plan defined over sixty discrete objectives to fight terrorism, covering foreign policy, home affairs, judicial cooperation, and financial and economic policy.

The crisis was seen as a test of the US' common foreign and security policy. In the first stage of the campaign, there were few if any significant differences between EU member states on how to tackle the terrorist crisis, and consensus was that they acted cohesively and rapidly in response to the threat. The immediate EU response to the September 11 attacks was impressive, but progress became bogged down in the following months. Nonetheless, the habits of intergovernmental cooperation created through the EU proved valuable support to counter the terrorist threat.

The United Nations has often been criticized, but events after the terrorist attack of September 11 show how essential it is to international peace and security. The UN Security Council, in particular, has proved its value in the present crisis. To combat terrorism, and specifically Osama bin Laden's network and the Taliban government of Afghanistan, a broad and diverse coalition is necessary. President Bush quickly realized that the active cooperation of other countries, including Muslim countries, was essential to the intelligence and policy work needed to fund terrorists and destroys their networks. The support of these countries was also important to avoid a severe political backlash against the use of military force in Afghanistan. To secure such cooperation and support, country-by-country negotiations were necessary, but they were not sufficient. The campaign against terrorism needed to be rendered legitimate in the eyes of the world – particularly in countries whose governments and people are suspicious of the United States. Unilateral American action could easily be portrayed as lashing-out by the powerful "hegemony" at the expense of the poor and the weak. To be legitimate, action had to be authorized collectively, in a public forum representing the whole world. No such forum exists except the Security Council of the United Nations. Its 15 members then included three Muslim countries –Bangladesh, Mali and Tunisia. Unanimous resolutions by the Security Council belie the claim that efforts against terrorism are anti-Muslim[74].

The Security Council has passed two unanimous resolutions on terrorism since September 11, 2001. Meeting in

New York the very next day, it adopted Resolution 1368, which unequivocally condemned the terrorist attacks on the United States, and called on the international community to redouble its "efforts to prevent and suppress terrorist acts." Resolution 1368 also referred to the "inherent right of individual or collective self-defense," in accordance with Article 51 of the United Nations charter. In effect, it declared that military action by the United States against those responsible for the attacks would be lawful[75].

On September 28, the Security Council passed a more specific and equally far-reaching Resolution1373. In the resolution it acted under chapter VII of the UN Charter, which gives the Security Council authority to order states to carry out "the measures decided upon by the Security Council." In other words, the measures enumerated in Resolution 1373 are mandatory. Resolution 1373 uses strong language. It calls upon all states to "deny safe haven to those who finance, plan, support or commit terrorist acts, or provide safe havens." It also calls upon all states to cooperate "to prevent and suppress terrorist attacks and take action against perpetrators of such attacks[76]."

Resolutions 1368 and 1373 build on two years of UN resolution on terrorism. In 1999 the Security Council called upon all states to fight terrorism and demanded that the Taliban turn over bin Laden to authorities in a country where he had been indicted. In December 2000 it specifically condemned the Taliban's sheltering and training of terrorists, and demanded, under the mandatory provisions of Chapter VII, that it "cease the provision of sanctuary and training for international terrorists." These resolutions, defied by the Taliban, established a record that justified focusing responses to the September 11 attack on that regime and on bin Laden. If the United Nations did not exist, obtaining such a collective endorsement of the struggle against terrorism would be impossible. Bin Laden and his supporters could more easily claim that attacks against them are "crusades by the hegemonic United States and its clients".

The devastating attacks on the citadel of capitalism and democracy rippled across the world, leaving almost no one unaffected by the images of destruction. The ripple effects of the implications of the September 11 attacks followed immediately on every front and the economic front has been the most important one. Even before the dust settles on the area where the World Trade Center used to stand, and the executive and legislative arms of the US government put together their response, mind boggling statistics and data relating to economic state of US, UK and the rest of the world started emerging.

The rise of risk across the world as far as human life and property is concerned makes the insurance cost zooming across the board. Since September 11 every life every where in the world looks insecure. Shipping industries has been badly hit because of higher insurance costs. The impact has been felt by companies that importing or exporting finished products, raw materials and machinery. War premium on cargo has gone up by as much as 80 percent. Global lines have imposed war surcharge in the range of $20-$150 per container for ships moving to Middle East and European ports. Exports to Dubai, an entry point to the region, were taken a hit since the attacks.

There was bloodbath on the markets in the aftermath of the attacks. Some $2.7 trillion of shareholder value had been wiped out. The Dow Jones recorded its biggest point loss in history the day Wall Street reopened after the attack and the week that followed was the worst since depression. The estimates ranged between direct losses to the US economy of $30 billion.

(The following data has been taken from Ned Davis Research Ink, New York)

Events	%gain/ loss	DJIA % gain 1*st*month	3*rd* month	6*th* month
Fall of France	-17.1	-0.5	8.4	7.0
Pearl Harbor	-6.5	3.8	-2.9	-9.6
Korean War	-12.0	9.1	15.3	19.2
Cuban Missile Crisis	1.1	12.1	17.1	24.2
FK Assassination	-2.9	7.2	12.4	15.1
Arab Oil Embargo	-17.9	9.3	10.2	7.2
Nixon resigns	-15.5	-7.9	-5.7	12.5
USSR in Afghanistan	-2.2	6.7	-4.0	6.8
Gulf War Ultimatum	-4.3	17.0	19.8	18.7
WTC Bombing	-0.5	2.4	5.1	8.5

All international airlines have imposed a per sector surcharge ranging from $1.25 for Singapore Airlines to $6 for Lufthansa, in order to recover the higher insurance costs. Air France and British Airways are taken similar measures. The worst hit airlines, the US Airlines demanded immediate financial assistance from the Federal Government. The US government readily provided $15 billion lumpsum grant to the US Airlines. Despite this, 60 thousands employee of airlines sector in US reduced to the unemployed status, which rise to three lakes in the subsequent period.

Except the Defense industry, all the other industries around world witnessed a cataclysmic effect of the September 11 attack. The then $9.1 trillion Gross Domestic Product of USA had a major influence on the world economy as it is true even today with its $11 trillion. The US economy is not only the largest but also it is the engine of growth for the rest of the world economy. Information technology boom received a severe jolt because of the attack and made a large number of people jobless all over the globe.

The British Government under the Churchillian Blair's energetic diplomacy in the early stages of the campaign helped to translate the outpouring of sympathy for the United States into a broad international coalition. British diplomatic initiatives also helped the government to develop a "positive agenda of engagement with Arab countries and the Islamic world; and helped Afghanistan, through the United Nation to establish a broadly based government representative of all groups in the country."

Between September 11 and the commencement of military strikes, the Prime Minister met several European leaders and visited President Bush in the United States. He attended an emergency meeting of the council of European Union in Brussels. He visited Pakistan and India in early October2001. Tony Blair visited India on 5th and 6th of October 2001 and talked with Prime Minister Atal Bihari Vajpayee. Blair made the following points to Vajpayee:

- Roofing out the Taliban from Afghanistan will ease the situation somewhat in Kashmir

- Whether it is Zahir Shah or the Northern Alliance, it is India's interest to prevent anarchy in the Pakistan-Afghanistan region and help create a situation to set up an alternative regime in Kabul

- The West needs Musharraf as a symbol of Islamic support however tenuous, to prevent the war from degenerating into an Islam versus Christianity war;

- India should fight the temptation of fishing in troubled waters. So it should not create a build-up on the western border while the Pakistan Army is busy on its eastern border[77].

Blair also visited Pakistan on 5th of October 2001, and appraised the Pakistani President Pervez Musharraf for the US war on terrorism on its border. Of all the Muslim countries the United States needed the cooperation of Pakistan and Central Asian Republic Tajikstan and Uzbekistan bordering Afghanistan most of its military campaign. The Taliban had risen from

Pakistan's madaras. They had been helped in every conceivable way by the ISI to fight its way to power in Afghanistan. The geopolitical position of Pakistan and its closeness to the ruling Taliban regime invited American attention more than any other Muslim state. Reports indicated that President Bush directly spoke to President Musharraf and asked him to choose between joining the war against international terrorism or be treated as an enemy, a country on par with Afghanistan. The refusal to cooperate with the United States could invite more stringent economic sanction driving Pakistan bankruptcy.

With the help of Britain and its Prime Minister Tony Blair, the United States made effort to enlist the cooperation of the Islamic world. Blair visited the Middle Eastern countries four times within a month and a half to seek their support. The British Foreign Secretary Jack Straw visited Iran, the first such visit in more than two decades, to persuade to join the war against global terrorism. But despite the fact that there was no love lost between the Taliban and Iran and that the latter was openly supporting the Northern Alliance, the Jack Straw's effort did not go far. Iran did not want to be seen in company of the United States fighting against another Muslim country. In October 2001, Prime Minister Blair visited Syria for the first time in thirty years to enlist its cooperation in gathering intelligence about Bin Laden and his organization. Here too the British Prime Minister drew a blank as the Syrian President Assad strongly criticized the military campaign in Afghanistan that began on 7 October 2001[78].

The United States has close relation with Saudi Arabia. The latter had permitted the United States to station its troops and set up communication and command centre in the country during the Gulf War. Yet deeply conscious of the widespread anger of the masses against the United States it too was unwilling to throw itself in the US led war against terrorism despite the fact that bin Laden threatened the very existence of the Saudi rulers. To demonstrate its distance from the US policy the Saudis made it clear that they would not support American strike against Arab country on the ground that terrorist organizations were known to operate from there. Even the Prime Minister Blair's personal visit to Saudi Kingdom did not produce open support for the war on terrorism in Afghanistan. Moreover, in a public snub, Saudi Arabian rulers declined to see him because of prevailing strong anti-west sentiment. After his visit to the Middle East Tony Blair concluded that the West was not winning the propaganda war and the message that the West was not at war with Islam was not getting through[79]. In order to reduce possible damages and hardening of opposition to the War, Prime Minister Blair welcomed Yasser Arafat in London and at the joint press conference supported the idea of a Sovereign Palestinian state side by side with Israel in peace and harmony. President Bush too came up with the statement that a Palestinian state had been always on the horizon of American policy. Its boundary could be settled through negotiations. However, on 7 November 2001 both Bush and Blair in a joint press conference declared that resolution of the Palestinian issue was not a condition for winning the war in Afghanistan.

Prime Minister Tony Blair visited Egypt on 9 October 2001, where he said the Middle East peace process was crucial to defusing tension in the wake of the US terror attacks. Speaking earlier as he flew to meet President Hosni Mubarak in Egypt, Mr. Blair said the UK, US and perhaps other countries were prepared to use their ground forces in Afghanistan. Mr. Blair's latest three-day tour to shore up support for military action ended as a new opinion poll suggests his popularity during the international crisis matches that of Winston Churchill in World War Two. During a break in their talks, both Mr. Blair and President Mubarak stressed the importance of reinvigorating the Middle East peace process as they pledged to stand united against terror. Meanwhile, the British Foreign Secretary held talks with Iranian, Egyptian and Israeli leaders and the Arab League[80]. Between 30 October and 1 November 2001, the Prime Minister also appointed Paul Bergne, a diplomat with experience in Central Asia, to be his "personal representative on Afghan affairs." Robert Cooper, another diplomat, was appointed to represent Britain in negotiations towards the future of Afghanistan in the UN and else where.

Mr. Blair, who spoke to Palestinian leader Yasser Arafat via telephone in Oman on 10 October 2001, said: "It is important that we put this peace process back on track so there aren't generations of people who then go and abuse the Palestinian cause to commit acts of terrorism." UK Foreign Secretary Jack Straw told the BBC on 11 October 2001 that the US and UK governments were agreed that no action would be taken against other countries, such as Iraq, at the moment. He said there would have to be as much evidence against other regimes as there was against Osama Bin Laden and the Taliban, before action was taken[81].

While in Oman on 10 October 2001 Mr. Blair met Sultan Qaboos of Oman, as well as some of the 20,000 UK troops currently involved in the biggest British military exercise since the Gulf War. Tony Blair's efforts to shore up the international coalition against terrorism suffered a setback on 11 October 2001 when it emerged that he had failed to secure a meeting with Saudi Arabia's leaders.

The prime minister spoke to crown prince Abdullah on 9 October 2001 about arranging a meeting during his two-day Middle East trip that ends on the night of 11 October 2001. Mr. Blair regards Saudi Arabia as a key member of the international coalition against terrorism. However, a British official said Mr. Blair could not find a mutually convenient time for the meeting. Mr. Blair wanted to hold talks on 11 October 2001 because he visited British troops in Oman on 10 October 2001. The British official acknowledged there could be political sensitivity in Saudi Arabia about Mr. Blair visiting the country while the military strikes on Afghanistan continued. However, the official said it was important to get across the argument that the action in Afghanistan did not amount to a conflict between the west and Islam.

A Downing Street spokesman said: "We did have discussions with Saudi Arabia about the possibility of including Riyadh on this trip. It simply was not logistically possible[82]." No Prime Minister before him has identified Britain so completely with a foreign power. The cheerleaders of the "war" on terrorism support their case with the sanctified precedent of the 1941 alliance between Winston Churchill and Franklin D Roosevelt. As Blair travels from Pakistan to Moscow to the Gulf, everyone believes he is speaking for an America whose own president lacks the communication skills international diplomacy requires.

Tony Blair began another audacious bid to reduce Middle East tension when he flew into Syria on 30 October 2001, which has a strained relationship with Israel and is home to US-blacklisted terrorist groups. Syria's sponsorship of three of the most feared anti-Israeli groups - Hizbullah, Hamas and the Popular Front for the Liberation of Palestine - presented a formidable obstacle for Blair's with the Syrian president, Bashar al-Assad. Blair had embarked on a three-day marathon tour designed to bolster the US-led international coalition against terrorism after September 11.

Blair was the most senior member of the coalition to go to the Middle East since the American Defence Secretary, Donald Rumsfeld, visited during the second week of October 2001 on the eve of the bombing. It comes at a time when the Israeli-Palestinian conflict threatens to throw off course the US and British strategy in the war against the Taliban and Osama bin Laden.

Prime Minister Tony Blair was forced to cancel plans to visit Saudi Arabia in the early October 2001 because of sensitivities in the kingdom. This remains problematic, with the

Saudi government calling for an early end to the bombing and concern over the number of Afghan casualties during Blair's visit to the region.

Blair's Syrian visit has been cleared with the US government, which has indicated it is willing to give President Assad an opportunity to join the coalition against terrorism. British officials tried to stop funding several groups classified by the US and Britain as terrorists, including Hizbullah, Hamas and the PFLP. The PFLP has its headquarters in Damascus, and claimed responsibility for the assassination of the Israeli cabinet minister Rehavam Zeevi a fortnight ago. Although Syria has condemned the September 11 attacks in New York and Washington, Mr. Assad refuses to accept that Hizbullah, Hamas and the PFLP are terrorists, arguing instead that they are freedom fighters.

On 25 October 2001, the Canadian foreign minister John Manley, on a visit to Damascus, conceded he could not reach agreement with the Syrians over the legitimacy of violence. Blair had also faced the same difficulty in his talks. Downing Street stressed that Blair was not traveling to the Middle East to deliver lectures or to carry a single blueprint for peace. The advantage and unique leverage with Blair was that he had full confidence of the US to negotiate with the Middle East, to enlist their support in the war against terrorism.

The Israeli government, normally skeptical about the visits of foreign dignitaries, described Blair as the most important visitor to the region since September 11 because of his high-profile involvement in the international coalition.

The Prime Minister and his Foreign Secretary took an active part in encouraging Russia's Vladimir Putin to see the aftermath of September as an opportunity to join the main stream of Western policymaking[83]. Elsewhere, the US administration was initially reluctant to involve the Group of Eight in the international counter-terrorism effort but at the UK's instigation's the US has broadened the remit of its Financial Action Task Force to include action to halt the flow of terrorist funding". On 29 September 2001 after an elaborate discussion on the counter-terrorism, G-8 Foreign Ministers released the statement as "G-8 Ministerial Statement on Combating Terrorism". That was as followed-

In the coming days, weeks and months, the United States and the G-8 will work in partnership in a broad coalition to combat the evil of terrorism. We will act jointly to expand and improve this cooperation worldwide. Those responsible for the recent attacks must be tracked down and held to account. We will mount a comprehensive, systematic and sustained effort to eliminate international terrorism — its leaders, its actions, its networks. Those responsible for aiding, supporting or harboring the perpetrators, organizers and sponsors of these acts will be held accountable. Given the events of September 11, 2001 it is imperative that we continue to develop practical measures to prevent terrorists from operating.

Our resolve is a reflection of the strength of the U.S.-G-8 relationship, our shared values, and our determination to address together the new challenges we face. The nature of our democratic societies makes it imperative to protect our citizens from terrorist acts, while at the same time protecting their individual liberties, due process, and the rule of law. The U.S. and the G-8 are committed to enhancing security measures, legislation and enforcement. We will work together to encourage greater cooperation in international fora and wider implementation of international instruments. We will also cooperate in global efforts to eliminate the ability of terrorists to plan and carry out future atrocities. We have agreed today that the United States and the G-8 will vigorously pursue cooperation in the following areas in order to reduce vulnerabilities and combating terrorism in our societies:

— Aviation and other transport security

- Police and judicial cooperation, including extradition
- Denial of financing of terrorism, including financial sanctions
- Denial of other means of support to terrorists
- Export control and non-proliferation
- Border controls, including visa and document security issues
- Law enforcement access to information and exchange of electronic data[84].

The United States and European Union (EU) have outlined several key areas for future cooperation in their effort to eliminate international terrorism. In a ministerial statement issued 20 September 2001, the two major powers said they would step up cooperation on aviation and other transport security, police and judicial activities, financial sanctions, export controls, border controls and exchange of electronic data.

The statement followed a same-day meeting between Secretary of State Colin Powell, Belgian Foreign Minister Louis Michel (Belgium currently holds the presidency of the EU), EU External Affairs Commissioner Chris Patten, and Javier Solana, secretary general of the EU Council and the high representative for the EU's Common Foreign and Security Policy. "The U.S. and the EU are committed to enhancing security measures, legislation and enforcement, we will mount a comprehensive, systematic and sustained effort to eliminate international terrorism — its leaders, its actions, its networks" the statement said[85].

On September 5, 2001, President Bush stated that America had "no more important relationship in the world" than that with Mexico. However, the 9/11 episode dramatically changed American perception and by September 20, the President invited Prime Minister Tony Blair to join him at a Joint Session of Congress, where he declared that "America has no truer friend than Great Britain[86]". Fear over the future of the "special relationship" before September 11 was probably exaggerated. However, the government's actions in the immediate aftermath of the attack did much to cement British-US relations at America's time of crisis.

It appear that having established Britain as America's most trusted ally in the war against terrorism the actions taken by the British government includes, to draw together and define an international coalition against terrorism, publicly and through multilateral fora. These actions ensured that, by the end of September 2001, Britain had "a seat at the table" in Washington and ensured that "the views of the Blair government are taken seriously." The government's articulation of campaign objectives also appears to have shaped coalition policy, seizing the moment of maximum support for counter-terrorist action to ensure that global action was taken to defeat the threat.

It was widely anticipated that after September 11 the US military reaction would be swift and extensive. After the al-Qaeda terrorist strikes against US embassies in Nairobi and Dar-es-Salem in August 1998, the Clinton administration had launched immediate missile attacks against the al-Shifa Chemical factory in Sudan, and against suspected terrorist targets in Afghanistan[31].

As Osama bin Laden involvements was assumed likely perpetrator of the September 11 attacks. Military strikes on bin Laden's terrorist network's bases in Afghanistan became the goal of US-UK military campaign. On 7th October 2001, British and American armed forces began a series of air and cruise missile attacks in Afghanistan. The attacks were launched against the terrorist camps of Osama bin Laden and the military installation of the Taliban regime[32]. By this stage, international legal grounds for such an attack had been established through Security Council Resolution 1368 and 1373.

On October 8, 2001, British Parliament was recalled for

the third time since September11. The Prime Minister's speech to the house was primarily to brief the Parliamentarians on the nature of the combined military campaign almost four weeks after the attacks on the World Trade Center and the Pentagon. The Prime Minister after paying "tribute to President Bush's statesmanship in having the patience to wait" explained that action had been delayed for three reasons: "First, we had to establish who was responsible. Once it was cleared that the al-Qaeda network planned and perpetrated the attacks were then wanted to give the Taliban regime time to decide their own position: would they shield bin Laden or would they yield him up? Thirdly, we wanted time to make sure that the targets for any action minimized the possibility of civilian casualties[33]."

Without trying the diplomatic route before military action, and without the clear and public articulation of coalition objectives and of responsibility for the terrorist attacks, global support for the operation would have been much harder to establish. Military action was taken with a remarkable high level of international endorsement. Islamic countries at the Asia-Pacific Economic Co-operation forum in October were generally supportive of the US-led campaign.

Operation Enduring Freedom, the military phase, began on October 7, 2001. Since then, coalition forces have liberated the Afghan people from the repressive and violent Taliban regime. As President Bush and Secretary of Defense Donald Rumsfeld have said, "this is a different kind of war with a different kind of enemy. The enemy is not a nation –the enemy is terrorist networks that threaten the way of life of all peaceful people."

The war against terrorism is the first war of the 21st century..... and it requires a 21st century military strategy. Secretary Rumsfeld and his team have worked with the British forces and other coalition allies' military to craft a cutting-edge military strategy. This was done, to minimize civilian casualties, partners with local forces, and brings destruction to the oppressive Taliban who supported the al-Qaeda terrorist network[35].

The coalition has achieved broad military success while putting fewer than 3,000 US ground troops on the ground in Afghanistan. In addition, Secretary Rumsfeld and the US military have shown a lightening quick ability to adapt to a distant, harsh and ever-changing battlefield. In some cases, US troops were conquering terrorists by welding together 21st century technology with 19th century tactics. Troops have chased terrorist on horseback while using mobile phones and global positioning systems to pinpoint targets for the Air Force. Bombers use 21st century targeting technology, and laser-guided and ground positioning system (GPS) guided smart bombs to. destroy specific targets, including centuries – old caves used as terrorist headquarters.

With in weeks the military essentially destroyed al-Qaeda's grip on Afghanistan by driving the Taliban from power. Taliban leaders surrendered major cities to opposition forces, including Kandhar, Kabul, Kunduz, and Mazar-e-Sharif. The military destroyed at least 11 terrorist training camps and 39 Taliban command and control sites. The Wall Street Journal reported on December 13 that as many as 50,000 terrorists from more than 50 countries may have received training in al-Qaeda camps in Afghanistan in recent years[30]. About 2.5 million humanitarian rations had been dropped to aid the people of Afghanistan. US Marines established a military base at Kandhar airport. Routes were being blocked to try to prevent the escape of al-Qaeda and Taliban members. Senior al-Qaeda and Taliban officials were either captured or killed. Friendship Bridge between Afghanistan and Uzbekistan was reopened to transport humanitarian aid by land. Minefields and roads were cleared to ensure delivery of aid and freedom of movement. Leaflet drops and radio broadcasts continues daily to convey the determination of the United States, provide truthful

information, and encourage the capture of Osama bin Laden[31].
Significantly, the Military action in Afghanistan represented a global coalition effort. In addition to the United States, military assets were being deployed from many other nations, including the United Kingdom, Australia, Canada, Czech Republic, France, Germany, Italy, Japan, New Zealand, Poland, Russia and Turkey[32]

THE ALLIANCE ON IRAQ WAR

During the period January 1- June 30, 2002, Baghdad continued to deny UN inspectors entry into Iraq as required by Security Council Resolution 687 and subsequent Council resolutions, and no UN inspections took place during the first half of 2002. Moreover, the automated video monitoring systems installed by the UN at known and suspect WMD facilities in Iraq were not operating during this period. Furthermore, Iraq has engaged in extensive concealment efforts and has used the period since it refused inspections to attempt to reconstitute prohibited programs.

More than ten years of sanctions and the loss of much of Iraq's physical nuclear infrastructure under IAEA oversight have not diminished Saddam's interest in acquiring or developing nuclear weapons. Iraq's efforts to procure tens of thousands of proscribed high-strength aluminum tubes are of significant concern. All intelligence experts agree that Iraq is seeking nuclear weapons and that these tubes could be used in a centrifuge enrichment program. Most intelligence specialists assess this to be the intended use, but some believe that these tubes are probably intended for conventional weapons programs[87].

Iraq has developed a ballistic missile capability that exceeds the 150 kilometer range limitation established under UNSCR 687. During the 1980s, Iraq purchased 819 Scud B missiles from the USSR. Hundreds of these 300 km range missiles were used to attack Iranian cities during the Iran-Iraq

War. Beginning in 1987, Iraq converted many of these Soviet Scuds into extended-range variants, some of which were fired at Tehran; some were launched during the Gulf war, and others remained in Iraq's inventory at war's end. Iraq admitted filling at least 75 of its Scud warheads with chemical or biological agents and deployed these weapons for use against Coalition forces and regional opponents, including Israel in 1991.

UNSCOM reported to the Security Council in December 1998 that Iraq also continued to withhold information related to its Chemical Weapons program. For example, Baghdad seized from UNSCOM inspectors an Iraqi Air Force document discovered by UNSCOM that indicated that Iraq had not consumed as many CW munitions during the Iran-Iraq war in the 1980s as had been declared by Baghdad. This discrepancy indicates that Iraq may have hidden an additional 6,000 CW munitions[88].

Iraq continued to pursue an unmanned aerial vehicle (UAV) program that converted L-29 jet trainer aircraft originally acquired from Eastern Europe. In the past, Iraq conducted flights of the L-29, possibly to test system improvements or to train new pilots.

Iraq aggressively continues to seek advanced conventional warfare (ACW) equipment and technology. A thriving gray arms market and porous borders have allowed Baghdad to acquire smaller arms and components for larger arms, such as spare parts for aircraft, air defense systems, and armored vehicles. Iraq also acquires some dual-use and production items that have applications in the ACW arena through the Oil for Food program[89].

In his State of the Union address on 29 January 2002, Bush announced that the US would take pre-emptive military action to counter threats to the US and its core allies. He stated that "I will not wait on events, while dangers gather. I will not stand by, as peril draws closer and closer. The United States of America will not permit the world's most dangerous regimes

to threaten us with the world's most destructive weapons[90]."
Bush's doctrine of pre-emption was formalized as a part of US
security strategy in the National Security Strategy which stated
that "while the United States will constantly strive to enlist the
support of the international community, we will not hesitate to
act alone, if necessary, to exercise our right of self-defence by
acting pre-emptively against such terrorists, to prevent them
from doing harm against our people and our country[91]." The
first operational use of the pre-emption doctrine would be Iraq
and the use of the strategy would lead to a deep crisis in
transatlantic relations and the "New-Old Europe" debate.

The 2003 US-led invasion of Iraq created a range of
diplomatic and strategic tensions in the transatlantic security
alliance and it exacerbated differences in the US over
cooperative versus militant multilateralism. Within the
administration, Secretary of State Colin Powell emerged as the
foremost proponent of cooperation, while Vice President Dick
Cheney and Secretary of Defence Donald Rumsfeld led the
drive for immediate action, even without strong international
support. Powell and the cooperationists initially held sway and
during the fall of 2002, the administration worked to develop
an international coalition and secure both UN backing and
bilateral support from the major European allies.

During this period, domestic anti-war sentiment grew in
states such as Germany and France, while domestic US support
for the war grew. On 10 October 2002, the US Congress
overwhelmingly passed a resolution authorizing the use of force
against Iraq, even if it meant unilateral and/or pre-emptive
action. Tensions mounted on both sides of the Atlantic. Former
US Secretary of State Madeleine Albright summarized the
situation as "European unease with American pretensions,
coupled with American doubts about European resolve" and
contended that the diplomatic conflict "creates the potential for
a long-term and dangerous rift[92]." A former Assistant Secretary
of State, James Rubin, observed that most European leaders

perceived that for the US "force had become an object in itself", and that Washington was using diplomacy simply to smooth the way for an invasion. Meanwhile, in Washington, there emerged a perception that the anti-war states, led by France, Germany and Russia, were actively working to undermine the American coalition and using diplomatic pressure to prevent states from supporting the US. There was an especially strong sense that Germany was using its chair position in the Security Council to block support for a UN resolution authorizing the use of force.

There was a growing awareness that the new and potential new members from East and Central Europe were decided pro-American at the governmental level and backed a coalition of atlanticist states within the alliance led by the United Kingdom. Eight NATO members issued an open letter in support of the US on 30 January 2003. The letter declared that:

We in Europe have a relationship with the US which has stood the test of time. Thanks in large part to American bravery, generosity and farsightedness, Europe was set free from the two forms of tyranny that devastated our continent in the 20th century: Nazism and Communism. Thanks, too, to the continued cooperation between Europe and the US we have managed to guarantee peace and freedom on our continent. The trans-Atlantic relationship must not become a casualty of the current Iraqi regime's persistent attempts to threaten world security. In today's world, more than ever before, it is vital that we preserve that unity and cohesion. We know that success in the day-to-day battle against terrorism and the proliferation of weapons of mass destruction demands unwavering determination and firm international cohesion on the part of all countries for whom freedom is precious[93].

In addition, ten Central and East European states, the Vilnius Ten, issued an open letter in support of the US which declared at one point:

Our countries understand the dangers posed by tyranny and the special responsibility of democracies to defend our shared values. The trans-Atlantic community, of which we are part, must stand together to face the threat posed by the nexus of terrorism and dictators with weapons of mass destruction.

At a pres conference on 22 January 2003, Rumsfeld made a series of comments which underlined the administration's policy of trying to develop a coalition of willing European states:

Now, you're thinking of Europe as Germany and France. I don't. I think that's old Europe. If you look at the entire NATO Europe today, the centre of gravity is shifting to the east. And there are a lot of new members. And if you just take the list of all the members of NATO and all of those who have been invited in recently – what is it? Twenty-six, something like that? – You're right. Germany has been a problem, and France has been a problem[94].

Rumsfeld's comments highlighted the manifestation of the older Atlanticist versus Europeanist debate with in the Transatlantic Alliance. A coalition of "Old European" Europeanist states, those that Rumsfeld considered to use "old" thinking, were led by France and Germany.

The divisions among the European states demonstrated the continuation of the Europeanist versus Atlanticist debate in transatlantic security. It also created a backlash against the pro-American states. The most striking example of this involved French President Jacques Chirac publicly berating East European states that supported the US Chirac called the pro-American stance of the East European governments "dangerous" and "reckless" and threatened that their policy positions could "only reinforce an attitude of hostility" in a not-so-subtle threat over future EU membership.

In an age where global issues threaten the very survival of states, as a country with an enormous scope of contacts and a vast network of influence, Britain is better placed than most countries to confront threats that emanate from anywhere in the world. The legacy of Britain's past as a powerful country with connections to countries of equal and greater status serves it well; the irony is that connections to the increasingly distressed lot of 'failed states', desperately poor and suffering states, some of them having become 'rogue countries', in far-flung places, have become more important. Therefore, the traditional role of the United Kingdom, that of building bridges, is more necessary and potentially more "profitable" in geopolitical terms than at any time in the post-World War II era.

With its privileged relations Britain maintains with continental Europe and the 'special relationship' the country values with the United States. The Euro bridge is built on proximity, shared history, the EU legal regime that incorporates economic, political and, recently, security cooperation, and developing relations with the new democracies of Central and Eastern European Countries (CEEC).

Britain has been able to manage the transatlantic relationship to its benefit, serving as balancer. British leaders have been able to trade off one relationship to enhance their influence in the other relationship, and the strategy has worked in both directions. The British are quick to admit, "this country's status as a leading member of the European Union adds to rather than detracts from its role as the premier ally of the United States". Britain has earned credit with the United States as a sponsor for US interests in Europe and around the world. After September 11, Blair logged incredible mileage in support of the war on Terror and in making approaches to countries, Pakistan, for example, with whom the UK could boast more historical knowledge than the United States. By the same token, successive Prime Ministers and politicians have served as interpreters of European perspectives to their counterparts in the US. Partly owing to Britain's ability to play the various relationships while maximizing influence in world events, British diplomats are credited with superior skills. Even as observer as critical as former US Secretary of State Henry Kissinger prized Britain's abilities. She was, he claimed, an example of a country which, through the exercise of outstanding diplomatic skills, enjoyed more influence than her physical power strictly warranted.

In an already radically changed security environment, Britain conducted its Strategic Defence Review (SDR) in 1998[95]. One of the main objectives at the time was to enable Britain to operate in a mobile, forward fashion, "to go to the crisis, rather than have the crisis come to us". The difficulty of being able to pin down future threats had already become apparent. The previous decade had seen two major crises emerge without prediction, Saddam Hussein's invasion of Kuwait in 1991 and the crisis of the former Yugoslavia that continued throughout the decade. For that mater, the collapse of the Soviet Union in the previous decade had not been predicted. Therefore, the SDR was cognizant that it needed to place priorities in the context of "a changing world".

The revitalization of NATO had succeeded despite the failure of the transatlantic relationship to find an early solution to the crisis of the Balkans and intervene to stop genocide. Before the ink was dry on the SDR, NATO would decide on its first military adventure and the first collective forceful humanitarian intervention in history in Kosovo where Europeans line up behind US leadership, despite grumbling, and the United States tolerated their input.

The SDR reflected certainly that Britain's interest were worth defending in another region. "we have particularly important national interests and close friendships in the Gulf". Of course, Britain's policy in the Gulf had a decade in which to unfold since the first war against Iraq in 1991, not to mention the UK had not withdrawn entirely from Iraq but patrolled no-fly zones in the North and the South alongside the United States.

1998 turned out to be a watershed year for British security, the result of a meeting Prime Minister Tony Blair had a St. Malo with French President Jacques Chirac. This marked the occasion when Britain decided to cooperate with EU plans to develop a security dimension. After this development, Britain sided with the efforts to give Europe an autonomous military capacity and the advent of Europe's Rapid Reaction Force. St. Malo redefined Britain's bridge to Europe, the weight of which had mainly been carried by NATO in military terms. The politics of this groundbreaking initiative were as important as the content.

NATO's endorsement of the Defence Capabilities Initiative (D.C.I) in 1999 has also had an impact on military planning in Britain. The DCI, adopted at the Washington Summit, was designed to stimulate European defence efforts to help them catch up with the US Revolution in Military Affairs. NATO's military intervention in Kosovo in 1999 had exposed the severe capabilities gap between the United States and its allies. Britain became resolute in closing the gap and in leading NATO members to do the same, to convince the United States of the continuing military value and relevance of the alliance. All of NATO did not share the same enthusiasm for the DCI which "had not been taken seriously be most European governments."

In 2002, the British added a New Chapter to the SDR to incorporate lessons learned in the intervening military actions in Kosovo, Sierra Leone, and Afghanistan. Although the SDR had put defence planning on the right track, especially in terms of thinking on the increased role for expeditionary forces and the need for greater spending, terrorism posed specific challenges. So did military cooperation with the United States, which the report refers as a Britain's "most important ally". The forward thrust of UK security, leaving behind a geo-specific emphasis, was again underlined, as well as the need for 'rapid reaction', having learned "opportunities to engage terrorist groups may only be fleeting".

Britain's 'special relationship' is special because no other European country or any European country, has a relationship with the United States that delivers the same benefits. When a new US President signals he is going to extend the benefits usually reserved to Britain to another country, the 'special relationship' is seen to be in decline by skeptics in the UK, the same ones who have long warned against depending on the United States.

Interesting, the same fears were raised at the outset of the Bush presidency. UK politicians were quick to notice the new administration's interest in upgrading relations within the hemisphere, as the Commons Foreign Affairs committee deliberately noted in 2000.

The President's earliest foreign visits were to Mexico and to Ottawa, while his first visit outside the Americas was to Madrid. As recently as 5 September, President Bush spoke of the United States as having "no more important relationship in the world than the one we have with Mexico[96]".

To the extent the relationship has waxed and waned according to the rapport US and British political leaders have been able to muster and maintain, the relationship is one vulnerable to politics, especially Presidential electoral politics in the United States.

Besides the transitory element of the exchange of political favor between British and US leaders, the relationship has durable content in security terms. The relationship has also waxed and waned in response to dangers in the world, or rather, perceptions of danger in the world. In fact, as the contemporary security relationship was forged during World War II, maintaining itself through NATO during the Cold War, common perceptions of danger in the world renews the primal *raison d'être*. However, this is not join the United States' anti-communist fight in Vietnam. As for the present threat of global terrorism, both countries leaders, US President Bush and UK Prime Minister Blair, personally, share the conviction terrorism is the greatest challenge history has presented to them.

The current ideology of the 'special relationship', that of good confronting evil and the sense of historical mission being understood by only a few, hark back to the Great War between democracy and fascism. The rhetoric both leaders utilize in relation to the terror threat has a definite Churchillian flourish. Oddly enough, memorializing wartime cooperation between the closest of allies, Blair presented a bust of Churchill, Bush's hero, on his first visit to the new American President. Blair embodies, by Bush's own estimation, so many of the qualities the president lauds. Loyalty, morality, and political realism, all exhibited by Blair, are in sync with the tone of Washington. That the British Prime Minister had to brave a course in face of so much dissent in Europe to support the United States in Iraq moved the relationship beyond 'special' and renewed its exceptionalism.

For the usually pragmatic British, the security relationship has yielded numerous, measurable, advantages, but not without costs. In terms of individual self-defence, Britain has benefited from intelligence cooperation, the closest that the United States has had with any country. Indeed, since September 11 and US-UK military cooperation in Afghanistan and Iraq, the countries' intelligence communities have developed even closer means for cooperation. The Commons Foreign Affairs Select Committee confirms "long-established mechanisms" that have been useful in the Afghanistan campaign, for example, "the placing of eighty British intelligence personnel in the United States central Command headquarters in Tampa, FL". This level of cooperation is no small gain in the war against terror as much as it depends on intelligence networks that span the globe. Furthermore, as long as the United States has superior technologies and has acquired capabilities in the collection of intelligence, partnership with the United States is critical if Britain wants to maintain an edge.

Theoretically, the asymmetry in power between the United States and Britain goes to the heart of whether the relationship is sustainable as one that is mutually beneficial. Nonetheless, the asymmetry of the relationship so far has motivated Britain to try to close the gap through continuous military cooperation with the United States over the last decade beginning with the Gulf War. Indeed, when one considers the decision of the UK to stand by the side of the United States in Iraq in the context of over a decade of military cooperation, one can see the policy as an extension of previous policy, not to mention in accordance with the SDR's identification of the Gulf region as a strategic priority. Stated in theoretical terms, British and American elites had an identity of interests in Iraq even though their publics may have needed to be brought up to speed.

The United States and Britain had been exchanging fire with Iraq since the first no-fly zone was created in Iraq in the North in 1991, initially with French participation; the French later withdrew and refused to join the zone added in the South. Ironically, Britain had used its 'special relationship' with the United States to convince the first Bush administration, intent on making a clean and quick exit from Iraq, to do something about Saddam Hussein's air assault on Kurds and Shi'ites who, at the end of the war and on the urging of Americans, had rebelled to overthrow the ruler. Thus, on the initiative of former British Prime Minister John Major, the first safe zone was established in the name of humanitarian intervention.

After September 11, the British and Americans had also expanded their joint presence in the region. With the United States, the Royal Navy had set up a headquarters in Bahrain to support the military operation in the first phase of the War in Afghanistan. The decision to establish this headquarters was a significant factor in the success of the UK maritime contribution to the Iraq operation.

Indeed, Afghanistan proved to be a good training opportunity for Iraq. Brigadier Dutton makes the point to the Commons Committee as to 'equipment performance' in Iraq, "most of this equipment was not unfamiliar because it had been acquired for the operation in Afghanistan the previous year". Anticipating Iraq, Britain had been the preferred partner in Afghanistan. An informed journalist recounted, "Though some 80 countries had made effort to help (in Afghanistan), only the British would participate in the first wave of strikes." Clearly, the temptation existed to continue with a winning strategy, to build in Iraq on the successes achieved in the war in Afghanistan, while much seemed to be in place. At least the success of the military campaign in Iraq reinforces the 'special coalition' prosecuting the next war together.

For weeks, amongst various United Nations Security Council members, there was disagreement about how to deal with the Iraq issue. There were disagreements between various permanent members on how any resolutions should be formulated and the objectives of them. The U.S. and U.K. were taking an openly hostile stance, while the other three (France, Russia and China) wanted a more measured approach, not convinced of the claims made by the other two, and not convinced of the need for military action, either. (It should also be noted that Russia, and France also have their own interests in Iraq, related to oil.)

On 8 November 2002, the controversial resolution, 1441 was adopted unanimously. Surprising for a lot of people was that even Syria, the Arab member on the Council also accepted the resolution. But 1441 was the result of a lot of political maneuvering (i.e. diplomacy). The U.S. was initially threatening to take unilateral action (with one or two allies), which would have been illegal according to international law under the United Nations. In order to ensure that the U.S. still took that path of the U.N., other members of the Council dropped various concerns and stances they had in terms of the resolution wording. As foreign policy expert and author, Phyllis Bennis *puts it*, for most of the U.N. Security Council members, vote to support the resolution "was not about constraining Iraq, it was about constraining the U.S. The message was: if the U.S. desires to launch a massive attack, it will have to return to the U.N. and win its approval. If the president makes war without U.N. backing, it will be violating the United Nations charter and international law."The final resolution then is seen as a successful diplomatic effort by the U.S. and U.K. interests. One of the key concerns raised by most states was that the resolution should not automatically mean war and that it should require further U.N. Security Council authorization. This aspect made it into the resolution, but with some controversy[97].

When the Resolution was adopted, the various member nations all gave the response. Almost all stressed at that time, (and was broadcast on major television news stations) repeatedly that there is no hidden trigger in the resolution for means automatic war. It was mainly because of this clause that all nations agreed to the resolution. *The "will of the United Nations" hardly represented one voice.*

So when we are reminded by the likes of Tony Blair, Jack Straw, Colin Powell and others of the "will of the United Nations" being expressed through this resolution, and that member states should therefore live up to their responsibilities and demand war, we should bear in mind that the resolution did not represent a common will, but a number of negotiated differences, and if anything, much of the "will" of the Security Council was to *not* have automatic war.The U.N. Security council would have to agree once weapons inspections completed and their report reveals a material breach. Even though later toward justifying war, British Prime Minister Tony Blair said a second resolution was not needed, on the day that 1441 was passed as he himself pointed out that it was: *"To those who fear this resolution is just an automatic trigger point, without any further discussion, paragraph 12 of the resolution makes it clear that is not the case*[98]*".*

Even the U.S. representative, John Negroponte, and the U.K. representative, Sir Jeremy Greenstock, confirmed this when he said "As we have said on numerous occasions to Council members, *this resolution contains no "hidden triggers" and no "automaticity" with respect to the use of force.* If there is a further Iraqi breach, reported to the Council by UNMOVIC, the IAEA or a Member State, the matter will return to the Council for discussions as required in paragraph 12."

UK representative Sir Jeremy Greenstock said "we heard loud and clear during the negotiations the concerns about "automaticity" and "hidden triggers" - the concern that on a decision so crucial we should not rush into military action; that on a decision so crucial any Iraqi violations should be discussed by the Council. Let me be equally clear in response, as a co-sponsor with the United States of the text we have just adopted. There is no "automaticity" in this resolution. If there is a further Iraqi breach of its disarmament obligations, the matter will return to the Council for discussion as required in paragraph 12. We would expect the Security Council then to meet its responsibilities"[99].

Most other Security Council members reiterated this. The same link above to the speeches has transcripts for the other members. Almost all reiterated that the resolution doesn't mean automatic war, but that another decision is needed by the Council. (Those that did not specifically mention that the resolution didn't mean automatic war did not say that it meant automatic war, either.) Taking just a few examples (the rest can be seen from the same source as above):

The French minister, Mr. Levitte, for example added, "France welcomes the fact that all ambiguity on this point and all elements of automaticity have disappeared from the resolution."

For Mexico, Mr. Aguilar Zinser said, "this resolution also constitutes progress, as it eliminates the concept of automaticity in the use of force in response to a serious violation without the explicit agreement of the Council."

Yet, well after those speeches, Bush, Blair and others in their governments have stated that 1441 doesn't require another U.N. resolution for war, even though almost all other U.N. ambassadors and ministers, including their own, said the opposite. This perhaps lends credence to those who argue that either the U.S. and U.K. were just going through the motions to attempt to get support on paper, and/or they did this to allow time to deploy their huge military machine in the Gulf, and that they intended to go to war anyway. The media rarely questions or challenges Bush or Blair when they make such assertions then. This allows propaganda to go unchallenged, thereby strengthening it. While the resolution does not automatically authorize war, it requires weapons inspections combined with very strict conditions for compliance. Yet many point out that the resolution leaves enough vagueness making it open to a lot of interpretation.

The U.N. resolution, its vagueness, and the 'diplomatic' goings on surrounding it, also highlights concerns that the U.S. and U.K. are pushing for their own geopolitical agendas, but now under the auspices of the United Nations. Furthermore, the credibility and authority of the U.N. in the area of international law and relations is seriously being questioned, and potentially undermined by two of the countries that helped create it in the first place.

In short, the leverage of aid, military assistance and the like help contributed to winning backing. As ordinary citizens, we might find it shocking to read such things, but in the world of geopolitics and "diplomacy", there appears to be little democracy in these processes. Power and influence wins out. So, just to get the U.S. on board, the resolution has been made to have "dangerous ambiguity."

Leading up to the resolution, the U.S. and British leaders had often implied that if the U.N. does not act, then they will. In the international arena, this is seen as quite threatening. An *article* from *The Nation* magazine described the Bush Administration tactics as "attempting to use UN resolutions improperly to justify an illegal pre-emptive war against Iraq". As the title of that article suggested, this was an attempt at "Subverting the UN".

Even well after that resolution had been passed, Tony Blair and others had pointed out on national television that they were prepared for action if the U.N. did not authorize war. Politicians such as Britain's Jack Straw and Tony Blair have repeatedly highlighted the U.N. resolution as representing the will of the international community to disarm Iraq, not as perhaps as others have seen it, as a last resort to try to get the U.S. in line with international law.

For the US, this position is quite clear: the UN is to be respected only in so far as it overlaps with plans set in Washington. US Secretary of State Colin Powell has stated the matter plainly: "If Iraq violates this resolution and fails to comply, then the council has to take into immediate consideration what should be done about that, while the United States and other like-minded nations might take a judgment about what we might do about it if the council chooses not to act." In other words, the US will subjugate itself to the UN - that is, force will subordinate to law - only when it is useful.

In the above passage, the note of instrumentality is crucial. For most nations, the U.N.'s existence is not questionable. Yet, for the U.S., it is to be used as and when needed, as has been seen for decades on all sorts of international issues. Hence, the U.N. resolution can also be seen as yet another *failure*, not success, by other states to hold their ground against U.S. and British political and "diplomatic" pressures.

But as well as indicating that if the U.N. does not act, the U.S. and U.K. will, some had long suggested that the U.S. and U.K. would act regardless. Even Bush's top security adviser, *Dr Richard Perle*, has *admitted* so back in November 2002. UK's Foreign Secretary, Jack Straw, and US Secretary of State, Colin Powell, had also stated such things. And possibly complicating matters is that in October 2002, the U.S. Congress had authorized Bush to invade Iraq without U.N Security Council authorization. Yet, this is illegal in international law.

The US plan to dethrone Saddam Hussein was subtly clear when the Bush administration published the vital document on US security "The National Security Strategy of the United States of America" in September 2002. This document clearly stated the possible action the US and its ally may opt to deal with Iraq. The National Security Strategy of the United States of America said –

"The United States possesses unprecedented— and unequaled—strength and influence in the world. Sustained by faith in the principles of liberty, and the value of a free society, this position comes with unparalleled responsibilities, obligations, and opportunity. The great strength of this nation must be used to promote a balance of power that favors freedom.

For most of the twentieth century, the world was divided by a great struggle over ideas: destructive totalitarian visions versus freedom and equality.

That great struggle is over. The militant visions of class, nation, and race which promised utopia and delivered misery have been defeated and discredited. America is now threatened less by conquering states than we are by failing ones.

We are menaced less by fleets and armies than by catastrophic technologies in the hands of the embittered few. We must defeat these threats to our Nation, allies, and friends.

This is also a time of opportunity for America. We will

work to translate this moment of influence into decades of peace, prosperity, and liberty. The U.S. national security strategy will be based on a distinctly American internationalism that reflects the union of our values and our national interests. The aim of this strategy is to help make the world not just safer but better. Our goals on the path to progress are clear: political and economic freedom, peaceful relations with other states, and respect for human dignity."

The National Security Strategy document made it clear about the action plan on which the US may rely upon to deal with states like Iraq. To achieve the above mentioned goals, the document suggested the following measures. The document stated the United States will:

- champion aspirations for human dignity;
- strengthen alliances to defeat global terrorism and work to prevent attacks against us and our friends;
- work with others to defuse regional conflicts;
- prevent our enemies from threatening us, our allies, and our friends, with weapons of mass destruction;
- ignite a new era of global economic growth through free markets and free trade;
- expand the circle of development by opening societies and building the infrastructure of democracy;
- develop agendas for cooperative action with other main centers of global power; and
- transform America's national security institutions to meet the challenges and opportunities of the twenty-first century.

The United States realized the reach and destructive capabilities of the international terrorist network with global reach only after the September 11 attacks on America. The National Security Strategy said:

"The United States of America is fighting a war against

terrorists of global reach. The enemy is not a single political regime or person or religion or ideology. The enemy is terrorism—premeditated, politically motivated violence perpetrated against innocents.

In many regions, legitimate grievances prevent the emergence of a lasting peace. Such grievances deserve to be, and must be, addressed within a political process. But no cause justifies terror. The United States will make no concessions to terrorist demands and strike no deals with them. We make no distinction between terrorists and those who knowingly harbor or provide aid to them".

The document further elaborated: "today our enemies have seen the results of what civilized nations can, and will, do against regimes that harbor, support, and use terrorism to achieve their political goals. Afghanistan has been liberated; coalition forces continue to hunt down the Taliban and al-Qaida. But it is not only this battlefield on which we will engage terrorists. Thousands of trained terrorists remain at large with cells in North America, South America, Europe, Africa, the Middle East, and across Asia."

The National Security Strategy offered a detailed plan to deal with rough states and tyrant. It made specific remarks on how the terrorist organizations and their perpetrators be tamed. The National Security Strategy of the United States of America" of September 2002 said: "We will disrupt and destroy terrorist organizations by:

- direct and continuous action using all the elements of national and international power. Our immediate focus will be those terrorist organizations of global reach and any terrorist or state sponsor of terrorism which attempts to gain or use weapons of mass destruction (WMD) or their precursors;

- defending the United States, the American people, and our interests at home and abroad by identifying and destroying the threat before it reaches our borders. While the United States will constantly strive to enlist the support of the international community, we will not hesitate to act alone, if necessary, to exercise our right of self defense by acting preemptively against such terrorists, to prevent them from doing harm against our people and our country; and

• denying further sponsorship, support, and sanctuary to terrorists by convincing or compelling states to accept their sovereign responsibilities. We will also wage a war of ideas to win the battle against international terrorism. This includes:

• using the full influence of the United States, and working closely with allies and friends, to make clear that all acts of terrorism are illegitimate so that terrorism will be viewed in the same light as slavery, piracy, or genocide: behavior that no respectable government can condone or support and all must oppose; supporting moderate and modern government, especially in the Muslim world, to ensure that the conditions and ideologies that promote terrorism do not find fertile ground in any nation;

• diminishing the underlying conditions that spawn terrorism by enlisting the international community to focus its efforts and resources on areas most at risk; and

• using effective public diplomacy to promote the free flow of information and ideas to kindle the hopes and aspirations of freedom of those in societies ruled by the sponsors of global terrorism.

Although the National Security Strategy document released in September 2002, the process to remove Saddam started much earlier. In the 1990s we witnessed the emergence of a small number of rogue states that, while different in important ways, share a number of attributes. These states:

• brutalize their own people and squander their national

resources for the personal gain of the rulers;

- display no regard for international law, threaten their neighbors, and callously violate international treaties to which they are party;
- are determined to acquire weapons of mass destruction, along with other advanced military technology, to be used as threats or offensively to achieve the aggressive designs of these regimes;
- sponsor terrorism around the globe; and
- reject basic human values and hate the United States and everything for which it stands.

The Strategy document said:

"At the time of the Gulf War, we acquired irrefutable proof that Iraq's designs were not limited to the chemical weapons it had used against Iran and its own people, but also extended to the acquisition of nuclear weapons and biological agents. In the past decade North Korea has become the world's principal purveyor of ballistic missiles, and has tested increasingly capable missiles while developing its own WMD arsenal. Other rogue regimes seek nuclear, biological, and chemical weapons as well. These states' pursuit of, and global trade in, such weapons has become a looming threat to all nations.

We must be prepared to stop rogue states and their terrorist clients before they are able to threaten or use weapons of mass destruction against the United States and our allies and friends. Our response must take full advantage of strengthened alliances, the establishment of new partnerships with former adversaries, innovation in the use of military forces, modern technologies, including the development of an effective missile defense system, and increased emphasis on intelligence collection and analysis."

It has taken almost a decade for the US to comprehend the true nature of this new threat. Given the goals of rogue states and terrorists, the United States no longer wanted to solely rely on a reactive posture as in the past. The inability to deter a potential attacker, the immediacy of today's threats, and the magnitude of potential harm that could be caused by the adversaries' choice of weapons, necessitated the US policy makers to act proactive. The US security strategy no more let the enemies of the US to strike first.

The National Security Strategy hinted pre-empt action against Iraq. It said:

"Traditional concepts of deterrence will not work against a terrorist enemy whose avowed tactics are wanton destruction and the targeting of innocents; whose so-called soldiers seek martyrdom in death and whose most potent protection is statelessness. The overlap between states that sponsor terror and those that pursue WMD compels us to action.

The United States will not use force in all cases to preempt emerging threats, nor should nations use preemption as a pretext for aggression. Yet in an age where the enemies of civilization openly and actively seek the world's most destructive technologies, the United States cannot remain idle while dangers gather."

The document "Iraq's Weapons of Mass Destruction - The assessment of the British Government" presented on 24th September 2002 at the House of Commons was based, in large part, on the work of the Joint Intelligence Committee (JIC). The JIC is at the heart of the British intelligence machinery. It is chaired by the Cabinet Office and made up of the heads of the UK's three Intelligence and Security Agencies, the Chief of Defence Intelligence, and senior officials from key government departments. For over 60 years the JIC has provided regular assessments to successive Prime Ministers and senior colleagues on a wide range of foreign policy and international security issues.

Its work, like the material it analyses, is largely secret. It is unprecedented for the British Government to publish this kind of document. But in light of the debate about Iraq and Weapons of Mass Destruction (WMD), Prime Minister Tony Blair wanted to share with the British public the reasons why he believe this issue to be a current and serious threat to the UK national interest.

The Prime Minister said:

"in recent months, I have been increasingly alarmed by the evidence from inside Iraq that despite sanctions, despite the damage done to his capability in the past, despite the UN Security Council Resolutions expressly outlawing it, and despite his denials, Saddam Hussein is continuing to develop WMD, and with them the ability to inflict real damage upon the region, and the stability of the world. Gathering intelligence inside Iraq is not easy. Saddam's is one of the most secretive and dictatorial regimes in the world. So I believe people will understand why the Agencies cannot be specific about the sources, which have formed the judgements in this document, and why we cannot publish everything we know. We cannot, of course, publish the detailed raw intelligence. I and other Ministers have been briefed in detail on the intelligence and are satisfied as to its authority. I also want to pay tribute to our Intelligence and Security Services for the often extraordinary work that they do."

The assessment of intelligence has established beyond doubt is that Saddam has continued to produce chemical and biological weapons, that he continues in his efforts to develop nuclear weapons, and that he has been able to extend the range of his ballistic missile programme. Giving his full approval to the report Tony Blair reiterated that:

"I also believe that, as stated in the document, Saddam will now do his utmost to try to conceal his weapons from UN inspectors. Saddam has used chemical weapons, not only against an enemy state, but against his own people. Intelligence reports make clear that he sees the building up of his WMD capability, and the belief overseas that he would use these weapons, as vital to his strategic interests, and in particular his goal of regional domination. And the document discloses that his military planning allows for some of the WMD to be ready within 45 minutes of an order to use them. I am quite clear that Saddam will go to extreme lengths, indeed has already done so, to hide these weapons and avoid giving them up."

In 1997, the UN inspectors declared they were unable to fulfill their task. A year of negotiation and further obstruction occurred until finally in late 1998, the UN team were forced to withdraw. The dossier's estimate on the basis of the UN's work that there were: up to 360 tonnes of bulk chemical warfare agents, including one and a half tonnes of VX nerve agent; up to 3,000 tonnes of precursor chemicals; growth media sufficient to produce 26,000 litres of anthrax spores; and over 30,000 special munitions for delivery of chemical and biological agents.

Due to the refusal of the Iraqi regime military action by the US and UK followed and a certain amount of infrastructure of Iraq's WMD and missile capability was destroyed, setting the Iraqi programme back, but not ending it. Tony Blair informed that the US and UK Governments taken every measure to restrict Iraq from developing WMD. He said:

"From late 1998 onwards, the sole inhibition on Saddam's WMD programme was the sanctions regime. Iraq was forbidden to use the revenue from its oil except for certain specified non-military purposes. The sanctions regime, however, was also subject to illegal trading and abuse. Because of concerns about its inadequacy - and the impact on the Iraqi people - we made several attempts to refine it, culminating in a new UN resolution in May of this year. But it was only partially effective. Around $3bn of money is illegally taken by Saddam every year now, double the figure for 2000. Self-evidently there is no proper accounting for this money.

Because of concerns that a containment policy based on sanctions alone could not sufficiently inhibit Saddam's weapons programme, negotiations continued after 1998 to gain re-admission for the UN inspectors. In 1999 a new UN resolution demanding their re-entry was passed and ignored. Further negotiations continued. Finally, after several months of discussion with Saddam's regime this year, Kofi Annan, the UN Secretary General, concluded that Saddam was not serious about re-admitting the inspectors and ended the negotiations. That was in July.

All of this is established fact. I set out the history in some detail because occasionally debate on this issue seems to treat it almost as if it had suddenly arisen, coming out of nowhere on a whim, in the last few months of 2002. It is an 11 year history: a history of UN will flouted, lies told by Saddam about existence of his chemical, biological and nuclear weapons programmes, obstruction, defiance and denial. There is one common consistent theme, however: the total determination of Saddam to maintain the programme; to risk war, international ostracism, sanctions, the isolation of the Iraqi economy, in order to keep it. At any time, he could have let the inspectors back in and put the world to proof. At any time he could have co-operated with the UN. Ten days ago he made the offer unconditionally, under threat of war. He could have done it at any time in the last eleven years. But he didn't. Why?

The dossier we publish gives the answer. The reason is because his chemical, biological and nuclear weapons programme is not an historic leftover from 1998. The inspectors aren't needed to clean up the old remains. His WMD programme is active, detailed and growing. The policy of containment is not working. The WMD programme is not shut down. It is up and running."

Prime Minister Blair elaborated how his Government along with the US administration failed to persuade Saddam

Hussein not to support clandestine WMD programme. He made it clear that:

"But let me put it at its simplest: on this 11 year history; with this man, Saddam; with this accumulated, detailed intelligence available; with what we know and what we can reasonably speculate: would the world be wise to leave the present situation undisturbed; to say, despite 14 separate UN demands on this issue, all of which Saddam is in breach of, we should do nothing; to conclude that we should trust not to the good faith of the UN weapons inspectors but to the good faith of the current Iraqi regime?

Our case is simply this: not that we take military action, come what may; but that the case for ensuring Iraqi disarmament (as the UN has stipulated) is overwhelming. I defy anyone on the basis of this evidence to say that is an unreasonable demand for the international community to make when, after all, it is only the same demand that we have made for 11 years and he has rejected."

During the debate in the House of Commons Prime Minister Tony Blair explained about the purpose of the British Government along with the United States. He explains that:

"Of course there is no doubt that Iraq, the region and the whole world would be better off without Saddam. They deserve to be led by someone who can abide by international law, not a murderous dictator. Someone who can bring Iraq back into the international community where it belongs, not languishing as a pariah. Someone who can make the country rich and successful, not impoverished by Saddam's personal greed. Someone who can lead a government more representative of the country as a whole, while maintaining absolutely Iraq's territorial integrity. We have no quarrel with the Iraqi people. Liberated from Saddam, they could make Iraq prosperous and a force for good in the Middle East. So the ending of regime would be the cause of regret for no-one other than Saddam."

On February 5, 2003, U.S. Secretary of State, General Colin Powell presented the case for a strike on Iraq. In what was regarded in many mainstream media circles as a "performance" he presented a plethora of information using a variety of media, from satellite photos, tapes of alleged intercepts of conversations between Iraqi military officers, information from defectors, slides and charts, etc. Though there was a lot of information provided, there were roughly three aims of the presentation: a) to show that Iraq possesses weapons of mass destruction, b) links with terrorists such as Al Qaeda and c) deception by Iraq of the U.N. weapons inspectors, and hiding weapons[100].

As detailed further above, all three of these themes have been questioned, and top officials have often said that for example, there is no evidence of nuclear weapons development (though there are some questions about chemical and biological weapons but much has been destroyed in prior years), that the links with terrorism is dubious.

Leading up to the presentation, a number of media outlets were pointing out that Powell himself said that he would provide no "smoking gun" but would nonetheless provide a compelling case. Iraq's denials will sound empty coming after all of this. This is not to say that Iraq may not be guilty as charged — but that the U.S. role in all of this is hardly above scrutiny either. It took eight weeks for the UN process to get underway. Six weeks had been spent by Washington agencies debating how to use the process to best effect.

Powell had shown satellite photos of alleged movement of mobile biological weapons laboratories and highlighted concerns about Iraqi officers moving equipment before UN inspectors got to the sites. However, as the Guardian reported, "Hans Blix said there was no evidence of mobile biological weapons laboratories or of Iraq trying to foil inspectors by moving equipment before his teams arrived."

Perhaps the following is a good summary of how Powell addressed the issue of an imminent threat: missing from the entire presentation was any serious talk about a threat posed by Iraq, either to the United States or even to any country in the region. Mere possession of WMD, even if established, is not exactly evidence of aggressive intent. And in fact Iraq has been the recipient of aggression frequently since the Gulf War (bombings by the U.S. and U.K., periodic invasions in the north by Turkey, virtual Kuwaiti annexation of Iraqi land in the south), but has not itself seriously threatened any.

The evidence about Iraq's intent to attack seems to run something like this - Saddam "gassed his own people" in 1988 therefore there is an imminent threat that he will attack us in 2003. The imminent threat is not, however, so severe as to keep us from having a full year of warmongering and bellicose rhetoric before we actually attack.

This conveniently ignores the central fact about Hussein's record of aggression. Without exception, his worse crimes were committed with full U.S. support, both material and diplomatic. The war on Iran, the massacre of Kurds in the Anfal campaign of the late 1980's, even the bloody suppression in 1991 of the "Iraqi intifada" all involved explicit measures of support from the United States - providing military intelligence, approving export of chemical and biological agents, providing "agricultural" credits, disarming rebels, and much more. The invasion of Kuwait was done in the deliberately fostered belief that the United States would not mind. Without U.S. support, Hussein knows well that he can only be a threat to his internal political enemies.

Powell did not deal with these facts, but essentially admitted the lack of any evidence of a real Iraqi threat when he fell back on the "pre-emption" argument - "should we take the risk that he will not someday use these weapons at a time and a place and in a manner of his choosing, at a time when the world is in a much weaker position to respond?" Of course, in the absence of concrete evidence, any country can make this argument against any other, which is why "pre-emption" is clearly not consistent with international law.

The United States has sought to remove Iraq's Saddam Hussein from power since the 1991 Gulf War, although achieving this goal was not declared policy until 1998. Iraq's obstruction of UN Weapons of Mass Destruction (WMD) led to growing Congressional call for overthrowing Saddam Hussein. In January 1998, an obscure, ominous-sounding right-wing policy group called Project for New American Century (PNAC), affiliated with Dick Cheney, Donald Rumsfeld, Paul Wolfowitz and George Bush brother Jeb Bush, urged President Clinton to invade Iraq. In addition to Clinton, the group lobbied GOP leaders in Congress to push for Saddam's removal. "We should establish and maintain a strong US military presence in the region, and be prepared to use that force to protect our vital interest in the Gulf – and if necessary, to help remove Saddam from power", the group wrote to Representative Newt Gingrich and Senator Trent Lott in May 1998. A formal Congressional push for a regime change policy began with FY supplemental appropriation (signed on 1 May 1998) that among other provisions, earmarked $5 million in Economic Support Funds (ESF) for the opposition and $5 million for a Radio Free Iraq, under the direction of Radio Free Europe/ Radio Liberty. The Radio service began broadcasting in October 1998, from Prague. A clear indication of Congressional support for a more active US overthrow effort was encapsulated in another bill introduced in 1998: the Iraq Liberation Act (ILA – signed into law on 31 October 1998). The ILA gave the President authority to provide up to $97 million in defence articles to opposition organization to be designated by the Administration. The Act's passage was widely interpreted as an expression of Congressional support for the concept of promoting an insurgency by using US air power to expand opposition-controlled territory. Indeed, the Iraq Liberation Act made the previously unstated policy of promoting regime change in Iraq, an official declared policy. A provision of the ILA states that it should be the policy of the United States to "support efforts" to remove the regime headed by Saddam Hussein. In mid-November 1998, President Clinton publicly articulated that regime change was a component of US policy toward Iraq. Thus by November 1998, the Clinton Administration clearly stated that the United States was pursuing a policy beyond containment to promoting a change of regime in Iraq.

Soon after the "Operation Enduring Freedom" campaign in Afghanistan, especially from January 2002, President Bush turned American attention and resources away from Al Qaeda to lead a crusade against Iraq's Saddam Hussein. Reports indicated that Bush had ordered the CIA and his senior military commanders to draw up details plan for military operation that could begin within months. To justify this policy shift, President Bush and his aides have argued that the campaign against Saddam is a natural continuation of the war against terrorism. In his January State of the Union address to the Congress President singled out Iraq, North Korea and Iran for seeking weapons of mass destruction. "States like these and their terrorist allies, constitute an axis of evil, arming to threaten the peace of the world," he said, adding the civilized world must act because the "price of indifference would be catastrophic". It was clear that the Pentagon and White House war lobby was at work on President. Vice-President Cheney along with Wolfowitz urged the President that war against Iraq was an urgent. He persistently warned that Saddam was stocking up on chemical and biological weapons.

It appears by August 2002 the President had approved the military intervention for removal of Saddam Hussein. A series of leaks from senior military brass who have growing increasingly distrustful of the adventurism of their civilian bosses marked the preliminary skirmishes in the conflict. The war of words burst into the open when the elder Bush's National Security Adviser Gen. Brent Scowcroft, issued a broad warning against the idea of going to war with Iraq in the editorial pages of the staunchly hawkish Wall Street Journal arguing that "war against Baghdad would likely to destroy international cooperation in the war against terrorism"., Scowcroft also warned that "war could well destabilize Arab regimes in the region".

Once the Bush administration had decided to launch military intervention in Iraq to remove Saddam Hussein, the administration engaged in preparing the public and the world to justify its actions. On 16 September 2002, President Bush unveiled the new National Security strategy of United States of America. It is something of hodgepodge, speaking about primacy and balance of power. It talks about organizing coalition but also about not hesitating to act alone in self-defence. The most important aspect of the strategy is the statement that codifies all the new aspect of exceptionalism. It adopts the doctrine of pre-emptive action – while warning others not to use pre-emption as a pretext for aggression – and, making not mention of the United Nations in this context, presumes that the United States is the sole judge of the legitimacy of its own or anyone else's pre-emptive strikes. The document emphasized the deadly threat posed by weapons of mass destruction – should they fall into the hands of rouge states that "reject basis human values and hate the US and everything for which it stands". It promises to maintain whatever military capability is needed to defeat any attempt by state to impose its will on the United States or its allies, and to dissuade potential adversaries for building up their own forces to equal or surpass American. Last but least, it reaffirms the determination to protect US national from the International Criminal Court. In sum, the Bush doctrine proclaims the emancipation of a colossus from international constraints (including from the restraints that the United States itself enshrined in network of international and regional organizations after Second World War. In this context, it amount to a doctrine of global domination.

Armed with doctrine of pre-emptive strike, claiming that the Security Council resolution 1441 gives the United States to take military action against Iraq, and Congress passing a resolution authorizing President Bush to use force on Iraq, the Bush administration even manipulated the intelligence evidence that Iraq acquiring fissile material for a nuclear weapons. This aspect found its place in President Bush's State of the Union address in January 2003. In July 2003, explaining the intelligence manipulation George Tenet, the Director of CIA testified before the Senate Intelligence Committee after the war in Iraq concluded and Saddam removed, said that adhoc committee called the Office of special Plans, set up by Deputy Secretary of Defence Paul Wolfwoitz, rewrote the intelligence information on Iraq that the CIA gathered and gave it to White House to help Bush build a case for war. It is surprising that the Pentagon and White House officials were so determined to launch the military campaign on Iraq, especially to obtain enlarge zone of Democracy that they did not bother when the European allies refused to support the war on Iraq. Thus the doctrine of pre-emptive strike proclaimed by America in the case of war on Iraq was manifestation of global domination even at the cost of emancipation from international constraints and allies counsel against war.

In the same speech as mentioned above, Tony Blair also claimed "Ridding the world of Saddam would be an act of humanity. It is leaving him there that is in truth inhumane." This implies regime change was not official British policy. But the claim of deposing Saddam Hussein can hardly be a humanitarian *act*: The main U.S. and U.K. position all along has been that Iraq poses imminent danger to the west for reasons related to weapons of mass destruction.

After threatening to take military action, the U.K.

convinced the U.S. to come to the U.N. and they put forth a hard resolution, 1441. This revealed no reason for war. Still looking for a reason for military action, and appearing (at least for now) to have exhausted the "imminent threat" or weapons of mass destruction type of argument, Blair seems only now to be playing the humanitarian argument. Given that this appears to be a shift in propaganda strategy, then the *act* can hardly be considered humanitarian, even if the *effect* were to be so (which itself is hard to know, given the past history of supporting other dictatorial regimes and puppets, as mentioned above).

When the U.S. and U.K. and others helped him acquire weapons of mass destruction, and supported him to wage a war against Iran where some 1 million people were killed, it would seem that in comparison, there was hardly any moral concern that it was "inhumane". Even if one were to argue that Blair was not in power then (ignoring for a moment a systemic level policy of successive U.S. powers and some of their allies), Blair does not acknowledge at all those past acts of supporting and arming a killer. This then makes it easier to imply that Saddam Hussein is a brutal person which will only be stopped if we now do something to save those people, and that protestors are not helping. It makes it easier to side-step that people criticized the U.S. support for Sadam Hussein in the first place as well.

And the issue of foreign-imposed regime change that this implies is also dangerous: it sends a dangerous message to other nations that if they don't agree with a leader of another country, they can depose of them. History suggests that deposing a foreign leader, by the powers of the time, has been accompanied with the installation of a puppet regime, and has not improved the state of the people of that nation, and in many cases made things much worse. In Latin America, democracy has been stifled due to support of dictators by America. In the Middle East, support of authoritarian regimes has contributed to anger, hatred, resentment, and fueling the fires of extremism, providing easy recruits to terrorist causes.

Blair also said he felt he had a "moral conviction" on his Iraq stance, suggesting an almost religious-like quality for himself sounds dangerously imperialistic. A number of critics of Bush and Blair have pointed out the double standards in their claims. This has been especially the case for allies that are far from democratic. For example, Saudi Arabia, where a lot of the suspected terrorists that planned the attacks on America in September 11, 2001, has a very authoritarian regime, long criticized by human rights groups and others. Israel has been a sore point for many, as they have nuclear weapons and are accused by human rights groups and others of countless abuses of human rights violations and military occupations of Palestinian areas. Turkey has for years had a harsh crackdown on Kurds. North Korea has recently increased hostility in its nuclear posture.

The journal, *Monthly Review*, looking at who has, and who has used weapons of mass destruction, *highlights* that the U.S. by far has more weapons, and has also used some of them. The article concludes that "the closer one looks at the question of suspected Iraqi weapons of mass destruction, in the context of the existence of such weapons in other countries, the more the Iraqi threat to world peace diminishes by comparison, while the threat represented by the United States looms ever larger."

Throughout the various sections under the geopolitics part of this web site, it has constantly been highlighted that the stances of various powerful nations, such as the U.S., to go against various nuclear weapons treaties, and against other treaties related to international security, rightly or wrongly, other nations may feel threatened and re-consider their military options, where possible. We have seen both India and Pakistan go nuclear, as well as Israel. Other nations are believed to be developing nuclear or chemical and biological capabilities to varying degrees. Considering Iraq in a much wider geopolitical context then perhaps it does not occur to leaders such as Tony Blair and George Bush, that perhaps there is a chance that some nations are becoming hostile, in part, because of their own actions (as well as the previous governments of these nations) either of supporting dictatorial and other non-democratic regimes, or, the use of aggressive politics and military in the international arena, in an almost systematic way. For far more detail and insight into this, see for example, the *Institute for Economic Democracy.*

Channel 4 News in UK also highlighted (February 18, 2003) another aspect of Blair's propaganda dishonesty: in that same speech, he read out a letter from an Iraqi woman supporting the war, making a passionate plea and highlighting understandable reasons a war is needed to get rid of Saddam Hussein. What Blair did not read out though, was another letter also sent by Iraqi women in exile, but arguing against war, and instead of supporting democratic movements and an uprising from within Iraq.

Despite the viewpoints one might have of how it should be done, that Tony Blair only highlighted one of the letters (the one that strengthened his argument) made for a propaganda speech, raising more concerns about dishonesty and trustworthiness of the Blair government. Many are therefore skeptical that the humanitarian concerns were genuine, and ask why other nations that are more of a direct threat, or potentially so, are not being dealt with in the same way.

Towards the end of February, 2003, George Bush gave a speech at the American Enterprise Institute, where he said, "A new regime in Iraq would serve as a dramatic and inspiring example of freedom for other nations in the region." This "Democracy Domino Theory" though sounding promising and full of hope is full of controversy.

Many nations in the Middle East did not receive it well.

At the same time, many have argued (including, for example, a group of Iraq women, exiled in Britain, appearing on public television, as mentioned above), that genuine democracy can only come from within, not installed from outside. A UN Sanctions Committee (heavily containing British and American influence) is the key implementers.

But further complicating matters, as reported by the *Los Angeles Times* has been that *according to a classified U.S. State Department Report, Bush's Democracy Domino Theory is 'not credible'*. Because, as argued above, the humanitarian card has been played so late, the justifications or goals for a war on Iraq do not seem concerned with humanitarianism as such, else that would have been the stated goals from the beginnings.

To many parts of the international community then, this sounds similar to imperial times where colonial rulers justified actions to save people from themselves. The irony often ignored in the mainstream is that the U.S., Soviets, as well as a few others were the ones that helped *support* a large number of corrupt, non-democratic regimes in the Middle East and elsewhere.

Often it has been heard on media reports that the "international community" feels this way or that way. Yet, the countries that make up the "international community" in the context of the Iraq crisis is often an unstated assumption of being other influential and powerful countries, such as France, Russia and occasionally China (the other three permanent members of the U.N. Security Council), plus occasionally other European countries, Japan and other key allies.

Public dissent in parts of that "international community" seems to be growing. For example, it appears that mass protests throughout Europe have contributed to a number of key nations also indicating that they are opposed to military action, or have highlighted the need to go the route of the United Nations.

German Chancellor Gerhard Schroeder said in a speech that "We will not take part in a military intervention in Iraq, and that is exactly how our voting behavior will be in all international bodies." France concurred. In countries such as Britain, Spain, France, Germany, Italy and Japan, there are extremely large percentages of the population against military action, in some cases even if there is a U.N. backing for such action. Even in Britain, Tony Blair suffered a major revolt, mostly from his own Labour Party, in what is the biggest revolt in recent times by the leader's own party. Tony Blair had put a motion forward asking Parliament for backing a UN effort to disarm Iraq. It did not explicitly mention war, but there was an ammendment put forward to say that the case for war is unproven. It was thought that of the approximately 600 parliament members, some 100 would vote for this, and the rest would successfully defeat this ammendement hence allowing for war. Instead, an unexpected 199, or an entire third of government voted for this ammendment, 120 or so of whom were from Blair's own Labour Party (with the rest including all members of the third major party, the Liberal Democrats, and a handful from the Conservative party as well). Blair won his backing by a vote of 393 to 199 mostly because of the large majority that Labour has in Parliament, and because most of the main opposition party the Conservatives, backed him, perhaps highlighting how far to the right Tony Blair has gone. (Most of the Labor Party did back Blair, some 254, but that some one third of his own party were against this is seen as extremely significant.)The positions of France, Germany, Russia, Belgium, China and others, in opposing immediate war have, to some extent, angered the U.S. and Britain, and have even led to rifts in NATO, where there has been disagreement on whether NATO should agree to defend Turkey if there is a war on Iraq.

Around the world, governments have raised concerns. So too have many ordinary citizens. In some cases, (for example, Britain and Italy), while the government may openly be supporting the Bush position, a large majority of people have been openly critical of their government and the U.S. war agenda. Indonesia, the world's most populous Muslim nation, has expressed concerns and doubts and has stated that it opposes possible war with Iraq.

Malaysia, another predominantly Muslim nation also expressed concerns of the implications of war and the reaction in Muslim countries, as reported by the *Gulf Daily News*, Bahrain. Some African countries have also said they are against a unilateral military strike. *The Namibian* reports that, "Namibia has said it is against military action against Iraq." After a summit of the African Union, the 53-nation union stated that it was firmly opposed to war. Even Iran, the longtime foe and neighbour of Iraq, feels that war with Iraq is unnecessary.

The Indian Prime Minister, Atal Behari Vajpayee has said that India does not favor an attack on Iraq. The secretary-general of the 22-member Arab League raises concerns about great instability in the region if the U.S. starts a war. Jordan is Iraq's largest trading partner, while also being an American ally. It also has *fears* ranging from economic consequences to domestic political problems and refugee influx concerns if war erupts. In Italy, opposition senators have denounced their government's support of Bush. George Bush's 2003 State of the Union Speech was met with much resentment around the world.

While American and British troops began to *prepare* for deployment in the Gulf French President, Jacques Chirac, suggested to his troops the importance of being ready, if need be. In March 2003, just before the onset of war, France even suggested that they would be ready to offer military assistance if Iraq used chemical weapons. This was met with some cynicism and humor in British and American circles, given France's hostility to war. And even if some governments are supportive of the American and British governments, large segments of society within those nations may be opposed to various aspects of the crisis.

Bush and Blair had proposed a second resolution to the Security Council, basically seeking authority for war. This resolution made six measurable demands. However, France and others said that the inspectors were working so there was no need for war at this time, so would oppose any war-requesting resolution (not *any* resolution, as simplified by the U.S. and U.K., making it appear that France were opposed to any concerted U.N. effort.)

Politicians supporting war of course are not going to analyze the negative side of their own proposed resolutions. Hence, often not mentioned was that at least one of the terms in the draft second resolution would be unacceptable whether the receiver of the demands was ruthless and despotic, or completely democratic and peaceful. This resolution was designed, then, as some would argue, to ensure Saddam Hussein would lose, and no-one would expect Saddam to surrender, hence, this resolution basically supported war.

IRAQ WAR OF 2003

The 2003 invasion of Iraq, termed "Operation Iraqi Freedom" by the US administration, began on March 20, 2003. It was originally coined "Operation Iraqi Liberation". The United States, the United Kingdom, Australia, South Korea, Italy and Poland supplied the vast majority of the invading forces, in co-operation with Kurdish forces. Many others supplied smaller troop contributions. Other nations also participated in part of a coalition force to help with the operation by providing equipment, services and security as well as Special Forces. The 2003 Iraq invasion marked the beginning of what is commonly referred to as the Iraq War.

On October 11, 2002, the United States Congress passed the "Authorization for Use of Military Force Against Iraq Resolution of 2002", giving U.S. President George W. Bush the authority, under US law, to attack Iraq if Iraqi President Saddam Hussein did not give up his weapons of mass destruction (WMDs) and abide by previous UN resolutions on human rights, POWs, and terrorism. On November 9, 2002, at the urging of the United States government, the UN Security Council passed United Nations Security Council Resolution 1441, offering Iraq "a final opportunity to comply with its disarmament obligations" that had been set out in several previous resolutions (Resolutions 660, 661, 678, 686, 687, 688, 707, 715, 986, and 1284), notably to provide "an accurate full, final, and complete disclosure, as required by Resolution 687 (1991), of all aspects of its programmes to develop weapons of mass destruction and ballistic missiles".

Resolution 1441 threatened "serious consequences" if these are not met and reasserted demands that UN weapons inspectors that were to report back to the UN Security Council after their inspection should have "immediate, unconditional, and unrestricted access" to sites of their choosing, in order to ascertain compliance. Significantly, the Resolution stated that the UN Security Council shall "remain seized of the matter" (United Nations Security Council Resolution 1441). The Iraqi government did what it was required in the 1441 resolution and presented a report of its weapons. The US government claimed that the report was false for not recognizing having the WMDs. It announced the invasion in the Spring of 2003. In his March 17, 2003 address to the nation, Bush demanded Hussein and his two sons Uday and Qusay to surrender and leave Iraq, giving them a 48-hour deadline[101]. This demand was reportedly rejected. Iraq maintained that it had disarmed as required. The UN weapons inspectors (UNMOVIC) headed by Hans Blix, who were sent by the UN Security Council pursuant to Resolution 1441, requested more time to complete their report on whether Iraq had complied with its obligation to disarm[102].

The International Atomic Energy Agency IAEA reported

a level of compliance by Iraq with the disarmament requirements (UN Security Council Resolution 1441; IAEA) Hans Blix went on to state the Iraqi government may have been hoping to restart production once sanctions were lifted and inspectors left the country, as speculated by senior Iraqi officials and a prominent defector, Gen. Hussein Kamel. The attempt of the United Kingdom and the United States to obtain a further Resolution authorizing force failed when France made it known they would veto further resolutions on Iraq. Thus, the Coalition invasion began without the approval of the United Nations Security Council, which United Nations Secretary-General Kofi Annan regarded as a violation of the UN Charter. Several countries protested. United Nations Secretary-General Kofi Annan said in September 2004, "From our point of view and the UN Charter point of view, it was illegal." Proponents of the war claim that the invasion had implicit approval of the Security Council and was therefore not in violation of the UN Charter. Nevertheless, this position taken by the Bush administration and its supporters has been and still is being disputed by numerous legal experts. According to most members of the Security Council, it is up to the council itself, and not individual members, to determine how the body's resolutions are to be enforced. Since 2003, chemical weapons containing mustard or sarin nerve agents have been found. Both of these nerve agents are classified by the United Nations as Weapons of Mass Destruction. However, these shells are also reported to have predated the original Gulf War. On August 22, 2006 President Bush admitted that Iraq had no WMDs.

Since the end of the Gulf War of 1991, Iraq's relations with the UN, the US, and the UK remained poor. In the absence of a Security Council consensus that Iraq had fully complied with the terms of the Persian Gulf War ceasefire, both the UN and the US enforced numerous economic sanctions against Iraq throughout the Clinton administration, and the U.S. and the UK patrolled Iraqi airspace to enforce Iraqi no-fly zones that they had declared to protect Kurds in northern Iraq and Shi'ites in the south. The no-fly zone was contested however by Iraqi military helicopters and planes on numerous occasions. The United States Congress also passed the "Iraq Liberation Act" in October 1998 after Iraq had terminated its cooperation with the U.N. in August, which provided $97 million for Iraqi "democratic opposition organizations" in order to "establish a program to support a transition to democracy in Iraq[103]." This contrasted with the terms set out in U.N. Resolution 687, all of which related to weapons and weapons programs, and made no mention of regime change[104]. Weapons inspectors had been used to gather information on Iraq's WMD (Weapons of Mass Destruction) program and to enforce the terms of the 1991 cease fire, which forbade Iraq from developing WMD. The information was used in targeting decisions during Operation Desert Fox, a US and UK bombardment of Iraq in December 1998 which was precipitated by lack of cooperation between Iraq and the UN weapon inspections team.

Notes from aides who were with Defense Secretary Donald Rumsfeld in the National Military Command Center one year later, on the day of the September 11, 2001 Terrorist Attack, reflect that he wanted, "best info fast. Judge whether good enough hit Saddam Hussein at same time. Not only Osama bin Laden." The notes also quote him as saying, "Go massive," and "Sweep it all up. Things related and not[105]." Shortly thereafter, the George W. Bush administration announced a War on Terrorism, accompanied by the doctrine of 'pre-emptive' military action, termed the Bush doctrine. From the 1990s, U.S. officials have constantly voiced concerns about ties between the government of Saddam Hussein and terrorist activities, notably in the context of the Israeli-Palestinian conflict. Through the Palestinian Arab Liberation Front (PALF), Saddam had offered $10,000 USD for families of "civilians killed during Israeli military operations" and, $25,000 USD for "families of suicide bombers[106]."

In 2002 the Iraq disarmament crisis arose primarily as a diplomatic situation. The Bush administration waited until September 2002 to call for action, with White House Chief of Staff Andrew Card saying "From a marketing point of view, you don't introduce new products in August." In October 2002, with the "Joint Resolution to Authorize the Use of United States Armed Forces Against Iraq", the United States Congress granted President Bush the authority to "use any means necessary" against Iraq, based on repeated Bush Administration statements to Congress and the public, which turned out to be incorrect, that Iraq possessed weapons of mass destruction. The joint resolution allowed the President of the United States to "defend the national security of the United States against the continuing threat posed by Iraq and enforce all relevant United Nations Security Council Resolutions regarding Iraq."

In November 2002, United Nations actions regarding Iraq culminated in the unanimous passage of UN Security Council Resolution 1441 and the resumption of weapons inspections. Force was not authorized by resolution 1441 itself, as the language of the resolution mentioned "serious consequences," which the majority of Security Council members argued did not include the use of force to overthrow the government; however the threat of force, as cultivated by the Bush administration, was prominent at the time of the vote. Both the U.S. ambassador to the UN, John Negroponte, and the UK ambassador Jeremy Greenstock, in promoting Resolution 1441, had given assurances that it provided no "automaticity," no "hidden triggers," no step to invasion without consultation of the Security Council. Such consultation was forestalled by the US and UK's abandonment of the Security Council procedure and their invasion of Iraq. The stated cause by the United Kingdom to forego further UN resolutions was notice supplied by France that they would block any further Security Council resolutions on Iraq.[30] Negroponte was noted as saying "one way or another, Mr. President, Iraq will be disarmed. If the

Security Council fails to act decisively in the event of a further Iraqi violation, this resolution does not constrain any member state from acting to defend itself against the threat posed by Iraq, or to enforce relevant U.N. resolutions and protect world peace and security."

There is still considerable disagreement among international lawyers on whether prior resolutions, relating to the 1991 war and later inspections, permitted the invasion. Richard Perle, a senior member of the administration's Defense Policy Board Advisory Committee, argued in November 2003, that the invasion was against international law, but still justified. At the same time Tony Blair's Attorney General Lord Goldsmith, while concluding that a reasonable case could be made that resolution 1441 required no further resolution of the UN, he could not guarantee that an invasion in the circumstances would not be challenged on legal grounds[107].

In the wake of the September 11 attacks and the seeming relative success of the U.S. invasion of Afghanistan in 2001, the Bush administration felt that it had sufficient military justification and public support in the United States for further operations against perceived threats in the Middle East. The relations between some coalition members and Iraq had never improved since 1991, and the nations remained in a state of low-level conflict marked by American and British air-strikes, sanctions, and threats against Iraq. Iraqi radar had also locked onto and anti-aircraft guns and missiles were fired upon coalition airplanes enforcing the northern and southern no-fly zones, which had been implemented after the Gulf War in 1991.

Throughout 2002, the U.S. administration made it clear that removing Saddam Hussein from power was a major goal, although it offered to accept major changes in Iraqi military and foreign policy in lieu of this. Specifically, the stated justification for the invasion included Iraqi production and use of weapons of mass destruction, alleged links with terrorist organizations, and human rights violations in Iraq under the Saddam Hussein government. Bush and his cabinet repeatedly linked the Hussein government to the September 11th attacks, despite the fact that there was no convincing evidence of Hussein's involvement. Saddam Hussein refused to allow weapon inspectors to search for weapons of mass destruction and prove that Iraqi government had nothing to hide. Because Hussein reneged his promise to cooperate with UN weapons inspectors for a second time, the United States and Great Britain began planning air strikes[108].

At the end of 2002, UN inspection teams returned to Iraq. At the time of the invasion, they had searched for alleged weapons for nearly four months without finding them, and were willing to continue. However, further delay in military action would have posed problems for an invasion due to seasonally rising temperatures, which would have made use of chemical protection gear unbearable as early as April and risen to around 48C (120F) in the summer. President George W. Bush stated that Saddam's weapons of mass destruction needed to be disarmed, and that the Iraqi people were to have control of their own country restored to them[109].

United States military operations were conducted under the codename Operation Iraqi Freedom. The United Kingdom military operation was named Operation Telic. Approximately 100,000 soldiers and marines from the United States, and 26,000 from the United Kingdom, as well as smaller forces from other nations, collectively called the "Coalition of the Willing," were deployed prior to the invasion primarily to several staging areas in Kuwait[110]. (The numbers when naval, logistics, intelligence, and air force personnel are included were 214,000 Americans, 45,000 British, 2,000 Australians and 2,400 Polish.) Plans for opening a second front in the north were abandoned when Turkey officially refused the use of its territory for such purposes. Forces also supported Iraqi Kurdish militia troops, estimated to number upwards of 50,000. Despite the refusal of Turkey, the Coalition conducted parachute operations in the north and dropped the 173rd Airborne Brigade, thereby removing the necessity of any approval from Turkey. (Later on, during the invasion, it was rumored that Turkey itself had sent troops into the Kurdish part of Iraq.)

The controversy around the war in Iraq has caused two American veterans' organizations to form: Vets for Freedom, a pro-war group, and Iraq Veterans against the War, an anti-Iraq war group.

ATTACK ON IRAQ

Prior to invasion, US-led Coalition forces involved in the 1991 Persian Gulf War had been engaged in a low-level conflict with Iraq, enforcing Iraqi no-fly zones. Iraqi air-defense installations were engaged on a fairly regular basis after repeatedly targeting and firing upon US and UK air patrols. In mid-2002, the US began to change its response strategy, more carefully selecting targets in the southern part of the country in order to disrupt the military command structure in Iraq. A change in enforcement tactics was acknowledged at the time, but it was not made public that this was part of a plan known as Operation Southern Focus.

The tonnage of US bombs dropped increased from 0 in March 2002 and 0.3 in April 2002 to between 7 and 14 tons per month in May-August, reaching a pre-war peak of 54.6 tons in September - prior to Congress' 11 October authorisation of the invasion. The September attacks included a 5 September 100-aircraft attack on the main air defence site in western Iraq. According to an editorial in The New Statesman this was "Located at the furthest extreme of the southern no-fly zone, far away from the areas that needed to be patrolled to prevent attacks on the Shias, it was destroyed not because it was a threat to the patrols, but to allow allied special forces operating from Jordan to enter Iraq undetected."

On March 20, 2003 at approximately 02:30 UTC or

about 90 minutes after the lapse of the 48-hour deadline, at 05:33 local time, explosions were heard in Baghdad. There is now evidence that various Special Forces troops from the coalition (led by the Australian SAS but including British SAS, the U.S. Army's Delta Force, U.S. Navy SEALs, and U.S. Air Force Combat Controllers) crossed the border into Iraq well before the air war commenced, in order to guide strike aircraft in air attacks. At 03:15 UTC, or 10:15 p.m. EST, U.S. President George W. Bush announced that he had ordered the coalition to launch an "attack of opportunity" against targets in Iraq. As soon as this word was given the troops on standby crossed the border into Iraq. These troops were led by the 4th bomb disposal unit which at the time had three R.A.F. regiment soldiers from 15th squadron on a tour.

Three weeks into the invasion, U.S. forces moved into Baghdad. Initial plans were for armoured units to surround the city and gradually move in, forcing Iraqi armor and ground units to cluster into a central pocket in the city, and then attack with air and artillery forces. This plan soon became unnecessary, as an initial engagement of armor units south of the city saw most of the Republican Guard's armor assets destroyed and much of the southern outskirts of the city occupied. On 5 April a "Thunder Run" of US armored vehicles was launched to test remaining Iraqi defenses, with 29 tanks and 14 Bradley Armored Fighting Vehicles rushing from a staging base to the Baghdad airport. They met heavy resistance, including many suicidal attacks, but were successful in reaching the airport. Two days later another thunder run was launched into the Palaces of Saddam Hussein, where they established a base. Within hours of the palace seizure, and television coverage of this spreading through Iraq, US forces ordered Iraqi forces within Baghdad to surrender, or the city would face a full-scale assault. Iraqi government officials had either disappeared or had conceded defeat, and on April 9, 2003, Baghdad was formally occupied by US forces and the power of Saddam Hussein was declared ended.

The fall of Baghdad saw the outbreak of regional violence throughout the country, as Iraqi tribes and cities began to fight each other over old grudges. The Iraqi cities of Al-Kut and Nasiriyah declared war upon each other immediately following the fall of Baghdad in order to establish dominance in the new country, and Coalition forces quickly found themselves embroiled in a potential civil-war. U.S. forces ordered the cities to cease hostilities immediately, and explained that Baghdad would remain the capital of the new Iraqi government. Nasiriyah responded favorably and quickly backed down, however Al-Kut placed snipers on the main roadways into town, with orders that Coalition forces were not to enter the city. After several minor skirmishes, the snipers were removed, but tensions and violence between regional, city, tribal, and familial groups continued into the occupation period.

General Tommy Franks assumed control of Iraq as the supreme commander of occupation forces. Shortly after the sudden collapse of the defense of Baghdad, rumors were circulating in Iraq and elsewhere that there had been a deal struck (a "safqua") wherein the US had bribed key members of the Iraqi military elite and/or the Ba'ath party itself to stand down. In May 2003, General Franks retired, and confirmed in an interview with Defense Week that the U.S. had paid Iraqi military leaders to defect. The extent of the defections and their effect on the war are unclear.

Coalition troops promptly began searching for the key members of Saddam Hussein's government. These individuals were identified by a variety of means, most famously through sets of most-wanted Iraqi playing cards. On 22 July 2003 during a raid by the U.S. 101st Airborne Division and men from Task Force 20, Saddam Hussein's sons Uday and Qusay, and one of his grandsons were killed.

Saddam Hussein was captured on December 13, 2003 by the U.S. Army's 4th Infantry Division and members of Task

Force 121 during Operation Red Dawn. The report of CNN World News on 29 September 2006 said - across the Tigris River from his opulent palaces, Saddam Hussein shuttered himself at the bottom of a narrow, dark hole beneath a two-room mud shack on a sheep farm. Having opted not to travel with security forces or an entourage that might bring attention to him, only a Styrofoam square, dirt and a rug separated the deposed Iraqi leader from the U.S. soldiers who routed him from his hiding place on that fateful Saturday night 13 of December 2003. "He was in the bottom of a hole with no way to fight back," said Maj. Gen. Raymond Odierno. "He was caught like a rat." Saddam's capture was based not on a direct tip, but a collection of intelligence gathered from the hostile questioning of Saddam's former bodyguards and family members. That intelligence prompted U.S. soldiers to go to Adwar, about 15 kilometers (nine miles) from Tikrit, Saddam's ancestral home. 'We realized early on in the summer... the people we had to get to were the midlevel individuals, his bodyguards... We tried to work through family and tribal ties that might have been close to Saddam Hussein," Maj. Gen. Raymond Odierno said. "Over the last 10 days or so, we brought in about five to ten members of these families, ... and finally we got the ultimate information from one of these individuals." After they received the "actionable intelligence" earlier Saturday, the 1st Brigade Combat team of the 4th Infantry Division, the Raider Brigade, was given the assignment to kill or capture Saddam in a mission dubbed Operation Red Dawn. Six hundred soldiers from the Raider Brigade prepared to move on two locations. They included cavalry engineers, artillery, aviation and special operations forces. Even with reliable information, U.S. forces initially failed to grab Saddam in raids on two targets near Adwar. But a subsequent cordon and search operation in the same area unearthed the ragged, bearded fugitive. Troops converged on a two-room mud hut squatting between two farmhouses with sheep penned nearby.

One room, which appeared to serve as a bedroom, was in disarray with clothes strewn about the area. The other room was a crude kitchen, Maj. Gen. Raymond Odierno said. Inside that shack, a Styrofoam plug closed Saddam's subterranean hideaway. Dirt and a rug covered the entryway to the hole, he said. U.S. forces encountered no resistance during Red Dawn. "I think the pressure had become so tight on him, (Saddam) knew he couldn't travel in large entourages so he didn't have any men with him, didn't have much of a security force," Maj. Gen. Raymond Odierno said. Saddam was armed with a pistol, but showed no resistance during his capture. "He was a tired man and also a man resigned to his fate," Lt. Gen. Ricardo Sanchez, commander of U.S. forces, told a news conference in Baghdad Sunday. Soldiers also recovered two AK 47 rifles, $750,000 in $100 denominations and a white and orange taxi in the raid. Troops took two other unidentified Iraqis affiliated with Saddam into custody. By 9:15 p.m., Saddam was moved to an undisclosed location and soldiers continued to search the area. "If you could see where we found him, he could have been hiding in a hundred different places, a thousand different places, like this all around Iraq," Maj. Gen. Raymond Odierno said. "And it just takes finding the right person who will give you a good idea where he might be, and that's what happened."

In the north, Kurdish forces opposed to Saddam Hussein had already occupied for years an autonomous area in northern Iraq. With the assistance of U.S. Special Forces and air strikes, they were able to rout the Iraqi units near them and to occupy oil-rich Kirkuk on 10 April 2003.

On 1 May 2003 George W. Bush landed on the aircraft carrier USS Abraham Lincoln, in a Lockheed S-3 Viking, where he gave a speech announcing the end of major combat operations in the Iraq war. Bush's landing was criticized by opponents as an overly theatrical and expensive stunt. The ship was returning home off the coast of southern California near the San Diego harbor. Clearly visible in the background was a banner stating "Mission Accomplished." The banner, made by White House staff and supplied by request of the U.S. Navy, was criticized as premature - especially later as the guerrilla war dragged on. The White House subsequently released a statement alleging that the sign and Bush's visit referred to the initial invasion of Iraq and disputing the claim of theatrics. The speech itself noted: "We have difficult work to do in Iraq. We are bringing order to parts of that country that remain dangerous[111]."

"Major combat" concluding did not mean that peace had returned to Iraq. Iraq was subsequently marked by violent conflict between U.S.-led soldiers and forces described by the occupiers as insurgents. The ongoing resistance in Iraq was concentrated in, but not limited to, an area referred to by Western media and the occupying forces as the Sunni triangle and Baghdad. Critics point out that the regions where violence is most common are also the most populated regions. This resistance may be described as guerrilla warfare. The tactics in use were to include mortars, suicide bombers, roadside bombs, small arms fire, improvised explosive devices (IED's), and handheld antitank grenade-launchers (RPG's), as well as sabotage against the oil infrastructure. There are also accusations, questioned by some, about attacks toward the power and water infrastructure.

Now that the invasion of Iraq is completed and Saddam Hussein captured, the occupation of Iraq with about 138,000 troops for the past 18 months is increasing proving a costly war. Already more than 1004 American soldiers have died, which is just the beginning. Moreover, failure to locate the WMD, insurgency in Fallujah, Karbala and Najaf and the grisly killing of American civilian and disgraceful Abu Gharaib prison episode have discredited Bush purpose of invasion of Iraq. Indeed it became major issue in the Presidential election when the Democratic Challenger John Kerry declared that in the pursuit of the war in Iraq "the President misled, miscalculated and mismanaged"; and also criticized that the war was "wrong war at wrong place and wrong time". By October 2004 the American nation was strongly polarized and was divided. On 30 October 2004 the Bin Laden released a video tape which broadcast on the Arabic language al-Jazeera network. Bin Laden declared that "your security is not in the hands of Kerry or Bush or al Qaeda. Your security is in your hands." This was Bin Laden, in his first videotaped address in three years. But it seems this videotape crucially among other reasons influenced the American electorate on the 2 November 2004 Presidential election. The American voters re-elected President Bush overwhelmingly and challenger Kerry lost. The victorious President Bush in the first press conference on 2004 November said: "I have earned capital in the campaign, political capital, and now I intend to spend it". He declared that he intend to spent it "winning the war on terror."

6
POSTSCRIPT

THE HUMAN COST OF IRAQI OCCUPATION

Who is bleeding – Iraq or America is not an easy question to answer especially when the body counts on both the side increasing. The US military casualties in Iraq since the war began are 4315 and still counting. The deaths since President Obama's inauguration (20 January 2009) are 87 and there is no sign of respite. Nearly 31354 personnel were injured since the war began and this is official figures the estimated injured persons may cross over 100000.

Although the figures are not any way near to the figure of Vietnam, critics have already started saying that the 2003 Iraq war is proving another Vietnam. There are many political casualties as well.

Colin Luther Powell was the first African American appointed as the Secretary of State. During his military career, Powell also served as *National Security Advisor* (1987–1989), as Commander-in-Chief, *U.S. Army Forces Command* (1989) and as *Chairman of the Joint Chiefs of Staff* (1989–1993), holding the latter position during the *Gulf War*. He was the first, and so far the only, African American to serve on the *Joint Chiefs of Staff*. The Vietnam War had a profound effect on Powell's views of the proper use of military force. These views are described in detail in the autobiography *My American*

Journey. The *Powell Doctrine*, as the views became known, was a central component of US policy in the *Gulf War* (the first U.S. war in Iraq) and *U.S. invasion of Afghanistan* (the overthrow of the *Taliban* regime in *Afghanistan* following the *September 11, 2001 terrorist attacks*). The hallmark of both operations was strong international cooperation, and the use of overwhelming military force. Powell was the subject of controversy in 2004 when, in a conversation with *British Foreign Secretary Jack Straw*, he reportedly referred to *neoconservatives* within the Bush administration as "fucking crazies." In addition to being reported in the press (though generally, the expletive was censored in the U.S. press), the quote was used by *James Naughtie* in his book, *The Accidental American: Tony Blair and the Presidency*, and by *Chris Patten* in his book, *Cousins and Strangers: America, Britain, and Europe in a New Century*. In a letter to Sen. *John McCain*, General Powell expressed opposition to President Bush's push for *military tribunals* of those formerly and currently classified as *enemy combatants*. Specifically, he expressed concern of Bush's plan to "amend the interpretation of Article III of the *Geneva Conventions*." He also pointed out that perception of the *War on Terror* may be losing moral support saying, "The world is beginning to doubt the moral basis of our fight against terrorism." In an interview in July 2007, Powell revealed that he had spent two and a half hours trying to persuade Bush not to invade Iraq, but that he did not prevail. At the Aspen Ideas Festival in *Colorado* Powell stated, "I tried to avoid this war. I took him [Bush] through the consequences of going into an *Arab* country and becoming the occupiers." Powell went on to say that he believed Iraq was in a state of *civil war*. "The civil war will ultimately be resolved by a test of arms. It's not going to be pretty to watch, but I don't know any way to avoid it. It is happening now." He further noted, "It is not a civil war that can be put down or solved by the armed forces of the United States," and suggested that all the U.S. military could do was put "a heavier lid on this pot of boiling sectarian stew."

But all said and done, Colin Powell not able to retain his position during the second tenure of the Bush Administration and he become the first scapegoat of Iraq war. Condoleezza Rice replaced Colin Powell as Secretary of State as President Bush wanted to wash some of the steins of Iraq invasion and the wrong done in the name of Weapon of Mass Destruction. Similarly, on the other side of the Atlantic, British Prime Minister Tony Blair had to resign from his post in the post Iraq invasion. *The war on terror was carefully woven into Blair's argument for action in Iraq,* even though there was no connection between al-Qaeda and Iraq until after the illegal invasion. Even the man who led the Iraq Survey Group after the invasion *thinks otherwise. A Parliamentary committee stated that Tony Blair inadvertently misled parliament. Beverly Hughes resigned after inadvertently misleading parliament* and the question of Iraqi invasion haunts Blair every now and then. Finally, Tony Blair proceeded with his resignation and handed over the baton into the hand of his Treasury Secretary Gordon Brown.

OBAMA AND BROWN

The international politics of recent years have seen resurgence and refashioning of the US-UK 'Special Relationship'. Widely seen as likely to expire with the end of the Cold War, the relationship revived following the 9/11 terror attacks on the United States. The longevity, sustenance and warmthness of US-UK 'special relationship' has always been a direct bearing on the personal rapport of the heads of the two states. The easy and understandable factors of this special relationship include simple inertia and the subtle effects of shared culture.

With President George Bush' Presidency receding to the history book and Prime Minister Tony Blair retiring on 27 June 2007, the future of US-UK Special Relationship again come into public debate. The anxiety about the future of their interpersonal relationship has already been surfaced.

Tony Blair's decision to step down as British Prime Minister on June 27, 2007 marks the end of an era in U.S.– British relations. Blair's extraordinarily close alliance with President George W. Bush defied all expectations and has been a major force on the world stage since the terrorist attacks of September 11, 2001. Blair's successor the Chancellor of the Exchequer, Gordon Brown, an uncharismatic, somber figure who is unlikely to set the world alight it seems. The Special Relationship will continue under Brown, but it will be a low-key affair with a greater emphasis on behind-the-scenes negotiations than high profile public displays of unity.

Blair rubbished the argument that the growing terrorism in the west is because of the presence of US-UK troops in the Iraq. He said that the 9/11 attacks predates the deployment of troops in the Iraq and Afghanistan. Under Blair's leadership, over 45,000 British military personnel participated in the liberation of Iraq, by any measure a huge contribution for a nation of Britain's size. More than 7,000 British troops are still based in southern Iraq, and 148 British soldiers have sacrificed their lives in the country. More than 5,000 British troops are engaged in military operations against the Taliban in southern Afghanistan as part of the NATO-led International Security Assistance Force (ISAF).

Under Blair, the British government failed to demonstrate to the British public that the Anglo–American alliance brings Britain tangible benefits and operates as a two-way street. Blair could do little to stem the tide of anti-Americanism among the British public, which became increasingly disillusioned with his support for U.S. foreign policy. The rise of anti-Americanism is not a temporary phenomenon but a dangerous long-term trend that will have far-reaching implications for both the Special Relationship and America's ability to project power on the world stage.

Today Britain is a hornet's nest of Islamic militants, with 400 to 600 al-Qaeda terrorist suspects in the U.K., some of whom have been trained in camps in Afghanistan and Pakistan. Blair's misguided belief that Britain can be both America's closest ally and part of a politically and economically integrated Europe was a key foreign policy failure. Roughly half of British laws now originate in Brussels, a shocking state of affairs that Gordon Brown may like to reverse.

GORDON BROWN AND U.S.-U.K. RELATIONS

Gordon Brown has never fundamentally transformed the nature of the Anglo–American alliance when he entered 10, Downing Street as the relation stood on a firm foundation. Brown, with a large base of support on the left of the Labour Party and whose ties to Washington are mainly to Democrats, has never matched the close friendship that Blair has developed with President Bush.

Gordon Brown's approach may be less sentimental than Blair's, based on a sharper-edged analysis of what he defines as the British national interest. This policy of Brown may lead to greater confrontation with Washington over issues such as international development assistance, poverty reduction, trade, and global warming. Brown has called for "a modern Marshall Plan for the developing world—a new deal between the richest countries and the poorest countries."

On his first tour to the United States after President Obama's inauguration, many, including some in his own party, believe that Mr Brown is taking too many hits for his own good and that he should retire. Two days in the American capital proved that he has no intention of standing down, and no intention of apologizing - for anything.

Brown mooted the idea to the President for a "global new deal" that would look at common banking rules, shutting down of tax havens, reform of the IMF and new fiscal stimulus. In the surrounds of the Oval Office Mr Obama went some way to agreeing with the Prime Minister's view, albeit in a more cautious manner than Mr Brown would probably have hoped. It was noted by the New York Times that "that phrase [global New Deal] was not repeated in public by Mr Obama".

British Prime Minister Gordon Brown's visit to President Obama at the White House marked the 897th time a British official has visited the White House without *trying to burn it down*. According to the British accounts, the chill descended on the American-British relationship soon after Obama was inaugurated, when someone at the White House advised the British Embassy to come collect their bust of Winston Churchill, which had graced the Oval Office under President Bush, but which apparently was no longer needed by Obama. Fragile British sensibilities were further bruised when, in a written statement announcing the prime minister's visit, Press Secretary Robert Gibbs referred to the "special partnership" enjoyed by the United States and Britain. That phraseology struck some Brits as sterile, perhaps invoking a sort of necessary, but loveless marriage.

CONCLUSION

The Anglo-American special relationship is extremely important to both the United States and the United Kingdom. It has also been an indispensable source of productive leadership for the international community.

To arrive at a conclusion the special relationship needs to be viewed realistically. There are occasions in the formation of the special relationship in which fundamental differences of principle or interest have strained the Anglo-American relationship. In some cases, these disagreements have been exacerbated by unrealistic expectations. The most well-known example is the 1956 Suez crisis. The comments of Lieutenant General Sir Hugh Stockwell, commander of the British 1st Corps during the planning for the French-British-Israeli operation, illustrate the degree of misunderstanding on the UK side – "as the British could fairly claim a "special relationship" with the Americans, by which they would hope to maintain the neutrality of the United States in the period of operation, Britain was the obvious choice for leadership". London was neither prepared for the intensely negative American response to the Suez invasion, nor for Secretary of State John Foster Dulles' subsequent explanation that the United States, which had extant defense arrangements with 44 other countries, "cannot have a hierarchy of relationships with allies around the world."

Gaining and retaining this special status has been a top priority for Britain since World War II. Indeed, Winston Churchill established this as a principle of British foreign policy even before the United States entered the war. In a statement before the House of Commons in 1940, he predicted that the two nations ". . . will have to be somewhat mixed up together" for the foreseeable future. He went on to reassure his colleagues, however, that "I do not view the process with any misgivings." Churchill was, nonetheless, an unsentimental realist who understood that if London wanted to be treated by the United States as primus inter pares, it would have to provide more than sage advice and accumulated wisdom. As a result, all British Governments since World War II have looked for ways to keep their nation militarily strong, not just as a good in itself but also as a means of sustaining the special relationship with the United States.

America's long-established policy towards Britain and Europe — one of downplaying the British-American "special relationship" in search of a broader and more fruitful "special relationship" with a united Europe has been based on three main points. The first was an assessment of America's ability to bind the continental European countries into a genuine trans-Atlantic community of interests. The second was a belief that greater European unity would lead to a larger European contribution to the continent's defense. And the third was whatever the vicissitudes of the European project, the U.S.

could rely in the last resort on Britain to put it all back on track.

Looking back, it is clear that the only periods when the special relationship between the U.S. and the UK has worked satisfactorily have been when it was based on effective mutual cooperation to the benefit of each country's national interest. Thus, unsurprisingly, British governments have wielded influence with successive American administrations in proportion to British contributions to American objectives. So in the early 1950s Clement Attlee was able to urge nuclear restraint on Truman — because British troops were engaged in combat by the side of the Americans in Korea. Likewise, Thatcher successfully urged caution about abandoning the nuclear deterrent in pursuit of Reagan's Strategic Defense Initiative on the eve of the 1985 Reykjavik Summit — because Britain was America's leading Cold War ally. Although British military contributions has diminished alarmingly in recent years that has been replaced by other important factors. Britain provides a vote on the U.N. Security Council, lends support to American leadership in NATO, and usually relied upon to act as a cheerleader in the European Union and British troops stay prepared to fight and suffer casualties.

Though, Britain is the greater beneficiary of mutual cooperation in security matters with the United States — simply because a medium-sized power can never bring as much to such a relationship as a superpower. But superpowers need reliable allies, and one quality the British have been shown to have in abundance within the trans-Atlantic alliance is reliability.

It is, at root, mutual trust that has traditionally allowed British and American forces to share the same battlefield. The growing gap between the two partners' military equipment threatens that friendship for technical reasons. And the inbuilt prejudices of the British foreign and security policy establishment are no help either. But British soldiers, unlike many of their European equivalents, are still psychologically equipped to fight; they are rigorously professional; and, again unlike most other European armies, they are undiluted by militarily ineffective conscripts. Although by the side of the U.S. defense effort, Britain's seems somewhat paltry but with the rest of Europe Britain appear positively militaristic.

At the heart of Anglo-American defense collaboration remains the nuclear weapon, though diplomats are too polite to mention that fact. Of course, all of NATO ultimately benefits from the American nuclear umbrella, but since 1961 Britain has enjoyed unique access to America's nuclear weapons technology. In any case, since then the British nuclear deterrent, though independent as regards control, has been dependent on America with regard to technology. The same still applies to Trident. This arrangement has allowed Britain to maintain a more effective nuclear deterrent. At the same time it has also given Washington unique leverage in influencing wider British policy.

Still more important, from a day-to-day security perspective, is U.S.-British intelligence sharing, which is indispensable alike to the mounting of British military and intelligence operations and the maintenance of British national security. It also gives the country a substantial strategic advantage over other medium-sized powers, particularly in Europe. For its part, Britain shares intelligence with the U.S. and other English-speaking countries that it does not share with the EU. The regular meetings of Britain's Joint Intelligence Committee are even attended by representatives of the CIA and of the Canadian and Australian intelligence agencies. Naturally, such procedures drive the Europeans wild. Enraged by allegations of commercial espionage centering on the Echelon intelligence-sharing program, one French member of the European Parliament exploded: "this is an Anglo-Saxon Protestant conspiracy. So much for Britain's commitment to European solidarity! Its real union is with America."

The underlying reason for Anglo-American closeness on intelligence is not, however, mere waspish prejudice, but rather a well-founded American suspicion that intelligence shared with the mainland Europeans is likely to be leaked to the press, sold to the highest bidder, or betrayed to America's enemies. And when the U.S. does find itself having to share intelligence with the Europeans, the outcome only confirms American fears — as when France was found to have passed vital information about NATO air strikes to the Serbs in Kosovo. (Evidence at the treason trial of Maj. Pierre-Henri Bunel in December 2001 suggested that his betrayal of secrets to the Serbs was the tip of a larger iceberg of double-dealing authorized by French military intelligence. There have also been strong suspicions of French complicity in the protection from arrest of indicted Serb war criminals like Radovan Karadzic).

The interpersonal relationship is highly beneficial for the United States and Britain. It is now a cliché to observe that English is already the global language of business. But it has taken a group of Anglo-American thinkers and writers to explore just what the dominance of English may mean. Language, they point out, is a medium not only for calculation but also for culture. In particular, the English language is a symbol of common attitudes and values. A powerful case can be made that the English-speaking world — or "Anglosphere" — has generated a uniquely successful civil society accompanied by a strong commitment to "individualism, rule of law, honoring contracts and covenants, and the elevation of freedom to the first rank of political and cultural values." This in turn has resulted in the enviable freedom, stability, and prosperity that characterize most of the Anglophone countries. The proponents of this view want to see such commonalities protected and promoted by institutional means in "trade, defense, free movement of peoples, and scientific cooperation."

With public expenditure running at a little less than 40 percent of GDP, the UK stands about midway between the American and European models. Britain is even closer to the U.S. when it comes to the government's interface with business.

As in America, British business expects to operate in an environment of low regulation and without routine use of kickbacks to state officials; the threat of mergers and takeovers is widely regarded as bracing and beneficial; and it is understood that the interests of shareholders and profits, not co-management with employees and industrial strategy, drive the system. The results confirm that while Anglo-Saxon capitalism generates growth and jobs, European capitalism swells debt and welfare rolls.

The shared approach as well as the shared language of Britain and the United States is also reflected in patterns of trade and investment. Britain is unlike the main continental European economies far more oriented towards exports to non-European Union countries. Britain is the largest overseas investor in the United States. The U.S. receives 44 percent of UK overseas investment and the U.S. provides 38 percent of UK foreign investment.

"As a leading European power she will speak with great authority to the US and her influence in Europe is likely to depend both on her own strength, military and economic, and on the extent to which she is known to enjoy influence and support in the US". This statement was issued by the Foreign Office not in 2004 or 2005 but in 23 March 1949 (Public Record Office,FO371/76384, Foreign Office, Her Majesty's Government, London), demonstrates a consistent line in British diplomacy, reflecting a determination by successive governments to play a distinctive role designed to enhance Britain's influence in both the US and Europe.

With the end of the Cold War and the departure of Margaret Thatcher and Ronald Reagan from the political scene, the 'special relationship' initially underwent a serious challenge. Claims that the Major government interfered in the election that brought President Clinton to office, difficulties over the Bosnia peace plans, and differences over Sinn Fein President Gerry Adams' visits to the United States in the mid-1990s clouded over the consistency of the special relationship.

The election of the Blair government in 1997, however, led to a renewal of close ties. Clinton and Blair developed a good working relationship and shared an ideological commitment to 'third way' political ideals. The American President also played a very constructive role in the Northern Ireland peace process and joint military operations in northern Iraq and Kosovo highlighted the value placed on the continuing diplomatic and defence relationship between the two countries. Despite the close personal ties between the two leaders, however, there were also some policy differences. Even during the joint air campaign in Kosovo the Blair government found it difficult to persuade the Clinton administration that a ground campaign might be necessary to bring about the final withdrawal of Milosevic's forces. There were also growing unilateralist trends in US foreign policy that caused increasing concern for Britain in issues like the International Criminal Court, the 1997 Kyoto Protocol on climate, the ban on land mines, the bio-diversity treaty, and the mechanism for the verification of the Biological Weapons Control Treaty.

These concerns were exacerbated, at least initially, by the election of George W. Bush as President of the United States in November 2000. In particular, there was anxiety that the loss of the close personal and ideological ties at the highest level would inevitably lead to an erosion of the 'special relationship'. Worries over American opposition to the new 'autonomous' European Rapid Reaction Force and apparent British concerns over even greater unilateralist tendencies in the United States raised question marks over the general convergence of Anglo-American interests which had taken place during the Blair/Clinton era. Blair's visit to Washington in February 2001, however, indicated that contemporary obituaries of the 'special relationship' were pre-matured. Blair put a lot of diplomatic effort into reassuring the new American President not only that the new European force would not undermine the NATO

Alliance but also that the United States could expect British support if it went ahead with its plans to develop a missile defence shield. At the same time, Bush pleased his visitors by using the term 'special relationship' to describe the continuing relationship with Britain.

The determination to maintain special relations was demonstrated even more dramatically in the aftermath of the attacks on the Twin Towers and the Pentagon in the autumn of 2001. Two things were noticeable about the reaction of the Blair government in the immediate aftermath of the attacks on September 11. First, the constant message of standing 'shoulder to shoulder' with the American government and the immediate offer of support, and second, the deliberate search to build a broad international coalition within hours of the atrocity occurred. The conventions of the past were immediately on display. Britain had to be seen to be the most supportive (and toughest) of America's allies. It was also important that Britain was prepared to aid the US in a practical and major way in its hour of need, including military aid in Afghanistan to topple the Taliban government in October 2001.

Much the same was true of Britain's involvement alongside the United States in the Iraq War in March 2003. Despite the debate over the legitimacy of the pre-emptive attack on Saddam Hussein's Iraq and the widespread condemnation both domestically and amongst the international community; the Blair Government was prepared to take considerable risks in support of its American ally. Although the British Government was supported by some of the newer recruits to the EU, it was prepared to go against the firmly held views of the French and the Germans thereby putting the futures of the UN, NATO and even the EU itself at risk. Apart from the fact that the government believed that this was the 'right' thing to do, ministers went out of their way during the conflict to indicate that at a time of growing unilateralism in the US support for the Bush administration in the war was the only effective way of trying to influence American policies in an increasing unipolar world.

The British role in the Iraq war clearly reflects a basic continuity in post-Second World War British foreign and defence policy. Amongst the decision-making elite there has been a more or less consistent and enduring belief that Britain's ultimate security and economic well-being depends on close ties with the United States. September 11 and the toppling of Saddam Hussein both appear to have confirmed the contemporary importance of this traditional policy. During the war against Iraq, in particular, great efforts were put into portraying the similarities between the Bush and Blair relationship and that of Churchill and Roosevelt.

As the events associated with the Iraq have shown, Britain continues to feel closer to the United States than it does to Europe. Both leading political parties also continue to see the 'special relationship' as an important instrument of foreign and, especially, security policy. Given the overwhelming contemporary preponderance of American power, it makes sense on the part of Britain to maintain the 'special relationship' as the key part of British foreign and defence policy.

As a result of the Iraq war there are those who argue that Britain has finally chosen the US over Europe and that this represents a 'profound' change in direction of British policy after decades of trying to act as the bridge between Europe and the United States. In practice, however, the 'bridge' concept has always been based on a British priority in favour of the US side of the bridge. It is true that there have been considerable efforts by British ministers since the war in Iraq to emphasize Britain's continuing commitment to the EU. Tony Blair and Jack Straw have both gone out of their way to argue that Britain would continue to refuse to make a choice between Europe and the United States. Though on some issues, like Iran and Kyoto, Britain sometimes sides with Europe than the US.

The importance of the UK for the American policy maker was partly based on the increased salience of military power—used in a very discriminating way—in the post-Cold War world. British forces repeatedly demonstrated in former Yugoslavia that in the context of "humanitarian intervention" their high competence was uniquely suited to the messy conflicts of the post-Cold War world. The degree of commitment on the part of the UK can be judged from the fact that Britain contributed up to 35 per cent of the army to operations at any one time. This is vital for the American policy-makers as and when they search for European military partners.

Nevertheless, the strength of the UK's military capabilities did not disguise the increasing difficulty of UK forces keeping up with technological developments within US forces. Operation Deny Flight in 1995 caused the RAF some real concerns in exposing how difficult it had become to interface forces with those of the United States in real operations. Operation Allied Force in Kosovo in 1999 made this abundantly clears and revealed the degree to which the UK was slipping behind the United States.

The U.S.-British alliance is a strikingly successful partnership of two great nations built on the solid foundations of a common heritage, culture, and vision. The two nations have fought alongside each other in seven major wars in the past 90 years, from World War I to the Iraq War of 2003.

Britain played a major role to support the US in the war to remove Saddam Hussein from power, deploying 45,000 combat troops to the Gulf. It was the largest British military deployment since the Second World War, representing over a third of the nation's armed forces. Over 10,000 British troops remain in Iraq, and the British currently administer the southern region of the country, including the city of Basra. Britain's continuing involvement in Iraq along with the US is critical for the country's transition. The British Army brings with it years of highly successful experience in peacekeeping in a wide range of theaters of operation, including Afghanistan, Bosnia, Kosovo, Sierra Leone, and Northern Ireland. The British possess an in-depth knowledge of Iraq and the region and have close diplomatic and historical ties with much of the Arab world.

Tony Blair played a more high-profile role on the international stage with regard to post-war Iraq. Blair was a pivotal figure before the war in developing the case internationally for taking military action to remove Saddam Hussein from power. He played a crucial role in building the broad-based international coalition of the willing that liberated Iraq. Washington was heavily dependent upon London in generating diplomatic support in Europe, which ultimately included Spain, Italy, Poland, and over 15 other European nations.

While the Iraq war was a huge military success, the strains of post-war administration and reconstruction have placed both the U.S. and British leadership under immense pressure. Since the end of hostilities in Iraq, the White House and Downing Street have faced mounting criticism over their handling of intelligence information in the lead-up to the Iraq war, as well as growing impatience over the pace of political reform and economic progress in Baghdad. There is also growing unease domestically, both in Britain and in America, over guerrilla attacks on coalition troops serving in the country and the growing cost of rebuilding the country.

Since the terrorist attacks on New York and Washington in September 2001, Britain has stood steadfastly with the United States in the war against terrorism. The U.K. was the first country to join with America in launching military strikes against the Taliban in Afghanistan. The British Prime Minister played an outstanding role in helping to build the international coalition in the fight against al-Qaeda. More than 1,500 British troops served with the International Security and Assistance Force in Kabul, which was led for the first six months by the U.K. A further 1,700 Royal Marines served alongside their U.S.

counterparts in the hunt for remnants of the Taliban and al-Qaeda.

To stem the flow of international terrorists flowing into the country from neighboring Arab states, the U.S. and U.K. coordinated efforts to pressure Saudi Arabia, Syria, and Iran to cease their support for terrorist groups and hand over Baathist leaders who may have sought safe haven in their countries. While increasing their coordination of anti-terrorist measures, London and Washington have enhanced intelligence cooperation between the U.S. Central Intelligence Agency and Britain's MI6. Britain and America continue to share intelligence through the Echelon electronic surveillance system while excluding other European nations, in particular France and Russia, both of whom provided Iraq with sensitive intelligence ahead of the coalition invasion. Echelon continues to be shared only by the United States, the United Kingdom, Australia, New Zealand, and Canada.

While the war on terrorism has brought even closer cooperation between the United States and Britain, there are potential pitfalls for the special relationship. The thorny issue of Europeans held by the United States on suspicion of involvement in al-Qaeda terrorist activities is a key issue of contention between the U.S. and British leaders. Tony Blair was under intense pressure from his own Labour Party to secure the suspects' return to Britain as over 200 British Members of Parliament have called for the United States to repatriate British Guantanamo Bay detainees to the United Kingdom.

While addressing British concerns over the continuing detention of European suspected terrorists at Guantanamo, President Bush is worry of making immediate concessions. It was extremely difficult for British or European courts to secure convictions against any of the suspected terrorists carries with it serious implications for the global war against terrorism.

For over half a century the Anglo-American "special relationship" has been a dominant force in world affairs. Today it is the engine of the global war on terror, and its enduring strength continues to confound and even infuriate leaders in continental Europe. Britain is the only nation the U.S. truly trusts as an ally; it is the British prime minister and not the German chancellor, the French president or the U.N. secretary-general, to whom the U.S. president looks first for partnership in addressing the big international security matters of the day.

An America without Britain alongside it would be weaker, more isolated, and less able to project power on the world stage. There is no realistic alternative to the Special Relationship. Its collapse would be damaging to America's standing as a global power and would significantly undermine America's leadership of the war on terrorism.

For Britain, any downgrading of the Anglo-American alliance would significantly harm British strategic interests, and result in the loosening of defense and intelligence ties, the further loss of national sovereignty within the European Union, the diminution of British global power, and a weakening of the two nations' close-knit financial, trade and investment relationships.

REFERENCES

1 Davis, Herbert A., (1969), An Outline History of the World, London: Oxford University Press, p. 199.

2 Griffith, Samuel (2002), American War of Independence, University of Illinois Press, Illinois, p. 72.

3 Longman, C.J. Bartlett (1992),The Special Relationship: A Political History of Anglo-American Relations Since 1945, London: Group United Kingdom Press, pg. 49.

4 Churchill, Winston (1946), as leader of opposition his speech at the Fulton, Missouri, on 5 March 1946 known famously as "The Sinews of Peace"

5 Ibid.

6 Reutor, Frank (1987), Trial and Triumph, Washington's Foreign Policy, Austin: Texas Christian University Press, p. 132.

7 Firzpatrick, John C. ed. (1940), The Writings of George Washington , Vol.35, Washington: Government Printing Office, p.234.

8 Walter LaFeber, Ed. (1965), John Quincy Adams' address of July 4, 1821, Chicago: Quadrangle Books, p. 45.

9 Kennedy, Paul (1988), The Rise and Fall of The Great Powers, London: Fontana Press, p.197.

10 Kurian, Nimmi (2001), The High Noon: Anglo-American Special Relationship under Thatcher and Reagan, New Delhi: Lancer's Book, p. 166-167.

11

12 Kurian, Nimmi (2001), The High Noon : Anglo-American Special Relationship under Thatcher and Reagan,New Delhi : Lancer's Book, p. 166-167.

13 Callaghan, James (1976), delivered a speech at 10, Downing Street, London on January 1976.

14 Rutherford, Malcolm (1986), "The Consultation Arrangement", The Times, London:17 April 1986.

15 Rutherford, Malcolm (1986), "The Consultation Arrangement", The Times, London, 18 April 1986.

16 Burt, Richard (1978), "Neutron Bomb", New York Times, New York, 9 April 1978.

17 Kissinger, Henry (1979), White House Years, London, Weidenfdd & Nicolson, p. 57.

18 EU Commission (2000), 2250th Council meeting-Agriculture-Brussels, 20 March 2000.

19 EU Commission, 2218th Council meeting-Agriculture-Brussels, 15 Nov. 1999.

20 Baldwin, Robert e., Carl B. Hamilton and Andre Sapir, eds. (1988), Issues in US-EC Trade Relations, Chicago: Chicago University Press, p. 256.

21 "The European Union A Guide for Americans", Delegation of the European Commission to the USA, Washington, DC 20037, www.eurunion.org. p. 10-13, visited on 13. 1.2006.

22 Kelleher, Catherine (1995), The Future of European Security: An Interim Assessment, Brookings Occasional Papers, Washington D.C, pg. 160-173.

23 White House (1994), A National Security Strategy of Engagement and Enlargement, Washington DC, July 1994.

24 Others claimed ownership, including the Germans, but

Kruzel clearly played a major role in its design and later in its implementation.

25 Talbott, Strobe (1995), Why NATO Should Grow, the New York Review of Books, 10 August 1995. Talbott wrote the article to counter the beginning of opposition to enlargement, particularly that of Senator Sam Nunn who had given a very critical speech in Norfolk, Virginia, on "The Future of NATO in an Uncertain World", 22 June 1995. Even earlier Secretary Christopher testified on the president's conviction to enlarge in testimony on 30 June 1994 before the Senate Foreign Relations Committee.

26 Holbrooke, Richard (1995), America, a European Power, Foreign Affairs, Vol. 14, No.2, April 1995, pg. 38-53.

27 Four Reasons why NATO Enlargement is in the U.S. National Interest, as agreed to by the Senate, Washington, DC, 16 December 1997.

28 Talbott also attempted to calm the fears of the Russians that NATO enlargement was directed toward them. Talbott, Strobe (1997), Russia Has Nothing to Fear, New York Times, 18 February 1997, A-25.

29 Apple Jr, R.W. (1997), Clinton's NATO: Keen on Growth, Murky on Mission, New York Times, 13 July 1997, Northeast Edition.

30 President Bush (2001), Remarks by the President in Address to Faculty and Students of Warsaw University, Warsaw, Poland, June 15, 2001.

31 British Defence Policy 1990-1991 (1990), Ministry of Defence Pamphlet, London, Ministry of Defence, April 1990.

32 Britain's Army for the 1990's (1991), Cm1595, London, Her Majesty's Stationary Office, (HMSO), July 1991.

33 Statement on the Defence Estimates (1994), Cm2550,

London, HMSO, April 1994.

34   Stable Forces in a Strong Britain (1995), Cm2800, London, HMSO, May 1995.

35   Statement on the Defense Estimates (1996), Cm3223, London, HMSO, 1996, para.101.

36   Tony Blair (1997), Speech to Parliament, Hansard Parliamentary Debates, 297, 9 July 1997, col. 937.

37   Hansard Parliamentary Debates, Commons, 297, 9 July 1997, col. 937.

38   A Higher Priority, The Times, 17 February 1997, 10.

39   Parliament Defence Committee (1998), Third Report NATO Enlargement, 18 March 1998, London, HMSO.

40   Hansard Parliamentary Debates, Commons, 316, 17 July 1998.

41   Ibid., col.684.

42   Ibid., col.687.

43   On 28 November 1995, the British and Irish Governments issued a Communiqué which announced the launching in Northern Ireland of a "'twin track' process to make progress in parallel on the decommissioning issue and on all-party negotiations." Subsequently the International Body formed with - Senator George J. Mitchell (Chairman), General John de Chastelain - Mr. Harri Holkeri with the specific task of 1) identify and advise on a suitable and acceptable method for full and verifiable decommissioning; and 2) report whether there is a clear commitment on the part of those in possession of such arms to work constructively to achieve that.

44   O' Clery, Conor (1996), The Greening of the White House: The Inside Story of How America Tried to Bring Peace to Ireland, Dublin, Gill and Macmillan, p. 215.

45   O'Clery, Connor (1997), Daring Diplomacy: Clinton's

Search for Peace in Ireland, London, Roberts Rinehart Publishers, pg. 87.

46 O'Clery, Connor (1997), The Irish Times, 17 March 1997, Belfast.

47 Clinton, Bill (2005), My Life, New York, Vintage, pg. 587.

48 US Department of State Dispatch (1993), US-UK Special Relationship: President Clinton and Prime Minister Major, 8 March 1993.

49 Holbrooke, Richard C. (1995), Testimony to US Congress. 104th Congress 1st Session, "Questions and Answers Submitted for the Record," House Committee on International Relations, Hearings held 15 March 1995.

50 On decommissioning the Report of the International Body known as Mitchell Report said in three point: 1) One side has insisted that some decommissioning of arms must take place before all-party negotiations can begin. The other side has insisted that no decommissioning can take place until the end of the process, after an agreed settlement has been reached. This has resulted in the current impasse. 2) The parties should consider an approach under which some decommissioning would take place during the process of all-party negotiations, rather than before or after as the parties now urge. Such an approach represents a compromise. If the peace process is to move forward, the current impasse must be overcome. While both sides have been adamant in their positions, both have repeatedly expressed the desire to move forward. This approach provides them that opportunity. 3) In addition, it offers the parties an opportunity to use the process of decommissioning to build confidence one step at a time during negotiations

51   On Friday, 10 April 1998 a comprehensive political agreement was approved at a plenary session of the talks. The two Governments signed immediately thereafter a new British-Irish Agreement committing them to give effect to the provisions of this multi-party agreement, in particular those relating to constitutional change and the creation of new institutions known as "The Good Friday (or Belfast) Agreement".

52   Baylis, John and Roper, Jon ed. (2006), the United States and Europe, London, Routledge Publication, pg. 81.

53   Dumbrell, John (2001), A Special Relationship: Anglo-American Relations in the Cold War and After, New York: Palgrave, p. 93.

54   Harris, Robin (2006), "America, The Hague, and Ante Gotovina: The Railroading of a Former U.S. Ally," The American Spectator, March 2006.

55   President Bush's address to a Joint Session of Congress and the American People September 20, 2001, Department of State Release. Prime Minister Tony Blair was also present on this occasion and Bush acknowledges his presence with these words, "America has no truer friend than Great Britain. Once again, we are joined together in a great cause — so honored the British Prime Minister has crossed an ocean to show his unity of purpose with America. Thank you for coming, friend."

56   Naughtie, James (2004), The Accidental American: Toni Blair and the Presidency, London: Public Affairs Publication, p. 191.

57   Coughlin, Con (2006), American Ally: Tony Blair and the War on Terror, New York: Ecco Publisher, p. 219.

58   Robins, Harris (2006), Beyond Friendship: The Future

of Anglo-American Relations, Washington: The Heritage Foundation, Web Memo No; 1081, Chapter 3.

59   Prime Minister Tony Blair's speech at the George Bush Senior Presidential Library, Texas, 7 April 2002, 10 Downing Street Release, Speeches of the PM.

60   Robins, Harris (2006), Beyond Friendship: The Future of Anglo-American Relations, Washington: The Heritage Foundation, Web Memo No; 1081, Chapter 3.

61   President Bush, Prime Minister Blair Hold Press Conference, Remarks by President Bush and Prime Minister Tony Blair in Joint Press, Crawford High School, Crawford, Texas, 6 April 2002.

62   Inside Echelon - The history, structure und function of the global surveillance system known as Echelon by Duncan Campbell 25.07.2000

63   www.GlobalSecurity.org's page on ECHELON visited on 28 January 2006.

64   U.S. Bureau of Transportation Statistics (2002), U.S. International Travel and Transportation Trends, 2002, Washington DC.

65   Pressure for Change (1999), Economic Research Service Publication, United States Department of Agriculture, Washington DC.

66   Rome Statute of the International Criminal Court, July 17, 1998, 37 I.L.M. 999, accessed on 20.9.2006, http://www.un.org/law/icc/statute/99_corr/cstatute.htm.

67   Rome Statute, Article 17(1) (a). The conditional nature of ICC jurisdiction is referred to as "complementarities" or "admissibility", accessed on 20.9.2006, http://www.un.org/law/icc/statute/99_corr/cstatute.htm.

68   Security Council Resolution 1497, U.N. SCOR, 58th Session, 4803rd, Meeting, 2003. See also Sean D. Murphy, "Efforts to Obtain Immunity from ICC for U.S.

Peacekeepers," American Journal of International Law, Vol. 96, 2002, pp. 725.

69 U.N. Charter, Articles 24(1) and 39, accessed on 20.9.2006, http://www.yale.edu/lawweb/avalon/un/unchart.htm.

70 U.S. Constitution, Article II, Section 2, clause 2, "He (the President) shall have Power, by and with the Advice and Consent of the Senate to make Treaties . . . ."

71 Blair, Tony (2001), The Prime Minister's Speech, House of Commons, British Parliament, London.

72 Bush, George (2001), President George Bush's address to the Congress, 23rd September2001, Dept. Of State Release.

73 Jean Schemo, Diana (2001), New York Mayer Rudi Giuliani Refused Arab Grants, The New York Times, 23rd October 2001.

74 Robertson, Lord (2001), NATO Press Information Service, Lisbon: 10th October 2001.

75 Ikenberry, John (2001), "American Grand Strategy in the Age of Terror", Survival, Vol.43, No.4/December 2001, p.20.

76 Resolution 1368 (2001), Adopted by the Security Council at its 4370th meeting, on 12 September 2001, accessed 4 June 2006 http://www.un.org/docs/scres/2001/sc2001.htm . The resolution said, Reaffirming the principles and purposes of the Charter of the United Nations, Determined to combat by all means threats to international peace and security caused by terrorist acts, Recognizing the inherent right of individual or collective self-defence in accordance with the Charter.

77 Resolution 1373 (2001), Adopted by the Security Council at its 4385th meeting, on 28 September 2001, accessed on 4 June 2006, http://www.un.org/docs/scres/2001/

sc2001.htm.

78 Press Release (2001), Government of India, Ministry of External Affairs, New Delhi 5 October 2001.

79 Editorial (2001), Blair's Visit to the Middle East, The Hindu, 01 November 2001.

80 Editorial (2001), Saudi Arabia Decline Blair's visit, The Hindu, 13 October 2001.

81 Seventh Report (2002), Foreign Policy Aspect of the War against Terrorism, House of Commons, London, 20th June 2002.

82 Straw, Jack (2001), UK Foreign Secretary's interview to BBC, 11 October 2001.

83 Press Release (2001), 10 Downing Street, London, 11 October 2001.

84 Putin's Initiative (2001), accessed on 24.6.2006, http:/www.publications.parliament.uk/cm200102/cmselect/cmfaff/384/38407.htmn.

85 Press Release (2001), U.S. Department of State, Office of the Spokesman, Washington DC, 29th September 2001.

86 Howorth, Jolyon (2001), "European Defence and the Changing Politics of the European Union: Hanging Together or Hanging Separately?" Journal of Common Market Studies, 39: 4, 765-789.

87 Bush, George (2001), President's address to the Joint Session of Congress, Washington DC, 20 September 2001, accessed on 26.6.2006, http://www.news.bbc.co.uk/foreign_policy/uk_us.stm. 31 Burke, Jason (2001), "War Against Terror", The Observer, London, 4th November 2001. 32 Editorial (2001), "US Attack on Afghanistan" The Hindu, New Delhi, 8th September 2001. 33 Blair, Tony (2001), PM's address to the House of Commons, Special Session, 8 October

2001, accessed 4 July 2006, www.explore.parliament.uk . 35 Chengappa, Raj (2001), "March on Kabul", India Today, 22 October 2001, New Delhi, p.37-39.30 Burke, Jason (2001), "US War on Terror", The Observer, London, 23rd December 2001.31 Chengappa, Raj (2001), "March on Kabul", India Today, 22 October 2001, New Delhi, p.37-39. 32 Dept. Of State Release (2001), "Global Support", accessed 5 June 2006 www.state.gov/.

88   CIA Unclassified Report to Congress on the Acquisition of Technology Relating to Weapons of Mass Destruction and Advanced Conventional Munitions, 1 January through 30 June 2002.

89   UNSCOM Chairman Butler's Report To UN Secretary General (1998), accessed on 2 September 2006, http://www.fas.org/news/un/iraq/s/butla216.htm .

90   CIA Unclassified Report to Congress on the Acquisition of Technology Relating to Weapons of Mass Destruction and Advanced Conventional Munitions, 1 January through 30 June 2002.

91   Bush, George (2002), President's State of the Union Address, Washington DC, 29 January 2002.

92   US National Security Council (2002), The National Security Strategy of the United States, 17 September 2002.

93   Albright, Madeleine (2003), "Bridges, Bombs, or Bluster?", Foreign Affairs, 82 (5), September/October 2003, p.49.

94   Aznar, Jose Maria; Barroso, Nose-Manuel Durao; Berlusconi, Silvio; Blair, Tony; Havel, Vaclav; Medgyessy, Peter; Miller, Leszek and Rasmussen, Anders Fogh (2003), United We Stand, 30 January 2003. The letter also stated that: "the real bond between the US and

Europe is the values we share: democracy, individual freedom, human rights and the rule of law. These values crossed the Atlantic with those who sailed from Europe to help create the United States of America. Today they are under greater threat than ever. The attacks of September 11 showed just how far terrorists – the enemies of our common values – are prepared to go to destroy them. Those outrages were an attack on all of us. In standing firm in defence of these principles, the government and people of the US and Europe have amply demonstrated the strength of their convictions. Today more than ever, the trans-Atlantic bond is a guarantee of our freedom. "

95   Rumsfeld, Donald (2003), "News Transcript: Secretary Rumsfeld Briefs at Foreign Press Centre," Department of Defence News Transcripts, 22 January 2003.

96   UK, Ministry of Defence (1998), The Strategic Defence Review, 1998, London: HMSO, online at http://www.mod.uk/issues/sdr.

97   UK, Foreign Affairs Select Committee (2001), Second Report on British-US Relations, 18 December 2001, accessed on 9.8.2007, http://www.publications,parliament.uk/cgi-bin/ukparl_hl?DB=ukparl&STEMMER=en&W.

98   Advancing US Interest Through the UN (2003), accessed on 2 September 2006,http://usinfo.state.gov/journals/itps/0597/ijpe/pj2bill.htm .

99   Blair, Tony (2002), Tony Blair's statement in response to the unanimous passing of UN resolution 1441, November 8, 2002.

100   Security Council 4644th meeting, Speeches delivered after adoption of U.N. Security Council Resolution 1441, United Nations document S/PV.4644, November 8, 2002.

101 Powell, Colin (2003), US Mission to the UN, Secretary of State Colin L. Powell to the UN Security Council, accessed on 14 September 2006, http://www.un.int/usa/03clp0205.htm .

102 Global Message (2003), accessed on 27 September 2006, www.whitehouse.gov.

103 Security Council Resolution (2002), "United Kingdom of Great Britain and Northern Ireland and United States of America: Draft Resolution", adopted as Resolution 1441 at the Security Council Meeting 4644, 8 November 2002.

104 Iraq Liberation Act of 1998, Enrolled as Agreed to or Passed by Both House and Senate, Library of Congress, accessed on 28 September 2006, http://thomas.loc.gov/cgi-bin/query/z?c105:H.R.4655.ENR.

105 Resolution 687 (1991) imposed obligations on Iraq as a necessary step for achievement of its stated objective of restoring international peace and security in the area, deploring the fact that Iraq has not provided an accurate, full, final, and complete disclosure, as required by resolution 687 (1991), of all aspects of its programmes to develop weapons of mass destruction and ballistic missiles with a range greater than one hundred and fifty kilometres, and of all holdings of such weapons, their components and production facilities and locations, as well as all other nuclear programmes, including any which it claims are for purposes not related to nuclear-weapons-usable material, deploring further that Iraq repeatedly obstructed immediate, unconditional, and unrestricted access to sites designated by the United Nations Special Commission (UNSCOM) and the International Atomic Energy Agency (IAEA), failed to cooperate fully and unconditionally with UNSCOM and IAEA weapons inspectors, as required by resolution

106 "Plans For Iraq Attack Began On 9/11", CBS News, 4, September 2002, accessed on 28 September 2006, www.cbsnews.com.

107 "Palestinians get Saddam funds", BBC News, 13 March 2003, accessed on 28 September 2006, www.bbcworld.com .

108 Security Council Resolution (2002), "United Kingdom of Great Britain and Northern Ireland and United States of America: Draft Resolution", adopted as Resolution 1441 at the Security Council Meeting 4644, 8 November 2002.

109 The 9/11 Commission Report (2004), Final Report of the National Commission on Terrorist Attacks Upon the United States, Section 10.3, Washington DC : United States Government Printing Office.

110 Bush, George (2003), President Bush Addresses the Nation, 19 March 2003, accessed on 29 September 2006, www.whitehouse.gov.

111 Schifferes, Steve (2003), US Names Coalition of the Willing, accessed on 29 September 2003, http://news.bbc.co.uk/2/hi/americas/2862343.stm. The US has named 30 countries which are prepared to be publicly associated with the US action against Iraq. Full list of coalition countries: Afghanistan, Albania, Australia, Azerbaijan, Bulgaria, Colombia, the Czech Republic, Denmark, El Salvador, Eritrea, Estonia, Ethiopia, Georgia, Hungary, Italy, Japan, South Korea, Latvia, Lithuania, Macedonia, the Netherlands, Nicaragua, the Philippines, Poland, Romania, Slovakia, Spain, Turkey, United Kingdom and Uzbekistan.

112 Bush, George (2005), "Text Of Bush Speech", Associated Press, New York, 1 January 2003.